BUILDING FROM WASTE

BUILDING FROM WASTE

RECOVERED MATERIALS IN ARCHITECTURE AND CONSTRUCTION

Dirk E. Hebel
Marta H. Wisniewska
Felix Heisel

Birkhäuser
Basel

ETH *zürich*

DARCH
Faculty of Architecture

(FCL)   FUTURE   未来
        CITIES   城市
        LABORATORY   实验室

Book design: Binocular, New York

Library of Congress Cataloging-in-Publication data
A CIP catalog record for this book has been
applied for at the Library of Congress.

Bibliographic information published by the
German National Library

The German National Library lists this publication
in the Deutsche Nationalbibliografie; detailed
bibliographic data are available on the Internet at
http://dnb.dnb.de.

This publication is also available as an
e-book pdf (ISBN 978-3-03821-375-8) and
EPUB (978-3-03821-932-3)

© 2014 Birkhäuser Verlag GmbH, Basel
P.O. Box 44, 4009 Basel, Switzerland
Part of Walter de Gruyter GmbH, Berlin/Boston

Printed on acid-free paper produced from
chlorine-free pulp. TCF ∞

Printed in Germany

ISBN 978-3-03821-584-4

9 8 7 6 5 4 3 2 1   www.birkhauser.com

CONTENTS

007   Introduction: Building from Waste
Dirk E. Hebel
Marta H. Wisniewska
Felix Heisel

021   City and Refuse: Self-reliant Systems and Urban Terrains
Mitchell Joachim

027   Hands off: Urban Mining! A Plea for the Re-evaluation
of Substandard Housing
Jörg Stollmann

DENSIFIED   033   Densified Waste Materials

RECONFIGURED   063   Reconfigured Waste Materials

TRANSFORMED   095   Transformed Waste Materials

DESIGNED   127   Designed Waste Materials

146   Organic Waste Design: A New Culture
of Designed Waste Products
Sascha Peters

CULTIVATED   151   Cultivated Waste Materials

Product Directory
172   Load-bearing Products
178   Self-supporting Products
180   Insulating Products
184   Waterproofing Products
187   Finishing Products

Appendix
193   Notes
195   Illustration Credits
196   About the Authors and the Contributors
198   Index of Products and Projects
199   Index of Manufacturers and Designers
200   Acknowledgements

1 Open landfill in Addis Ababa, Ethiopia.

INTRODUCTION

BUILDING FROM WASTE

Dirk E. Hebel
Marta H. Wisniewska
Felix Heisel

Our economic system is based on the principle of the exhaustion of natural resources for the purpose of production, entailing the fabrication of waste. This system functions at the expense of our social integrity and environmental sustainability. Images of the urban poor searching steaming landfills for valuable items are iconic representations of our modern life-style. In a dramatic way, the garbage sites show the entanglement of economic success and rapid urbanization with social segregation into "haves" and "have-nots". It is also telling that this image is almost exclusively to be found in urban agglomerations, where by far the majority of non-organic waste is produced. Instead of being included in a metabolic cycle and flow model of goods and resources, waste is considered within a dead-end scenario of a linear process; to be literally buried from view – out of sight, out of mind – as a formless substance that has no value and is therefore covered by thick layers of earth or burned to ashes.

Looking, by contrast, at the waste products reveals a completely different story. It is the story of a resource that is being wasted. 1.3 billion tons of municipal solid waste are generated every year by cities worldwide. This amount is expected to grow to 2.2 million tons by 2025, i.e. within the next ten years. Unsurprisingly, the 34 OECD countries (members of the Organization for Economic Cooperation and Development) produce more solid waste than the other 164 nations together. China is on a fast track to break this record; the World Bank estimates that China will produce more than half of the total of solid waste worldwide by 2025.[1] Looking at the map of the most waste-generating nations in the world, two readings are possible: either to see them as the biggest polluters, following the traditional understanding of waste; or to see them as countries with an enormous richness of resources. The latter perspective requires a different view of garbage production.

Marc Angélil and Cary Siress, in their article "Re: Going Around in Circles, Regimes of Waste", acknowledge this huge potential: "Waste and its meticulous handling are valued as gifts, offered by society to itself. Where we turn the parable's missed opportunity to our advantage, a modified economy would be set into motion. Perhaps then we would come full circle in being sustained by the constant transformation of matter and energy at hand, without beginning and without end."[2] Referring to Georges Bataille,[3] the authors talk of waste as a gift that needs to be freed from its "pejorative stigma". Their call to understand waste as part of societies' wealth follows, in fact, also an economic principle: waste production is an investment that needs to be returned. So far, this investment is deadlocked and we seem to have lost the key to how to open its potential and benefit from it as a life-long revenue. Once the waste is produced – i.e. when a natural resource is transformed into a product with a limited life span – society should be able to make a profit of its constant reformulation. Instead, today the beneficiaries of the way we treat waste as a result of the exploitation of natural resources are to be found in a black spot of our economic system; they are another by-product, so to say.

SHADOW ECONOMY

Strangely enough, criminal organizations have had a strong interest and bond to garbage for a very long time. It seems that our way to suppress waste and enclose it in our subconsciousness generates a legal vacuum where space can be claimed by outlaws. For decades, the Italian Mafia has been deeply involved in the waste business. Contracted by the public authorities, they dump the waste that has been collected and supposedly treated, on open land without any protection system, mixed with toxic and other contaminated substances. They even export the garbage to other locations, where rules, regulations, and ethics are less rigid than in Europe. The bill has to be paid by the people living close to the garbage sites and by the immediate natural environment. An extreme case is an area north of Naples, also known as "Land of Poison". In 1997, one of the

Municipal solid waste
kg / person / day

■ >2.50
■ 2.00-2.49
■ 1.50-1.99
□ <1.49
□ No data

heads of the Casalesi Mafia clan, Carmine Schiavone, gave testimony to a parliamentary investigation committee in Rome. His confession was so outrageous that the Italian government kept it classified until 2013: "'We are talking about millions of tons,' Schiavone, formerly head of administration for the Mafia organization, told the parliamentarians. 'I also know that trucks came from Germany carrying nuclear waste.' The operations took place under the cloak of darkness and were guarded by Mafiosi in military police uniforms, he said. He showed Italian justice officials the locations of many of the dumpsites because, as he put it in 1997, the people in those areas are at risk of 'dying of cancer within 20 years'."[4]

Another example: the largest export good of the United States of America to China is trash.[5] This has to do with the growing problem of finding landfill spaces or new locations for incineration plants. There are countries that happily accept the trash from other societies, especially when they are paid for it. Their understanding of environmental protection or human health is less distinct. In the case of Ghana, one of the main recipients of e-waste from all over the world, people move from rural areas to scrap sites next to harbour zones to strip and burn electronic wastes in order to collect valuable metals such as aluminium and copper. To get to the metal inside, the plastic casings are burned on

2 Global map of per capita solid municipal waste production.

Known and suspected
routes of e-waste dumping

Source of E-Waste
Known Destination
Suspected Destination
No data

LINEAR ECONOMY

The dominant economic model for our current waste management has been phrased by Annie Leonard, the author of the film and book *The Story of Stuff*,[9] as "Take, Make, Waste". This is not *per se* an unsustainable principle, as it permits that the resource "taken" would become the outcome of "wasting". But this is not the case. In fact, we follow a linear process where the outcome of our consumption is not valued as a resource, but seen as a product excluded from the cycle of our economic system – belonging neither to the natural resources nor to the desired products.

open sites, releasing thick, black toxic fumes containing ingredients known to be carcinogens. According to Al Jazeera,[6] people working in the business make between two and three US Dollars a day, just enough to survive. The Basel Convention E-Waste Africa Programme[7] estimates that approximately 40,000 tons of e-waste went to Ghana in 2010, compared to the total for Africa of around 230,000 tons. This prosperity trash of Western societies will continue to be shipped to Western Africa, as long as the Northern nations do not conceive of it as a rich resource.

Why does our society accept these circumstances? The answer is very complex. The potential of waste to be a substance of value or even a resource for our economy is somehow banned from our awareness. Therefore, we usually do not ask what happens to it after it has left our home. Furthermore, the business of illegal waste disposal has become a powerful global economic player, as the example from Italy shows. The environmental organization Legambiente claims that the business of black-market waste was over 16 billion Euros in Italy alone in 2012 generated from more than 11.6 million tons of illegally disposed waste substances.[8] Compared to the Gross Domestic Product of the same year, this represents almost 1% of Italy's economic power.

Absurdly enough, we pay our local authorities to collect our trash, confirming that it has no value nor is seen as a resource by us. Today, of the approximately 251 million tons of municipal solid waste generated in the USA per year, only around 87 million tons are recycled. The remainder, roughly 164 million tons, ends up in incineration plants and landfills.[10] This waste of waste is at the same time a dissipation of natural resources, considering alone the energy, water, and other materials that were needed (and wasted) to produce from virgin resources the items later discarded. The production of a plastic bag requires crude oil not only as the raw material but the same quantity of oil to produce the energy needed for

3 Global map of e-waste dumping routes.

the manufacture of the bag. In total, one kilogram of CO_2 is emitted for the production of five average-sized plastic bags.[11] Almost half of this amount could be saved if we were to start recycling our plastic waste materials instead of locking them away or burning them to ashes, emitting even more CO_2 and toxic fumes. Numbers are even higher in other industries. Recycling steel saves 75% of energy compared to the process generating it from scratch. And to produce 1 ton of paper, 98 tons of natural resources are needed. But large amounts of paper waste still end up as trash, even though the recycling of this material is one of the easiest processes we know and could be part of a circular understanding of the stock and flow of materials.[12]

CIRCULAR ECONOMY

What we describe today as a circular or metabolic economy has been rooted for decades in the thinking of economists and surprisingly enough also architects. In the USA, landscape architect John T. Lyle developed a theoretical concept in the late 1970s in which communities are envisioned that base their daily activities on living within the limits of available renewable resources and without causing environmental degradation. His work and vision, developed together with his students at Cal Poly Pomona University, found widespread interest due to the studies of Walter R. Stahel, co-founder

Linear metabolism – cities consume and pollute at a high rate

Circular metabolism – cities minimize new inputs and maximize recycling

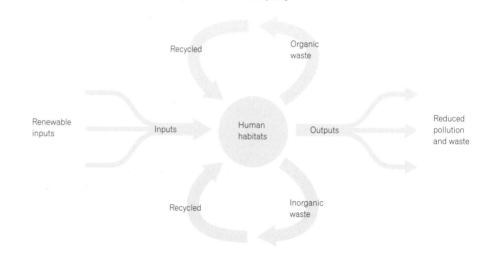

Illustrations based on: *Cities for a Small Planet* (Richard Rogers, 1996).

of the Product-Life Institute in Geneva (and Graduate of the Department of Architecture at the Federal Institute of Technology (ETH) in Zurich in 1971). Stahel had become a pioneer in the field of sustainable thinking by promoting the "service-life extension of goods", and one of the first to introduce the three R's to product life cycles: Reuse, Repair, and Remanufacture (which, in the meantime, have been renamed and given a fourth sibling – see further below). In his 1982 paper "The Product Life Factor"[13] he advocated the development, and application in the industry, of new sustainable strategies and

4 Linear metabolism – inputs equal outputs.

5 Circular metabolism – minimized inputs and outputs due to the concept of a circular economy.

policies in economic terms. His ideas were an important contribution to a model that we call today a circular economy. Industries around the world adopted the concepts of reuse and service-life extension of products as a strategy for waste prevention in order to decouple our prosperity from the exploitation of natural resources.

It is also Walter R. Stahel who is credited to have first coined the term "cradle to cradle", an expression later turned into a well-known principle by the architect and former student of John T. Lyle, William McDonough. Together with the German chemist Michael Braungart, the Cradle-to-Cradle framework was developed to introduce the idea that all materials used in the industrial and commercial production processes should be acknowledged as constituents of a continual circular growing process. Imitating a natural metabolic life cycle, the authors developed a model of a technical metabolism of the flow of industrially produced materials. The key idea is very obvious: products should be designed in such a way that they can become part of a continuous recovery and reutilization process. They act as nutrients in a global metabolism, without ever being discarded as useless substances that are of no value. Following McDonough's and Braungart's argument, systems need to be installed that constantly recover the economic

value stored in industrial products, and an awareness of the social responsibility to do so must be developed. By taking natural processes as a model, the Cradle-to-Cradle concept displays a distinct similarity with the principles of biomimicry. Here, nature is used as an ecological standard to measure the sustainability of our economic actions. Biomimicry means that we do not ask what we can extract from our natural surroundings but instead seek to find out how we can learn from nature to turn the abundance of renewable energies into a circular metabolism of growth and economic surplus – without wasting or polluting a single element inside this system.

Roland Clift, Professor Emeritus of Environmental Technology in the Centre for Environmental Strategy at the University of Surrey, and Julian Allwood, Senior Lecturer in Engineering at the University of Cambridge, claim in their article "Rethinking the economy"[14] that so far all attempts at improving the energy efficiency of industrialized processes focus on an inappropriate parameter: instead of the energy input, what should be targeted and reduced are the materials circulating in the industrial realm. Clift and Allwood plead the case for a system change to create closed-loop processes with waste serving as the main input source. Thus the formerly unwanted and undesired substance becomes the key element for

an "industrial ecology". At the same time, a process of natural capital restoration would be initiated that evolves towards the desired decoupling of the creation of material wealth and the exploitation of natural resources.

The American MacArthur Foundation estimates that a change to a circular economy model would save materials, i.e. natural resources, in the value of over one trillion US Dollars.[15] In this spirit, in recent years the European Union has introduced a system called "extended producer responsibility", which turns around the question of who has to take care of our waste: producers or consumers? The Europeans think that the producers are the ones who can do the most. Since it is the manufacturers who decide on the design of products, it needs to be made their responsibility of how to deal with these at the moment when they leave their first life cycle. "The EU's directive on 'end-of-life vehicles' not only obliges manufacturers to accept vehicles that are no longer wanted, but also requires them to recycle or re-use 80% of the parts by weight, a proportion that will rise to 85% by 2015. The manufacturers can farm out the job, but only to authorised firms."[16] Examples from other industries show that this political tool can force designers and engineers to think way ahead of the first death of their product, constructing it in such a way that it can become the resource for yet another life cycle.

WHAT A WASTE?

In order to perceive of waste as an opportunity for the architectural production process, it seems necessary to reconsider its definition, introduce our own conceptual understanding of it, and explain how this approach has become the base for the selection of the materials and applications that we put together in this publication.

Waste, as we see it, can be defined as unwanted or undesired materials. These

6 Victor Papanek: *Design for the real world*, book cover of first edition of 1971 (New York: Pantheon Books).

materials include man-made as well as natural matter. In general, when we use the term "waste" in this book, we refer to so-called solid waste in contrast to waste that is produced in the form of energy or radiation emitted to the atmosphere or ground. We do include in our argument airborne particles as well as waste discharged in sewage systems, both of which could be transformed into new building substances. Yet what is waste to one person is not waste to another, which makes the definition of the term highly complex. It requires a careful and differentiated recognition of the enormous differences in various cultures and social perceptions. Victor Papanek, in his book *Design for the real world*,[17] refers to Frances Fitzgerald, an American journalist who wrote about the cultural differences concerning the theme of waste between American troops and the native population in South-East Asia during the Vietnam War: "... while they (the Americans) saw themselves as building world order, many Vietnamese saw them merely as the producers of garbage from which they could build houses."[18]

"Desire", contrariwise, describes a sense of longing for something, which apparently is absent when we think of items that we do not want around us anymore or that are useless or even nauseous to us. The definition of waste, therefore, includes emotions and feelings that are not to be measured in objective terms. Aesthetic and other senses play an important role and the sheer thought that something is made out of waste might trigger negative emotions in various cultural groups. This fact makes it hard to think of waste as a future building material. But in our view, waste, in a prospective way, should count among the renewable resources of our planet.

WASTE THROUGH THE TIMES

From man's earliest days, through their mere presence on earth, through every activity in their struggle for survival, through their production of culture and goods, human beings have produced waste. It is known that the Mayan Indians in North America collected waste in special locations, organized in a monthly rhythm; when necessary, the solid waste was burned or covered with a layer of earth, which resulted in a constant rise of ground levels in their settlements. Indeed, the development of solid waste is strongly connected to the evolution of human settlements into urban conglomerates. In a first attempt of establishing a waste management system, the ancient civilization of Greece organized dumpsites outside its cities, which had to be located at a certain prescribed distance from the city walls – authorities were afraid that enemies could use the piled-up waste as an access ramp to invade the city. This issue also triggered reactions in the city of Rome to introduce rules and regulations for a first waste collection and managment system.[19]

Until the 19th century, little changed in the way waste was treated. In the Middle Ages, waste was usually simply thrown out of the window, sometimes justified by a belief that the waste (including human faeces) would be eaten by stray dogs and other animals. Even when this was actually the case, the filth attracted rats, which developed diseases that also infected human beings. The bubonic plague, cholera, or typhus drastically affected the European populations and changed political landscapes in the Middle Ages. Wars resulted from these unstable conditions. William Worrell and P. Aarne Vesilind describe in their book *Solid Waste Engineering* an historical incident that triggered an awareness of the connection between the devastating diseases in European cities and the unhygienic and filthy conditions resulting from the lack of a waste management system: "The 'Great Sanitary Awakening' in the 1840s was spearheaded by a lawyer, Edwin Chadwick (1800–1890), who argued that there was a connection between disease and filth. The germ theory was not, however, widely accepted until the famous incident with the pump handle on Broad Street in London. The public health physician, John Snow (1813–1858), suspected that the water supply from the Broad Street pump

was contaminated and was the cause of the cholera epidemic. He removed the handle and prevented people from drinking the contaminated water, thus stopping the cholera epidemic and ushering in the public health revolution."[20]

Most waste products of former times were of biological nature. This was about to change with the rise of the industrial revolution. The composition of solid municipal waste changed dramatically during the 19th and 20th centuries. While organic waste diminished steadily, product waste such as chemically harmful substances, as well as manure and urine generated by horses used for transportation, were on the rise, hazardous to the health of workers in the emerging fabrication sites and their homes. By the turn of the 20th century, waste was understood to be the biggest problem for authorities in urban settlements. The answer was seen in machines that collected the waste from public streets or processed it, such as the "Destructor", an incineration plant in Nottingham, England. In the USA, sorting machines were invented and first recycling ideas were developed for metals and other valuable materials. But the most popular way of getting rid of waste was still the open landfill, used for the co-disposal of industrial processed waste as well as solid municipal waste. Almost every community in Europe and the USA had one or several

of those sites, mostly unprotected against seepage of hazardous substances into the groundwater.

The 1970s and 1980s saw a tremendous change in the public opinion about existing waste management systems. People started to demand the closing of wild and open landfills and pressured authorities to build new and better controlled plants to prevent the contamination of groundwater and the surrounding environment. This development was also due to a new character or quality of waste, which started to be a hazard no longer only in terms of bacterial contamination, but also by nuclear radiation.

During the 1980s and 1990s, recycling programmes started to emerge in the industrialized world. Waste was no longer seen as a merely unwanted or useless substance, but as a resource for new products. Many nations, for example, have come to recycle the remains of waste incineration as landfill material used to reclaim land from the sea. Private recycling companies started to enter the markets of most developed countries, attracted by the incredible potential of collecting solid waste materials to recycle them for a circular industrial production process. Today, most industrialized nations dispose of organized recycling concepts in their communities, even though reuse rates seem to have been stagnant since the late 1990s. The convenience of collection processes created yet another phenomenon known as the "throw-away society", also called a "take-make-waste" mentality. As citizens continue to rely on the existing recycling processes, the focus has shifted from the reduction of waste to consumption. So what is currently taking the centre stage is the realization that more and more of our daily consumable products, due to their chemical composition or their limited durability, are not designed to be recycled.

WASTE AND MODERN ARCHITECTURE

In the early 20th century, architecture adopted a new terminology that responded directly to the filthy and unhygienic conditions resulting from the absence of waste management in European cities. Modern architects, gathering around key figures like Le Corbusier, the Dutch group of De Stijl, or the Bauhaus protagonists in Weimar and Dessau, used definitions of "clean", "pure", or "healthy" to describe their designs. The tenor was that our built environment should act as a "healing machine" against diseases resulting from unhygienic conditions. Architecture should be devoted to rationalization, optimization, and cleanliness as the discipline's spatial and material contribution to the modern project of a rational society. Architects began to see themselves as sociologists and agents of social hygiene,

establishing a process of mental, physical, and aesthetic cleansing and deodorization. In an ideological partnership of architects, engineers, doctors, and politicians, public health became the key issue of urban reform programmes. At its meetings between the late 1920s and the late 1950s, the Congrès International d'Architecture Moderne (CIAM) developed an ideal alternative to the dark, dirty, filthy, tuberculosis-ridden European city towards a green, open, healthy, light, and therefore modern environment. The opposition of the "sick" and the "healthy" city dominated the architectural and urban discourse of the Modern Movement for decades. But this rhetoric was based on a one-dimensional understanding of health, an understanding that presupposed the possibility of abolishing crises, waste, or sickness by means of design. Architecture and urbanism were assigned the role of a prosthesis on the way towards an ideal condition of the human body, a kind of spatial and aesthetic treatment.

Following this argument, Le Corbusier developed visionary scenarios for cities like Paris or Zurich, erasing the existing inner-city structures and replacing them with high-rise constructions. The designs detached both the buildings and the humans living in them from the supposedly poisoned grounds, reducing contact with the ground to the sole element of the columns. It is no coincidence

that the buildings are to a large extent conceived to be white, the colour of an antiseptic state, with façades and roofs stripped of ornaments and any design elements that could disturb the pureness and therefore healthiness of his architectures. The profession's mandate to create order in a state of hygienic crisis became imperative. The problem of waste and the history of architecture seem to have become intertwined at the latest from this moment onwards. A similar mindset and the ensuing designs are to be found around the world until today, following a strategy that uses architecture to form barriers or borders to separate human beings from their own waste.

While in the meantime the concept of an ideal body that is only healthy when free of diseases, has been substituted by the idea of the body as an open, self-regulating system, waste is still perceived as an unwanted and "value-free" condition. As a self-regulating system, the body continuously oscillates between the extremes of healthy and sick, so that disease is understood as the necessary and integral precondition of defining health. In a way, the state of being sick is a motivation for our organism to change and develop and, by overcoming conditions of crisis, to define new, dynamic levels of a balanced status quo. George Canguilhem put it this way: "The healthy man does not flee from the problems posed by sometimes sudden disruptions of his habits, even physiologically; he measures his health in terms of his capacity to overcome organic crises in order to establish a new order."[21] Could a disease be in fact the true incentive for a constructive adaptation and therefore the precondition for human development? Could waste, in a similar sense, become an integral part of our architectural design philosophy instead of excluding it from the creative process?

This book tries to test this option by introducing alternative approaches to how architecture can be "modern" without falling into the trap of a linear thinking of separation and exclusion. We introduce new materials – and structures and buildings that come with them – that take waste not as a threat but as an opportunity.

WASTE AND SOCIETY

The science that studies the question of trash composition is called "garbology". In many instances it overlaps with the discipline of archaeology when it comes to determining the paths of social change, use of different materials and techniques, spiritual preferences, as well as nutrition compositions, which can all be traced through the analysis of the waste that a given civilization produced at a certain moment in time. Today, the rather young discipline of garbology is used to assess solid waste and figure out new ideas

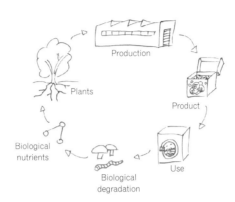

Biological cycle
for products for consumption

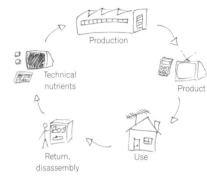

Technical cycle
for products for service

for waste management, for the formation of waste is changing radically. Urbanization and financial status of diverse societies tend to determine the type of waste generated. As people grow wealthier and move towards urban conglomerates, the percentage of inorganic substances in their waste increases, while organic substances account only for a decreasing share. In rural areas, by contrast, the biological and compostable components of waste still reach up to 85%, according to the Worldwatch Institute.[22]

The challenge for our society is more and more how to minimize our production of inorganic waste, and how to convert those inorganic substances in our garbage that are perhaps unavoidable into a resource. This is the essence when we talk about

a minimum- or even zero-waste society, following the four R's: Reduce, Reuse, Recycle, and Recover. This hierarchy of waste management, as it is often called, aims for a total circular metabolism in order to avoid any disposal at all. In the past two decades, this thinking has altered the behaviour of the younger generations in our society. It has become fashionable, for example, to buy accessories made out of reused truck canvases or other throw-outs. While this trend aims mostly at the reuse of materials and products, it could easily be expanded to apply also to the other three R's, leading to a society without waste production. A definition of such a zero-waste philosophy was developed by the *Zero Waste International Alliance* in 2004: "Zero Waste is a goal that is ethical, economical, efficient and visionary,

7 Cradle to Cradle is a registered trademark of McDonough Braungart Design Chemistry, LLC (MBDC).

to guide people in changing their lifestyles and practices to emulate sustainable natural cycles, where all discarded materials are designed to become resources for others to use. Zero Waste means designing and managing products and processes to systematically avoid and eliminate the volume and toxicity of waste and materials, conserve and recover all resources, and not burn or bury them. Implementing Zero Waste will eliminate all discharges to land, water or air that are a threat to planetary, human, animal or plant health."[23]

This definition introduces a socially responsible alternative to the present "take-make-throw" model. It places not only the producer, but also the consumer into an ethically active role to reuse waste products as a resource and to avoid waste production based on an unsustainable lifestyle.

As discussed above, the Cradle-to-Cradle concept aims in the same direction. In their book *Cradle to Cradle. Remaking the Way We Make Things,*[24] William McDonough and Michael Braungart suggest a logic of production based on a completely closed resource cycle, in contrast to a Cradle-to-Grave ideology that has been the dominant system in our societies so far. To emphasize their argument, they extended the four R's to a list of seven: Reduction, Reusing, Recycling, Recovering, Rethinking, Renovation, and

Regulation. Especially the last term in this enumeration, extends the responsibility from the manufacturers and consumers also to political decision-makers. By introducing new regulations, so the authors' hope, new thinkers and designers will enter the stage who start to see waste as what it should be: an incredible resource for the production of new goods. This holistic framework, incorporating ecologic, industrial, social, and economic principles, aims to create efficient systems that will ideally lead to a waste-embracing society, for more waste means more opportunities.

All of those models, whether successful or not at the present stage, comprehend waste not as a final and definite output of society that needs to be done away with, but as a renewable resource for a continuous doing and creating. The question at stake is: are we able to use this knowledge to change the nature, design, composition, or character of products lest they be seen as waste after their first life cycle?

URBAN MINING

Urban mining is a rather young phenomenon, embracing the process of reclaiming compounds and elements from wasted or at least undesired products or buildings that contain high levels of valuable materials. In their text "Mine the City", Ilka and Andreas

Ruby describe the contemporary shifting awareness that raw materials are not to be found anymore in a "natural" realm, but more and more in the "cultural" domain of buildings: "The material resources of construction are becoming increasingly exhausted at the place of their natural origins, while inversely accumulating within buildings. For example, today there is more copper to be found in buildings than in earth. As mines become increasingly empty, our buildings become mines in themselves."[25] In their view, the city is to be seen as a container of buildings and mines at the same time, much needed for its own reproduction.

Thomas E. Graedel of the Yale School of Forestry and Environmental Science combines his analysis of urban mining with the question of how much energy can be saved by recycling the wasted materials found in landfills or buildings. For him, buildings do not only store the materials to be recycled, but together with these a large amount of energy that could be reactivated. He argues that the reuse of aluminium that could be recycled from buildings needs only 5% of the energy originally used for its production. "Aluminium is extensively employed in buildings, but it does not remain permanently in place. Buildings are remodelled periodically, and even deconstructed, thereby freeing the aluminium for recycling. Therefore, it is not inaccurate to regard

Concrete, currently the most-used building material worldwide,[28] can play a vital role in this game. Francesco di Maio, a researcher at the Delft University of Technology, believes that "instead of transporting aggregates from far away, we can use local buildings as a source for aggregates."[29] He researches the option to recuperate aggregates like sand, pebbles, and small rocks on the one hand, and cement on the other, which would have the immense advantage that no additional CO_2 were to be released into the atmosphere, while original cement production is highly energy-consuming and CO_2-emitting. Tests have shown that concrete made out of recycled aggregates shows material qualities superior to those of samples made out of virgin aggregates.

Urban mining demonstrates a potential and possibility of how waste products can be resourced at the end of their first life span when entering a second, by being transformed, reshaped, remodeled, or reconfigured. But it also opens up the question of whether the consideration of the waste state of a product should not become the starting point of its design proper.

BUILDING FROM WASTE

The title of this book combines two terms that so far have been understood as separated entities, one – the waste – usually being

this aluminium as 'urban ore' and cities as 'urban mines'."[26]

Open urban landfills, which became illegal in most developed nations in the early 2000s or even before, were often transformed into parks or other public facilities after their closing. They currently undergo a complete renaissance, not as waste collection facilities, but as valuable sources for metals and rare earths. In Germany alone, 8.4 billion Euros were saved in the year 2009 by recycling valuable matters from waste products, and according to the Cologne Institute

for Economic Research, this amount can easily double by 2015.[27] However, opening up former landfills will also change our urban landscapes and many inhabitants are afraid of the health hazards emanating from dangerous substances formerly sealed with thick layers of soil. Therefore, it is the buildings that increasingly move into the focus of attention as containers of materials to be recovered, since the recycling of their components – instead of wholesale demolition – bears high potentials of regaining valuable materials, such as copper or aluminium, as described above.

8 The Rhyolite house, Death Valley, NV, USA, has been built out of 50,000 discarded glass bottles, a cheap construction resource in the desert. There is no distinction here between waste and supply. Photograph by Tom Kelly, 1926.

produced by the other – building – either through the act of production, construction, application, inhabitation, transformation, adaptation, or demolition. Following this logic, waste is a result of any human action and interaction, bringing natural raw materials – understood so far as our sole form of resources – from one stage of being into another, by applying various forms of skills and energy. In this sense, waste was seen for centuries as something specific that neither belonged to the family of natural resources nor to the one of finished products. Waste was a by-product, unable to be categorized in our dialectic understanding of raw vs. configured.

The book at hand tries to unfold the possibility of understanding waste as an integral part of what we define as a resource. We would thereby acknowledge its capacity to

figure as the required substance or matter from which to construct or configure a new product. And at the same time, the product could be seen as the supply source for other artefacts, after its first life span. This metabolic thinking conceives of our built environment as an interim stage of material storage, or to say it in the words of Mitchell Joachim, one of the contributors to this book: "The future city makes no distinction between waste and supply."[30]

If the prognoses of the Worldwatch Institute cited at the beginning of this introduction prove correct, namely that the world's growing population and prosperity will make the annual production of municipal solid waste double by 2025, its volume most probably increasing from today's 1.3 billion tons to 2.6 billion tons per year,[31] will we be able to activate this material for urban construction? If so, the concept of a circular metabolism could emerge whereby the city constantly produces the very matter it needs to grow without exploiting natural resources. Concepts for future cities call for architects and designers to think, work, and create in a holistic, circular spirit, incorporating ecologic, industrial, social, and economic principles that would allow them to create efficient systems whereby materials live through several states of formation and use over their entire life span, without ever being seen as waste matter.

Although various techniques and ideas were developed in recent decades of how to transform waste into desirable and therefore valuable goods, most of today's construction materials are still based on the knowledge, ideas, technologies, and cultural understandings developed in the age of industrialization, with an uncritical view towards the question of sustainability and availability of resources. As a first step, how can we categorize waste? We could do the obvious and sort it along material characteristics such as biological waste, plastic, glass, paper, etc. But is this the right way when talking about alternative building materials? We think it makes more sense to sort waste according to the types of processes that turn the unwanted into something valuable. Following such criteria of how to process waste, we have categorized the methods and procedures into five chapters: Densified, Reconfigured, Transformed, Designed, and Cultivated. The latter two might sound strange at first sight, but indeed we think that they hold the highest potential: dealing with the waste phase of a product from its conception onwards; and pursuing the promising idea that waste might become so attractive that it makes sense to grow more of it. By introducing this somewhat unconventional cataloguing system, we intend to unveil the hidden potentials of waste materials for future building products. Their use, continued reuse, and capacity of substituting other materials could become

9 New cultivated materials, grown from mushroom mycelium by Ecovative.

crucial factors in creating identity and local spirit as well as resource efficiency, and in making urban systems resilient by introducing local value chains and decreasing the dependency on foreign imports.

Starting on this positive note, it is also obvious that not all waste materials are suitable for such an approach. Chemical, medical, or even radioactive waste products need special treatment and are not part of our investigation. Nevertheless, the majority of waste products hold the potential we are looking for, especially household waste. In this sense, investigating the potential of refuse products as a resource for new construction materials could be a key factor for future sustainable building concepts.

This publication submits an inventory of current architectural projects and materials that can be seen as exemplary and at the cutting edge of this development. We do not address here the mere and simple recycle aspect of waste materials (sometimes known as adaptive reuse[32]). Recycling takes given objects as found in their context and re-applies them in different contexts and with different functions with little or no physical modifications. By contrast, our aim is to introduce an alternative way of thinking – food for thought – to a community of architects, builders, engineers, environmentalists, and economists, but

also to entrepreneurs who would consider capitalizing on one of the biggest resources available in our cities today: waste.

In the course of our research we realized more and more that thinking about waste as a resource for building materials is indeed a new concept and that there are few projects that have already used such products in a fully developed way. We decided therefore to emphasize this struggle for the new and showcase not only existing buildings and structures but also products and prototypes that have not yet found an application at the time of writing, even though they have the potential for success. Within the realm of research and development, we concentrated on applied research projects, leaving aside purely theoretical ones. A physical presence, and may it only be as a prototype or as a temporary construction, was a requirement for a product to be included here. We are of course aware of the fact that the emerging market for products made from waste is highly dynamic and that manufacturers and designers may change their product lines as mentioned here in very short time.

A dual reading and guiding system categorizes all products in two different ways. The five chapters as mentioned above give an overview of new construction materials produced out of waste and their application in building structures. This reading surveys

the products and applications according to their inherent properties. This is followed by a product directory structured according to the functions of their applications, allowing the reader to browse easily and efficiently for possible alternatives to common solutions. In addition to these two systematic approaches, three invited contributors and specialists in the field give insight in their daily work: Mitchell Joachim as an educator, researcher, and inventor of new ecological design strategies; Sascha Peters as an investigator of emerging alternative materials and author of several books about the subject; and Jörg Stollmann, an academic researcher and designer in the urban realm.

We hope that this book provides on overview for a wide range of professional readers, both practitioners and innovators in the field, and that this contemporary outline of knowledge, ideas, and research is able to play a vital role for future building concepts.

1 History and future of
garbage in New York City.

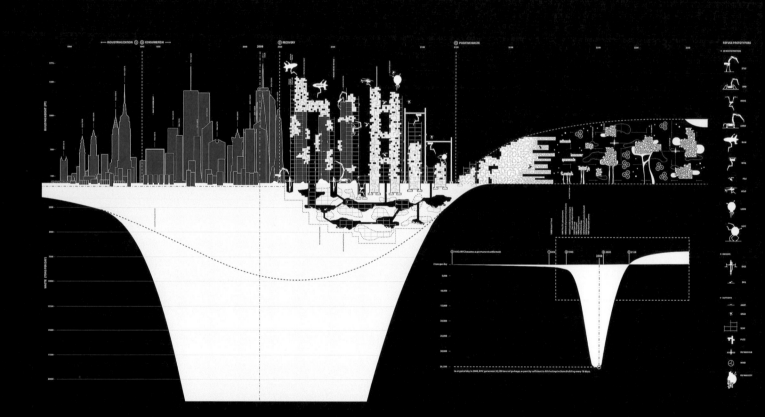

CITY AND REFUSE

SELF-RELIANT SYSTEMS AND URBAN TERRAINS

Mitchell Joachim

What is the key objective for ecological cities? A primary assertion for the city to come is that all necessities are provided from inside its physical borders. In this intensified version, all vital commodities for its population are provided by the city itself. In this city, food, water, air quality, energy, waste, mobility, and shelter are radically restructured to support life in every form. Infrastructure is celebrated as the new centre of the city.

This strategy includes the replacement of dilapidated structures with vertical agriculture and the merging of housing with road networks. Former streets become snaking arteries of liveable spaces embedded with renewable energy sources, soft cushion-based vehicles, and productive green rooms. The former street grid provides the foundation for up-to-the-minute networks: by re-engineering the obsolete streets, we can install radically robust and ecologically active smart pathways.

These considerations are not just about a comprehensive model of tomorrow's city, but are meant to provide an initial platform for discourse. Urban designers must expect that the future will necessitate marvellous dwellings to be coupled with a massive cyclical resource net.

RAPID RE(F)USE, 3D FABRICATED POSITIVE WASTE ECOLOGIES

In this context, imagine our colossal municipal landfills turning into sensible resource sheds to build our future urban and peri-urban spaces. Now that the bulk of humanity has chosen to settle in urbanized areas, waste management needs a radical revision. What kind of effort is required to reuse the landfill's bountiful contents? For hundreds of years we designed cities to generate waste. Now it is time that we begin to design waste to regenerate our cities. What are the possibilities for urban environments when our aged infrastructure has been recalibrated? How might urban intensification and waste mix?

Terreform ONE's supposition is to reallocate resource streams to flow in a positive direction.[1] In this case, waste is not faintly recycled through infrastructural mechanisms but instead up-cycled in perpetuity.

America is the lead creator of waste on the earth, making approximately 30% of the world's trash and tossing out 0.72 tons per US citizen per year.[2] Ungracefully, our American value system is somewhat distressed. It seems that value has devolved into rampant waste production: mega-products scaled for super-sized franchise brands, big-box retail, XXL jumbo paraphernalia, and so on. The US mindset is thus encapsulating a joint race for ubiquity and instantaneity. Where does it all end up? Heather Rogers, in her investigative book *Gone Tomorrow*,[3] affirmed that throwing things away is unsustainable. The first step we must take is reduction – meaning a massive discontinuation of objects designed for obsolescence. Then we need a radical reuse plan.

One such dilemma lurks in New York. New York City is currently disposing of 32,840 tons of waste per day.[4] Previously, most of this

discarded material ended up in Fresh Kills on Staten Island, before operations were blocked. Manhattan's inhabitants discard enough paper products to fill a volume the size of the Empire State Building every two weeks. Terreform ONE's Rapid Re(f)use and Homeway projects strive to capture, reduce, and redesign New York's refuse infrastructure. The initiative supposes an extended city reconstituted from its own junked materials. The concept remakes the city by utilizing all the trash entombed in the Fresh Kills landfill. Theoretically, the method should produce, at a minimum, seven entirely new Manhattan

Islands at full scale. New York City's premier landfill was once started by Robert Moses and driven by apathetic workers and machines.[5] Now, guided by a prudent community with smart equipment, we must reshape it.

How could this work? Outsized automated 3D printers could be modified to rapidly process trash and to complete the task within decades. These potential automatons would be entirely based on existing techniques commonly used in industrial waste compaction devices. To accomplish this job, nothing drastically new needs to be invented. Most technologies are intended to be off-the-shelf. Instead of machines that crush objects into cubes, compaction devices could benefit from adjustable jaws that would craft simple shapes into smart 'puzzle blocks' for assembly. The blocks of waste material could be predetermined, using computational geometries, in order to fit domes, archways, lattices, windows, or whatever patterns would be needed. Different materials could serve specified purposes: transparent plastic for fenestration, organic compounds for temporary decomposable scaffolds, metals for primary structures, and so on. Eventually, the future city would make no distinction between waste and supply.

Admittedly, this meta-design theme is not entirely novel. At approximately the same time that Rapid R(e)fuse was initiated, the

2 Every hour New York City produces enough waste to fill the Statue of Liberty.

trash compaction and distribution device. His name is an acronym: Waste Allocation Load Lifter Earth Class. Left behind by mankind, he toils with trillions of tons of non-recycled inner-city trash. Not only is WALL-E a highly advanced rubbish manager, he also is a mechanized and inventive architect. He accomplishes his immense tasks while remaining completely adorable. Not easy to do.

WALL-E's life is a tale of an ultramodern trash compactor in love. Ceaselessly, he configures mountains of discarded material. Why pyramids of trash? WALL-E's daily perpetual feats seem almost futile. Disney omits exactly why he is programmed to pile refuse; and there is the shortcoming.

FUTURE WASTE AND PAST CITIES

Collaborators at Terreform ONE were interested in exploring a deeper motivation for stacking refuse. Similar to the Disney film, what if the refuse was refabricated to become real urban spaces or buildings? If it is plausible to adapt current machinery, how much material is available? At first sight, any sanitary landfill may be viewed as an ample supply of building nutrients. Heavy industrial technologies to compact cars into lumber or to automatically sort out garbage are readily available. Other technologies, which would make possible the articulation of specific

feature film *WALL-E* was conceptualized.[6] The film profoundly infused Terreform ONE's research agenda.

EXCURSION TO DISNEYLAND

Inspired by an equal interest in fictional productions of tomorrow such as Disney's *Tomorrowland*, Terreform ONE visited the Walt Disney Imagineering (WDI) headquarters in Glendale, Southern California. The group had prepared a presentation that would unpack a comprehensive view of its version of the future: a world free of carbon

loading in the atmosphere and abundant in self-sufficient lifestyles. As architects invested in an ecological future vision, the team had meticulously crafted cities within the rubric of a socio-ecological domain – rethinking the design of entire systems, from doorknobs to democracies.

When Ben Schwegler, mastermind and chief imagineer, pulled back the proverbial curtain to reveal WALL-E, the group was crestfallen. Disney had beaten them to it. WALL-E was perfect – almost: a tightly packaged, solar-powered, curious, obedient, evolved robotic

3 A spectacle of smart infrastructure highlights in the new downtown.

forms, are also available if scaled in larger sizes. 3D printing has exhaustive capabilities if adjusted to larger scales. This is where Terreform ONE's city began.

The envisioned city would be derived from trash; not ordinary trash, but "smart refuse". A significant factor of the city composed from smart refuse is "post-tuning", as unitized devices would not immediately adapt. Integration into the city texture would be a learning process. In time, the responses would eventually become more attenuated to the needs of the urban dweller. This city is envisioned from trash, but each individual component would be enhanced with a modicum of CPU power. Brief durational events would endow these "smart units" with experiences needed for their evolution.

The main objective for the city of Rapid R(e)fuse is to establish a smart, self-sufficient, perpetual-motion urbanism. It has been advocated that perpetual motion cannot exist. Perpetual motion defies the laws of thermodynamics and energy conservation, since it would necessitate a machine that produces more energy than it consumes. Cities, unlike machines, are similar to a complex ecology.[7] Ecology is capable of achieving a continuous harmonious state, or even further, a positive intensification. If ecological models are productively everlasting, urban models can logically follow. What if the Rapid R(e)fuse city was like an instrument that produces more energy from renewable sources than the energy it consumes? In this case, nothing can be thrown away. Every bit would be a vital piece of stored energy, poised to be reused in a cyclical nutrient stream.[8] Rapid R(e)fuse is imagined as a city without a tail pipe; a city that not only has zero impact, but a positive contribution towards the natural surroundings.

John Fitzgerald Kennedy once declared: "Our problems are man-made, therefore they may be solved by man."[9] The matter posed on the table is not only about solving our ecological issues, but also about returning to a system of perpetuity. This is the only possible future for a truly breathing, interconnected, metabolic urbanism. Cities have passed the age of industrialization and entered the age of recovery. After this great cleansing, we may transition into in a greater order: "positive waste". Here is an order that captures our socio-ecological needs: not utopia, but a place where everything is precious and nothing is disposed.

ENVISIONING ECOLOGICAL CITIES

How should urban design foresee new instrumentalist technologies for cities? For 150 years, the innovation of the elevator has done more to influence urban design than most urban designers. Elevator systems had incredible success in the creation of compact and greener cities. Imagine what the advent of the jet pack will do for cities. Urban design is greatly altered by such devices. For instance, automobiles have defined limits in cities for almost a century. Unlike the elevator, however, the car has arguably caused more problems than it has solved. Perhaps it is time for urban design to rethink technologies to fit cities, not constrain them. As a wide-ranging discipline, it can effortlessly illuminate the technological potentials for cities. Urban design will successfully situate itself through the production of future macro-scaled scenarios predicated on innovative devices.

Physicist and polymath Freeman Dyson has said that the best way to comprehend our near urban future is to examine science fiction, not economic forecasts. In his experience, sci-fi is good for decades of technological fulfilment. Unfortunately, economic forecasts are only accurate within five to ten years. Most of these predictive economic models are quantity-based and find it difficult to extrapolate the qualifiers associated with creativity. Sci-fi is a phenomenal way to chronicle our plausible urban future that should not be dismissed by urban designers. Dyson is certain that the urban era of information will soon transition into "the age of domesticated biotechnology."[10]

In his novel *Infinite in All Directions*, he states: "Bio-tech offers us the chance to imitate nature's speed and flexibility." He envisions a realm of functional objects and art that humans will "grow" for personal use. According to a *New York Times* article on Dyson, "The Civil Heretic", he also believes that climate change is profoundly misstated. "He added the caveat that if CO_2 levels soared too high, they could be soothed by the mass cultivation of specially bred 'carbon-eating trees.'"[11] He is not concerned with predicting the future but rather with expressing the possibilities. These expressions are founded along societal desire lines as a kind of relevant optimism. Therefore Dyson measures the wants of civilization and advances our expectations.

At some level, urban design engages this position that promises a better tomorrow. Numerous practitioners and urbanists mildly suffer from this invariable search for direction and clairvoyance. Alex Krieger strongly asserts that the broadly defined vocation is more of a scrupulous sensibility than an exclusive authority.[12] The profession is torn between many incompatible agendas, weighty theories and oversimplified applications, ivory towers and new urbanism, developer brands and radical ecologies, and vernacular forms and futurology. One of my research group's chief directives is about shrewdly locating the intersection of

technology and urbanism, especially under the rubric of ecology. Our projects range from highlighting the possible effects of self-sufficient cities to studying flocks of jet packs. These ideations keep us thriving as urban design researchers. It is our supposition that the prospective ecological city is about extreme solutions to an extreme predicament. Our future fundamentally depends on the immensity our solutions envision.

We foresee strategies for people to fit symbiotically into their natural surrounds. To achieve this, all things possible are considered. We design the scooters, cars, trains, and blimps, as well as the streets, parks, open spaces, cultural districts, civic centres, and business hubs that comprise the future metropolis. For centuries cities have been designed to accommodate the theatre of our human desire. We have joined the ranks of those delivering a new sense of the city, one that privileges the play of nature over anthropocentric whims. We are constantly vying for a profound clairvoyant perspective. We desire to preview a likeness of our collective future yet untold.

Our foresight of ecological design is not only a philosophy that inspires visions of sustainability but also a focused scientific endeavour. The mission is to ascertain the consequences of fitting a project within our natural environment. Solutions are

derived from numerous examples: living material habitats, climatic tall building clusters, and mobility technologies. These design iterations succeed as having activated ecology both as a productive symbol and an evolved artefact. Current research attempts to establish new forms of design knowledge and new processes of practice at the interface of design, computer science, structural engineering, and biology.

4 View of clean tech industrial water park (top); site with five retrofitted dry docks for green manufacturing (bottom).

1 Berlin Kreuzberg,
Mariannenstraße 39–41:
three buildings erected
in 1964 by two private
proprietors via the *Aufbauprogramm* (reconstruction
programme).

HANDS OFF:
URBAN MINING!

A PLEA FOR THE RE-EVALUATION
OF SUBSTANDARD HOUSING

Jörg Stollmann

The term 'urban mining' describes the potential to comprehend our cities as resource reservoirs. Those reservoirs can be tapped in order to retrieve materials for the production of new goods, including the city itself. In the same way as we have excavated natural building and construction materials from beneath the earth crust for the longest time, lately we have started to mine former landfills in and around our cities. In this process we unearth solid waste materials, mostly valuable metals or rare earths, and it is assumed that the occurrence of such substances is by now higher in human-made dump sites than in the natural realm. The second field for urban mining is the building stock proper. Since the material resources used in the building sector have been accumulated in our cities for centuries, they are more and more exhausted at their places of origin. The mines of the future are therefore not underground, they are to be found in our built environment.

In recent decades the life expectancy of buildings has been shrinking due to a predominantly economic valuation of architectural objects. Once the investment costs are written off and revenues are earned, the buildings become ambiguous from an economic point of view. Often high maintenance costs and low rent levels minimize the profit and make a demolition and replacement worthwhile. This is the moment in the process when the building rubble can become part of an urban mining process. But there is another alternative strategy in the context of urban mining that has not been conceptualized yet: the strategy of keeping the old structures and spatial arrangements in place as long as possible. Beyond their economic productivity for the owner, buildings have social, cultural, and ecological values that contribute to a city's and a society's resilience. More importantly, beyond the property owner's economic motives, there is a societal, macroeconomic accounting, which shows the building stock in a different light: as a resource for affordable housing.

Taking a closer look at the post-World War Two building stock in Berlin, Germany, this essay proposes a mind shift by introducing an understanding of urban mining as a strategy of re-evaluating buildings in relation to the livelihood of the urban. A key idea of this approach is to understand substandard housing as an adequate, although temporary, reservoir of affordable housing, of which almost every city worldwide disposes in abundance. This means considering substandard housing not as waste but as a resource for urban resilience. The urban housing stock can be made part of a process of constant transformation and adaptation, without ever ending up as waste. While this would respond to the need for decent housing for the economically weaker urban population, there are of course many more agendas and stakeholders at play. Therefore, the question of transformation versus replacement requires innovative and considerate governance measures and has to be supported by the adequate rules and regulations, incentives for the owners, and ideally, a different tenant-based subsidy programme. Instead of demolition, one could say that a "consummation" of those buildings might make sense. For this purpose they need to be left alone: "Hands Off – Urban Mining!"

THE BERLIN HOUSING CRISIS AND THE INVISIBLE HOUSING RESOURCE

Berlin is facing a housing crisis. With a growing city and a backlog in housing construction, the market has failed to provide for the livelihood of Berlin's citizens. Unaware of shrinking housing resources until a few years ago, a recent report of the Investitionsbank Berlin indicates that a yearly minimum of 10,000 new apartments are needed. Due to the high demand, rents are increasing;[1] at the same time, Berlin is

expected to grow to a very large extent in low-income population. It is expected that one out of three Berliners will depend on basic security benefits and aid money.

In 2001, the federal government's social housing programme was replaced by a number of benefit and subsidy programmes delegated to the states, the Länder. In the case of the poorer states like Berlin, this decision entailed the termination of any new building activity for the low-income sector. At the same time, subsidized apartments continuously reach the end of their public co-financing timeframe and subsequently increase in rent. As a consequence, entire inner-city neighbourhoods are facing rents that do not match their household income by far. Experts and the politically engaged public alike are advocating new public funding programmes to subsidize at least 30% of the new construction to be affordable for low-income groups. Another request is to sell or better even lease state-owned land for affordable housing construction below market prices. Yet as the Berlin state budget is in deficit, both strategies are not very likely to be implemented consistently enough to meet the demand.[2] So where will Berliners with lower incomes live in the near future?

Tracing the areas where the rents (exclusive of heating) still meet the basic social security benefit standard[3] via satellite photography,

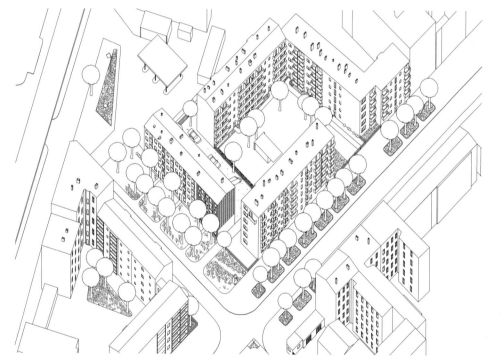

2 The buildings were erected on war destruction sites within the perimeter of the Berlin urban block. Pre-war buildings stock's rubble was recycled as a building material.

an invisible Berlin comes into sight: the housing stock that was built shortly after World War Two. Nearly one out of six apartments in Berlin date back to the period of the 1950s and 1960s. They were built expeditiously at the time, as after the war Berlin citizens were either cohabiting crowded apartments that had withstood the massive bombing or had retreated to self-built shacks and *Schrebergarten* sheds in the periphery. On closer inspection, most of those post-War buildings are plain and ordinary, almost invisible compared with the originally ornate pre-war façades. On their shabby fronts, next to the main door, they often carry a brass emblem depicting the Berlin Bear, the engraving *Aufbauprogramm* (reconstruction programme) and the year of their erection. This reconstruction programme was the first post-war governmental initiative to generate extensive housing fast, especially in the part of the city that was to become West Berlin after the building of the Berlin Wall in 1961.

The reconstruction programme focused on filling in urban gaps and building on wastelands by supporting private, mostly smaller investors. Mostly four to five-story residential blocks, few high-rises and a number of building estates were fitted into the existing Berlin building block structure and between the Gründerzeit development. Other than the outstanding examples of architectural and urban design of this period, like the

1957 Interbau Hansaviertel, most of the buildings supported by this programme were cheaply built. At the time of construction, the buildings were considered resourceful in the use of material and space, for instance by reusing rubble of the World War Two destructions. Today, these buildings are waste in the eyes of the real estate developers because of their mediocre material quality, low ceilings, and constricted floor plans. What is more, these buildings do not meet the current energy regulations; the insulation of walls and windows and the technical infrastructure are far below standard. For a long time, while the Berlin housing market

was stagnating, an extensive renovation was too expensive in relation to the expected rent. Only today, the backlog in housing brings this option back and would in fact make it economically feasible.

There are two perspectives to critically re-evaluating this housing stock and to rethinking an alternative to destruction or luxury refurbishment. From the individual perspective of the occupant, the buildings have increasingly taken on a role as a safeguard from being forced to move out and leave the neighbourhood for the urban edge. From the other perspective of the advocates

3 While Mariannenstraße 39 was renovated in the 1980s, Mariannenstraße 40 and 41 have not been remodeled since their original construction.

With a rent in the realm of 4.80 Euro/m² (not including operating expenses and heating), rents are at about half the price of average rents in this neighbourhood.

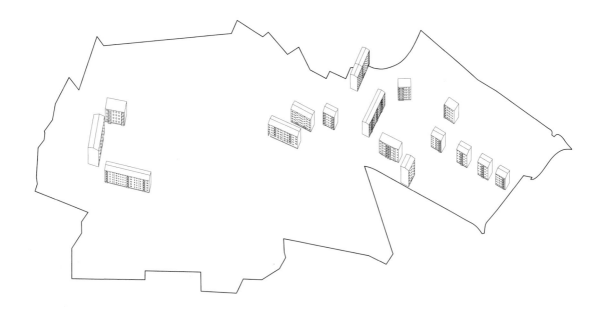

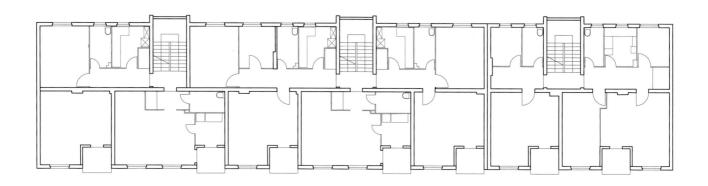

4 16 buildings in the neighbourhood, identified on a field trip in 2013, are comparable to Mariannenstraße 39–41 in building construction and present condition.

5 Reconstructed floor plan according to the 1964 construction permit.

of an inclusive city, they provide affordable housing in the inner city and thus allow for a wide social mix – a traditionally strong characteristic of Berlin's urbanity, which is being challenged or has already been lost in neighbourhoods like Prenzlauer Berg and Mitte. Both perspectives point in the same direction: one should not waste this potential.

In order to assess the buildings' real value for an inclusive urbanity infinitely more data would be required.[4] A rough estimation for Berlin could be derived from the figure of 272,000 apartments implemented between 1952 and 1968.[5] The Association Competence Centre for Large Housing Estates[6] in Berlin has repeatedly pointed out this "academic void" of missing data and is currently preparing a first report as a starting point for further research on the topic as a basis for developing new scenarios for what to do with this immense resource.

HANDS OFF – URBAN MINING!

Urban mining, understood as the maintenance and adaptation of the existing substandard urban building stock, will be consequential to urban governance policies. Private and public property owners have to be stimulated to cautious renovation measures that prevent the buildings from degeneration while having minimal effect on the rent (inclusive of heating). Instead

of subsidizing primarily new building activities – as was common and is planned to do again – new political instruments and financial incentives should be established to attract public as well as private investors to push for a rethinking of how to handle the neglected building stock of the 1950ies and 60ies. One option could be the founding of housing cooperatives or associations, where the tenants become fully or partially owners of their own apartments. This should be combined with new subsidy programmes for the active transformation of living space could be initiated to help the individual tenants – instead of financing investor lead programmes. To implement both strategies on a larger scale, a new set of rules and regulations will have to be established. Even mixed models, whereby the public purse invests in the structural and infrastructural components and private investors or the tenants themselves in the added value spatial arrangements, would be conceivable. All of these options have one principle in common: they prevent the destruction of the existing buildings and enable the tenants to determine how expenses and gains will be negotiated.

Such a no-waste urban mining approach to the existing built fabric would not least entail a revised understanding of building conservation. The object to be protected would be conceived as liveable unit of space, anchored in a historical, cultural, and social environment and as being a part of a human support structure of the city. The priority would indeed be on conservation, but in the sense that the building's material condition or design value would rank second. In a broader view on the matter, however, conservation would become a moving target and waste would take on the character of being just a transitory state within a metabolic understanding of the urban landscape.

DENSIFIED WASTE MATERIALS

CASE STUDIES

Airless p. 36
Ubuntublox p. 40
Corrugated Cardboard Pod p. 42
PHZ2 p. 44
NewspaperWood p. 46
Enviro Board (E-Board) p. 50
Strohhaus p. 52
Strawjet p. 54
Sustainable Emerging City Unit (SECU) p. 56
Decafe Tiles p. 60

The most obvious and direct way to process waste materials into building construction elements is densification. The garbage press, today a standard equipment in solid waste management and already introduced in England in the 19th century, is mainly intended to reduce the volume of refuse through compacting. The principle of these machines is always the same: waste products often come as a loose mix with a low bulk density. The handling of this type of waste is difficult and in order to cope with it, waste recycling companies have developed special methods to transform loose solid waste substances into units that are easy to handle. One option is to place the material in a mould and compress it into manageable bales, which are then striped in order to keep them from dissolving. Alternatively, the loose stuff is pressed into small pellets uniform in shape and with a much higher bulk density compared to the incoming material. Many plastics, sorted or unsorted, lend themselves to densification and are subsequently fed into an extrusion process to create the new products. Pellets produced out of waste resources such as sawdust, wood chips, bark remains, recycled paper, textile residues, or even manure, have lately become an important energy source for heating systems worldwide. They are known as Recycled Densified Fuel (RDF) products. In both ways of processing, the original material remains unchanged in terms of chemical composition; it is also neither disintegrated nor manipulated in its physical form, or mixed to form composits.

On a popular level, Pixar's cinematic take on the garbage press and the theme of waste materials is the animated movie *Wall-E* (Pixar, 2008), which playfully demonstrates the potential of compressed waste blocks for the construction sector. Wall-E is relentlessly collecting trash into his belly, pressing it to condensed little bricks which fall literally out of him. Towards the end of the sequence, activating these added values of new material properties, the small robot builds a series of skyscrapers out of its creator's leftovers, constructing a new city skyline out of garbage.

The chapter "Densified Waste Materials" addresses products and processes based on the principle of compressed refuse. The act of pressing stores energy in the system, resulting in a higher state of material properties. The ensuing reduction of volume is not the main goal, rather a tool to activate a specific potential within a specific waste product. Straw, for example, an agricultural by-product still considered waste in many societies, contains starch, which when activated by pressure turns into a natural glue usable in straw panels, columns, beams, and many other products. One could argue that straw is not a genuine waste product; yet the ubiquitous habit of burning it on

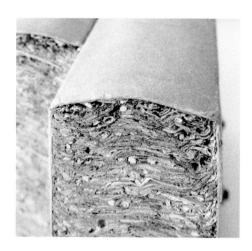

the fields after the harvest creates harmful substances that are emitted into the air, turning the material into a waste problem. Another objection would be that straw and other organic materials are biodegradable and can be composted to enrich the soil, hence should remain part of an organic life cycle. We see a potential in abstracting these from the regular cycle for a limited period, using them as a building material before feeding them back into the earth's natural metabolic system.

Several products emerging from a densification process are introduced here. Most of them share one specific property: they have exceptional insulation characteristics, thermally as well as acoustically. This is a result of their very high degree of compactness, which also usually results in a remarkably

high fire resistance due to the elimination of air in the material. Both straw and paper show this potential in compressed form, despite their rating as "easy inflammable" in a loose material configuration.

Nevertheless, all of the presented products require waterproofing in one or the other way. No water or moisture should reach the material during construction or after implementation. It needs either special design provisions or else an immense material thickness to protect these products' properties.

Similar to straw, paper materials can be pressed into very strong and durable packages and used as construction elements. The Corrugated Cardboard Pod project activates waxed cardboard materials, which are taken out of the waste stream and pressed into larger bales. Due to their original surface treatment, they resist water penetration and therefore decomposition. The cardboard contains no ink or other chemical liquids which could harm the immediate environment or users of buildings – an important consideration when thinking of recycled paper for the construction process.

In an almost ironic way, the materials introduced here do allow for a "wasteful" handling and application, since they are cheap, available in huge quantities, as well as easy to access and manage. They store

an overcapacity of materiality and properties, something to which architects and designers are not used anymore, since efficiency and slimness became mandatory parameters of the contemporary design process. "More" material to be used in the act of building could actually mean "less" waste.

Similar to compression, negative pressure – in other words a vacuum condition – can be used to create construction elements. A temporary pavilion structure in Zurich utilizes PET bottles enclosed in a preformed membrane. The induced additional friction between the bottles, resulting from the membrane pressing the bottles together in a vacuum, ties the PET elements into a closed structural system. We all know this principle from peanut packages, where this technology has been in use for decades. But it did not enter the design concepts of architects, designers, or engineers. This might change in the future, since many waste products could be used in this context. An additional benefit is that the membrane functions not only as a barrier between the two different air pressure conditions, but also as a protection layer for the contained.

The process of densification neither alters nor changes the utilized refuse product. Consequently, densified waste materials can be seen as a temporary material storage for future construction elements or the

1 Compressed straw waste can easily be densified to create load-bearing construction panels.

"regrowing" of materials: after deconstruction, straw could be decomposed, bottles reused, transformed, or reconfigured. In this sense, the processes described here belong to the family of long-term strategies. As long as the materials are not mixed with others or glued together or changed in any other form, they can easily be sorted and recycled again after use in a densified product.

The methods described here are emphatically low-tech, resulting in a wide range of applications and possible production locations, requiring a minimum amount of energy to produce them. Since waste is a universal challenge, densification can be a feasible solution for developing and developed regions alike, creating building elements close to the site of construction. Current urbanization rates show that the majority of future cities will be built in developing regions. Most of the countries concerned have no or little access to heavy industry products such as steel, cement, or machinery. The use of waste materials and a continuous research and development effort geared towards their recovery for, and sustainable application in, the building process may be a viable option to avoid the current dependency from importing outside resources. It would also open up entrepreneurial thinking and making use of the biggest resource that these countries can provide today: people and their brain power.

Given the specific method of production, the products presented in this chapter are mainly structural building elements or insulation panels. Combining both applications, depending on the context and the local raw material, densified waste materials could provide the construction material for entire buildings. The selected case studies show this potential in various ways.

2 Discarded PET bottles
form a vacuumized
structural building element.

AIRLESS

Polyethylene Terephthalate (PET) is one of the most common consumer plastics worldwide, best known in products for containing food, such as bottles or jars. PET bottles form the most obvious part of the yearly production for the consumer. Intended to be recycled in a circular economy mentality, in reality the majority of PET products worldwide end up as waste. This happens despite the fact that PET products are typically easy to be recycled, forming granulates or flakes that can be turned into new products. By contrast, when PET is discarded, many problems arise: PET products are extremely long-lasting and hardly degradable. Once PET has entered the food cycles, for example floating as fine aggregates in the oceans, it remains for a long time in our environment and may harm organisms like fish and ultimately human beings. Incineration is no real alternative, as it produces toxic by-products that are harmful for our environment and health.

New technologies may allow to pursue the strategy of extending the PET waste products recycle process and store the material for a certain time in our built environment. Following this approach, Airless uses empty PET bottles by packing them into prefabricated arch-shaped and airtight foil tubes that are vacuumed once they are completely filled. This process creates a lightweight and extremely efficient load-bearing element that can be used to create large-span spatial structures. The ensuing system can be controlled according to various parameters: the higher the negative pressure resulting from the vacuum condition, the higher is the friction between the bottles, resulting in a more rigid system. The maximum load capacity of such elements depends also on the quality of the bottles used. Closed bottles, containing still some amount of air, have a higher resistance against vacuumization and also against pressure, they are harder, while open bottles form a softer system with less capacity to absorb external forces.

The design of such load-bearing structural elements requires a complex understanding of the shrinkage process. Tests showed that the vacuumized system shrinks in height and diameter by around 7% in relation to the original cut of the vacuum tube. This has to be taken into account when designing the details and especially the connection points to non-shrinking elements, such as membranes or pressure members.

1 Discarded PET bottles can be the base for an alternative construction method. Placed into airtight tubes, the system is vacuumized and forms a structural rigid building element.

2 The resource: discarded PET Bottles of all sizes and types.

PROJECT DATA

RESOURCE
Discarded PET bottles

MANUFACTURER
Luft & Laune, Zurich,
Switzerland

DESIGNER
Assistant Professorship
of Architecture and
Construction Dirk E. Hebel,
ETH Zurich/FCL Singapore,
Singapore, and Zurich,
Switzerland

PRODUCT DIRECTORY
Load-bearing, page 173

PRODUCT DATA

STANDARD SIZE
Custom

STANDARD THICKNESS
Custom

DENSITY
53 kg/m^3

FIRE RATING
Fire-retardant B1
(DIN EN 13501) for
vacuum foil tube

PRESSURE
22–25 mbar

3 Vacuumized arches
with PET bottles inside.
Prototype of Airless built
at ETH Zurich in 2014.

3

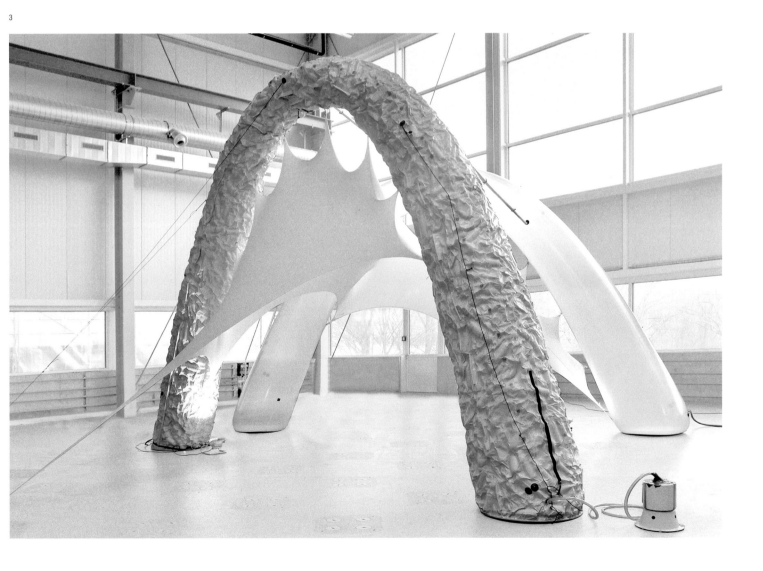

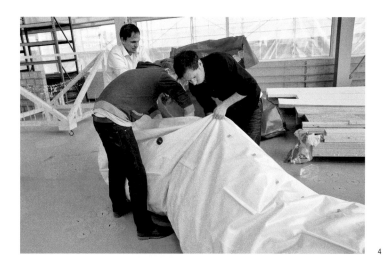

4

5

6

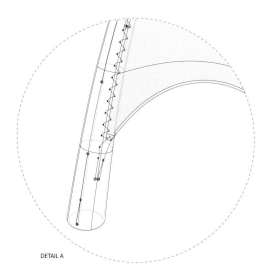

DETAIL A

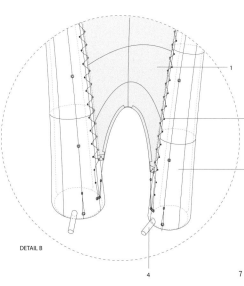

DETAIL B

4   7

4 As a first step, the empty PET bottles are put in place inside the tubes.

5 The arch is vacuumized lying on the floor, before being raised to its final vertical position.

6 Vacuumized structure: once the air is sucked out from the tubes, the compressed bottles create a robust structural system through friction.

7 Connection details between the tubes and a membrane. The arches are equipped with special hooks that allow for easy interlacing of the fabric strings.

1   membrane
2   thread eye connection
3   foil tube
4   vent

8 The Airless arch system can be constructed out of various foil types, addressing different functional and aesthetic properties.

8

9

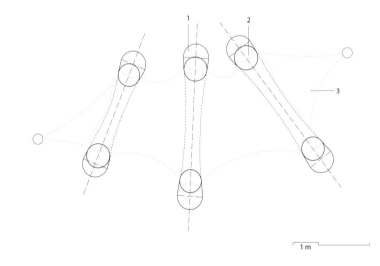

9 Plan view of one of countless possible arrangements. The membrane, however, is designed for specific configurations.

1   foil tube
2   PET bottles
3   membrane

10 Cross section of a possible arrangement, showing a membrane structure connected to the arches.

1   foil tube
2   PET bottles
3   membrane

1 m

10

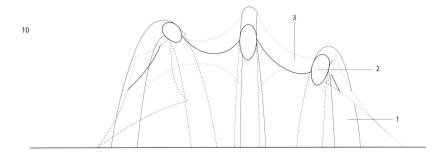

UBUNTUBLOX

After the 2010 Haiti earthquake, the *New York Times*[1] reported that the government of the island estimated that more than 280,000 buildings were destroyed and an even bigger number was damaged or cut from any infrastructural support. In the aftermath of the destructive event, the fence-builder and inventor Harvey Lacey developed a simple press to mechanically condense widely available plastic waste into building blocks for shelter housing, called Ubuntublox. The hand-operated apparatus was built locally and with the exception of some screws, all material was sourced on Haiti. The device is intended to be simple to use and to be transported by a single person, the homebuilder himself.

While the press worked well from the beginning, questions about the material arose. First prototypes made from unsorted plastic waste proved successful from a structural point of view, yet on the economic side the material used was too valuable: at a weight of about 3 kg per block, the required plastics could be redeemed at conventional recycling centres for about 35 to 70 USD cents (the price being a function of the fluctuating market price of oil, since plastic is a petroleum product). In a 2.00-USD-per-day economy, a typical occurrence in developing nations, the plastics from three building blocks

were equal to a day's wage. Therefore, the project started concentrating its efforts on materials with no value: film and foam plastics.

In an attempt to collect film and foam plastics for a library project in Custin, a small village outside Cavillione in Haiti, the team realized that not nearly enough of this material was available for free for such a construction. As a suitable substitute, an organic waste product was discovered: discarded vetiver roots. Vetiver roots are distilled into essential oils, the number one export product from Haiti in terms of earning. The leftovers from the extraction process are usually burned but unfortunately, they mostly smoulder if no accelerant is used. In Haiti, people use motor oil to speed up this process, which of course seriously contributes to air pollution. But vetiver roots turned out to be a very good raw material for Ubuntublox. Naturally insect and fungi-resistant, the material can be easily compacted and is widely available. Due to the natural fibre and rough surface of the compressed material, the finished blocks can also easily be plastered to give the house any desired outer finish. Up to this day, the press remains an easy-to-use and easy-to-maintain apparatus that can be operated by a single worker wherever a suitable material can be found.

1

1 Densified Ubuntublox made from organic waste material derived from vetiver roots provide an organic building material.

2 The press is designed to allow one person to transport and operate it.

1   plastic waste or
    vetiver roots
2   wires
3   threaded rod
4   wire notches in ram
5   compression wheel
6   metal lids
7   spacing for wires in
    back construction

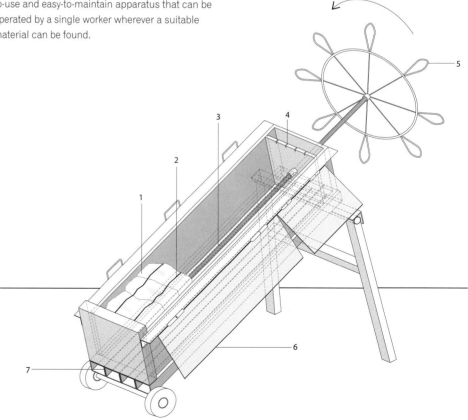

2

3 Ubuntublox made from discarded plastic waste are used to build a small test house. The system is reinforced with steel rods for structural stability.

4 The first prototype of Ubuntublox used unsorted plastic at the Community Centre in Port-au-Prince.

3

4

PROJECT DATA

RESOURCE
Plastic waste or
vetiver roots waste

MANUFACTURER
AND DESIGNER
Harvey Lacey, New York
City, NY, USA

PRODUCT DIRECTORY
Load-bearing, page 175;
Insulating, page 183

PRODUCT DATA

STANDARD SIZE
200 mm × 400 mm

STANDARD THICKNESS
200 mm

DENSITY
225 kg/m³

THERMAL INSULATION
Very high, no scientific
information

FIRE RATING
No information
(under testing)

SPECIAL PROPERTY
Insect-repelling

CORRUGATED CARDBOARD POD

Corrugated cardboard is well known for its lightweight character and high rigidity. The material is named for its fluted inner layer that is usually placed on one or in between two sheets of linerboard. This sandwich composition makes the material resistant to impacts and attractive for use for shipping boxes. Corrugated packaging is the biggest application industry for the material with nearly 1,500 box plants in the USA, according to the American Association of Independent Corrugated Converters. Cutting the unfolded box shape out of the boards produces large amounts of waste: there is an average of 22 tons of disposal of this highly engineered product in a box factory per day. The production remains, especially those impregnated with wax, are usually pressed into bales and sent to incineration plants or landfills for decomposition, as the recycling of the material would often be more costly than producing it anew.

The Corrugated Cardboard Pod, an experimental housing project constructed in 2001 at the campus of Auburn University, explores the possibility to activate this vast waste material pool for the building sector. The structural capabilities, thermal mass potentials, and insulation values convinced the designers to explore the waste cardboard bales as potential unconventional building elements. In a first prototypical building, the bales are incorporated in both the foundation system and the wall structure, using them as load-bearing elements.

The use of the boards in bundled bales rather than loose material allows for an efficient and modular construction approach. The cubes are placed in a running-bond pattern, derived from masonry. Due to the friction resulting from the rather high weight and rough surfaces of each bale, there is no need for any additional support or reinforcement. The gaps between the bales are sealed with a mixture of Portland cement, soil, and cardboard shavings. A heavy timber ring beam is installed on top of the walls to give support for the roof structure. Additionally, cross-bracing cables are installed to stabilize the building.

Since its construction, the Pod has served as a material testing ground at Auburn University, allowing students to conduct hands-on empirical research, especially on questions of durability and maintenance.

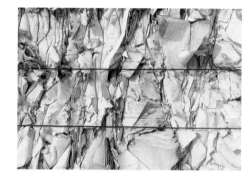

1 Cardboard scraps, when pressed into bales, provide an efficient and easy-to-handle construction material.

2 The rectangular shape produced by a regular garbage press allows for an easy use as a building block.

3

3 The cardboard bales function as load-bearing, insulating, and finishing material all in one.

4 The cross section shows the use of cardboard bales in wall structures and also as foundation elements.

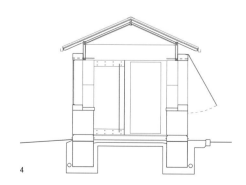

4

5 The Corrugated
Cardboard Pod, a temporary
student housing project
built by students of the
Rural Studio at Auburn
University, AL, USA. Due
to the friction resulting
from the high weight
and rough surface of the
bales, there is no need
for additional support or
reinforcement.

6 Ground floor plan.
The cubes are placed in
a running-bond pattern,
derived from masonry
construction.

5

6

PROJECT DATA

RESOURCE
Discarded corrugated
cardboard

MANUFACTURER
Corrugated cardboard
box plants, USA

DESIGNER
Rural Studio,
Auburn University,
Newbern, AL, USA

PRODUCT DIRECTORY
Load-bearing, page 175;
Insulating, page 183

PRODUCT DATA

STANDARD SIZE
800 mm × 2000 mm

STANDARD HEIGHT
700 mm

DENSITY
approx. 400 kg/m³

FIRE RATING
No information

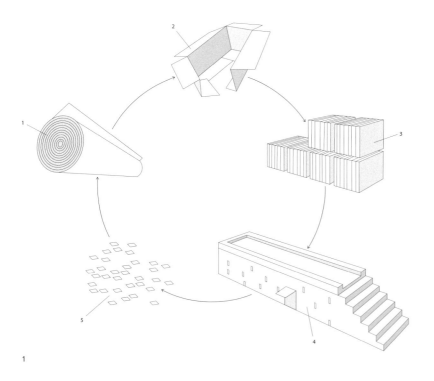

1 Recycling process of discarded cardboard scrap: the paper building blocks can be fed back into the regular process after use.

1   cardboard production
2   cardboard box
3   pressed cardboard bales
4   architectural application
5   reclaimed cellulose

2 Cardboard paper is usually pressed into bales for recycling, in order to save space in collection facilities.

1

2

PHZ2

Discarded cardboard is typically pressed into bales because this allows more material to be stored in collection facilities before recycling. This densification process potentially prepositions the substance for use by architects and builders.

According to the German Pulp and Paper Association (VDP), almost two thirds of all paper including cardboard and pasteboard is recycled in Germany. This equals more than 16 million tons of material per year, which is mostly used in recycled paper products in the packaging and newspaper industry. The PHZ2 project activates this enormous potential for the building sector.

The densified bales, held together by metal straps, possess an extremely high compressive strength capacity. The bales are easy to stack and can form wall elements of up to 30 m in height without any additional support. Furthermore, their mass of approximately 500 kg per unit endows them with astonishing sound insulation qualities. In terms of thermal insulation, walls with a thickness of

1 m or more and made out of corrugated as well as flat cardboard show highly appreciated properties.

The winning scheme of the architects proposed a temporary structure for start-up companies at the Zollverein World Heritage Site in Essen, Germany. The innovativeness and aesthetics of the material choice but also the fact that the building was 40% below the cost of a comparable structure in conventional materials convinced the competition jury. For construction the bales were placed one next to another, forming rows similar to a masonry system. Adhesive paste was used to level the top surface of a finished row and connect to the next layer. No additional structure or anchoring was needed, since the material was heavy enough to withstand wind forces. Drilling tests showed that it was possible to bolt other materials such as a wooden roof structure into the cardboard bales. The roof was covered with a cement board deck, extending the public areas of the Zollverein onto the building.

With the support of the Fraunhofer Institute it was established that rain would not penetrate the walls, as only the first 8–10 cm were affected by even heavy precipitation and the façade dried out in short time, so that no additional sealing of the vertical gaps was required. Shortly after construction the colour of the south-west façade started fading. While the original printed cardboards gave the building a rather wild and colourful appearance, the aging process produced more subtle and homogeneous shades of white, which was equally appealing.

It was unfortunate that the planners and authorities decided against an additional fire protection of the bales or the overall building, which could have been achieved with special impregnations or using sprinkler systems. This omission was due to the temporary character of the building, which was planned to be recycled at the end of 2011. In April of that year the structure was destroyed by fire.

3

4

PROJECT DATA

RESOURCE
Discarded cardboard

MANUFACTURER
Paper recycling facilities,
Oberhausen, Germany

DESIGNER
Dratz & Dratz Architects,
Oberhausen, Germany

PRODUCT DIRECTORY
Load-bearing, page 175;
Insulating, page 183;
Waterproofing, page 186

PRODUCT DATA

DIMENSIONS PER
WASTE PAPER BALE
1,400 mm × 1,100 mm ×
800 mm

WEIGHT PER WASTE
PAPER BALE
Approx. 500 kg: Total weight
of 550 waste paper bales
as used in the building:
Approx. 275,000 kg

PAPER TYPE
Packaging cardboard
B19 (> 70% corrugated
cardboard)

FIRE RATING
Fire-retardant F30
(DIN EN 13501)

COMPRESSION STRENGTH
< 630 kPa

FLOOR AREA
185 m²

3 PHZ2 was a temporary
structure to house start-up
companies at the Zollverein
World Heritage Site in
Essen, Germany.

4 The paper house
accommodated a multi-
functional event space,
a bar, and small service
rooms.

5 The plan view reveals how
the layout of the building
is determined by the
dimensions and structural
properties of the paper
bales.

6 The elevation shows the
elongated shape of the
building with the stairs in
front, allowing the public
space to flow towards the
structure.

5

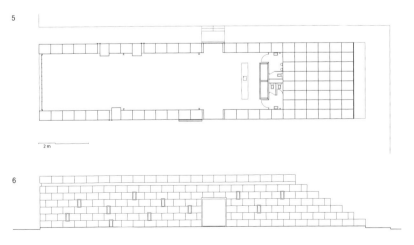

2 m

6

1

2

NEWSPAPERWOOD

According to the European Environment Agency, the Netherlands belongs to the top five recycle nations in Europe: approximately one million tons of paper and cardboard solid waste is recycled every year. With more than 60%, the recovery rate of this resource is extremely high, making recycling an important factor for the production of new paper. Roughly one third of the overall paper of Dutch newspapers comes from this recycling process.

NewspaperWood aims to tap into this material metabolism and add another cycle by converting wastepaper into a composite material with wood-like properties and aesthetics. In an emphatic sense, the process suggests a reversal of the traditional production: from paper to a wood-like substance. Designer Mieke Meijer together with the company Vij5 developed a new procedure and special machinery. Paper waste is soaked with glue and wrapped along a linear axis in a radial movement, successively forming a roll of paper layers reminiscent of a tree log. The layers of paper that appear when cutting a NewspaperWood log remind one of the annual growth rings of a tree.

The material can be cut, milled, drilled, nailed, and sanded; all in all it can be treated like any type of wood. Sealed from the outside, it can be turned into a waterproof substance. Applications span from façade to decorative elements and anything that could be built out of wooden boards.

NewspaperWood does not aim to be a large-scale alternative to wood, nor to transform all paper waste into a new substance. The main goal is to introduce an alternative strategy for transforming a surplus of wasted material into something valuable by using it in a different context and form of application. As a basic resource, newspaper misprints and the excess print run of yesterday's newspaper already provide enough supply to implement this strategy. Ubiquitous availability of newspapers minimizes the transport requirements for the product, taking the resource out of the already existing system of paper recycling. At the end of its lifespan as a building material, the designers suggest to reintroduce it once again into the same cycle. Consequently, the glue utilized in the production process must be free of solvents and plasticizers.

1 NewspaperWood is produced out of rolled-up newspaper sheets, creating a wood-like appearance when cut lengthwise.

2 The boards can be sanded and varnished to achieve various appearances.

3 The boards can be milled, sanded, drilled, and cut like wood.

3

PROJECT DATA

RESOURCE
Discarded newspapers

MANUFACTURER
AND DESIGNER
Mieke Meijer with
Vij5, Eindhoven,
The Netherlands

PRODUCT DIRECTORY
Finishing, page 189;
Self-supporting, page 179

PRODUCT DATA

MAXIMUM DIMENSIONS
140 mm × 380 mm

MAXIMUM THICKNESS
Custom

FIRE RATING
Fire-retardant
(DIN EN 13501),
varying depending
on finishing

HANDLING
Can be cut, milled,
sanded, and drilled
like any other wood

4 Newspaper sheets are rolled up and glued together, forming a log, then cut into any desired shape.

4

5

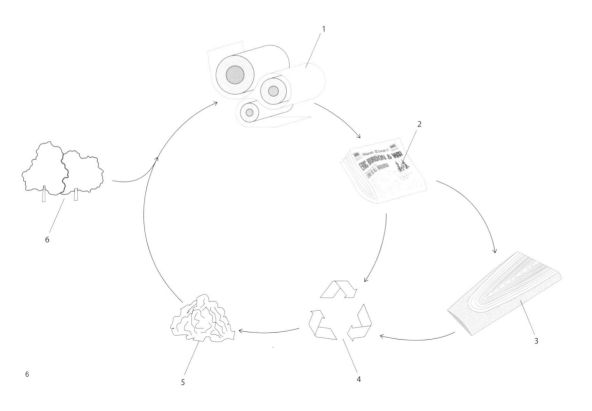

5 The boards need drying before they can be used.

6 NewspaperWood and its by-products can be reintroduced in an existing paper recycling system once discarded.

1 paper production
2 newspaper
3 newspaper wood
4 paper recycling
5 reclaimed cellulose
6 new cellulose

6

1 Wasted straw is the resource for new organic construction boards.

2 Straw bales are being unfolded in the Enviro Board Mark II Mill.

3 Two sheets of paper are applied to each side of the board for protection and additional structural strength.

4 Model house in Calusa, CA, USA, using E-board in a lightweight steel frame structure.

5 The panels can be modified after installation using common wood-working tools.

1

ENVIRO BOARD (E-BOARD)

The production technology of Enviro Board Corporation is capable to manufacture approximately 200,000 construction boards every year from 7,000 metric tons of straw. About 46% of all solid waste products worldwide (the number reflects data of 2009)[2] can be classified as organic substances coming from agricultural production. Among these, over 500 million metric tons of wheat straw are produced every year, representing an enormous resource for the construction sector. Enviro Board Corporation has developed a technology that is able to convert a variety of such agricultural waste products – for example rice or wheat straw – into versatile building panels. Burning the remains of agricultural production, as practiced in most grain-producing regions and cultures, not only contributes to the re-fertilization of the ground but also releases harmful pollutants as well as CO_2 into the atmosphere. By using the straw as the main substance in building products,

combustion and the resulting emissions can be avoided.

The process begins in the fields, where straw is collected, baled, and transported to the factory. Once the round bales arrive at the main extruder portal, they are unfurled and fed into the production line. A computer-controlled actuation system provides the compression required to press the material into panels. Once compacted, durable and waterproof papers are applied on all surfaces using ecologically sound glue. After the panels have cured and cooled, they are cut to length and immediately placed into a light steel wall-frame system.

With their steel wall-frame edge protection, the panels lend themselves to modular and off-site prefabrication. Preconstructed wall systems can be transported to the sites and quickly

assembled in a variety of applications, such as interior and exterior walls, floors, ceilings, and roofs. The panels are easy to handle also by unskilled labourers, which reduces construction time significantly compared to traditional methods. For use as an exterior building element, the boards are typically waterproofed with a moisture barrier and covered with any conventional outdoor surfacing material including stucco, vinyl, shingles, or stone. As straw is also an excellent acoustic insulator, the material reduces noise by 65 dB.

The boards have proven suitable for many commercial applications, especially those in which annual energy costs are a determining factor. At the time of writing, applications include warehouses, cold-storage facilities, large retail stores, office buildings, multi-tenant housing, high-rises, and even a symphony hall.

2

3

PROJECT DATA

RESOURCE
Straw waste

MANUFACTURER
AND DESIGNER
Enviro Board Corporation,
Camden, NJ, USA

PRODUCT DIRECTORY
Load-bearing, page 177;
Insulating, page 181

PRODUCT DATA

STANDARD SIZE
2,438 mm × 813 mm and
3,658 mm × 813 mm

STANDARD THICKNESS
57 mm

DENSITY
Approx. 300 kg/m³

SOUND INSULATION
57 mm = 65 dB

FIRE RATING
Fire-retardant B2
(DIN EN 13501)

4

5

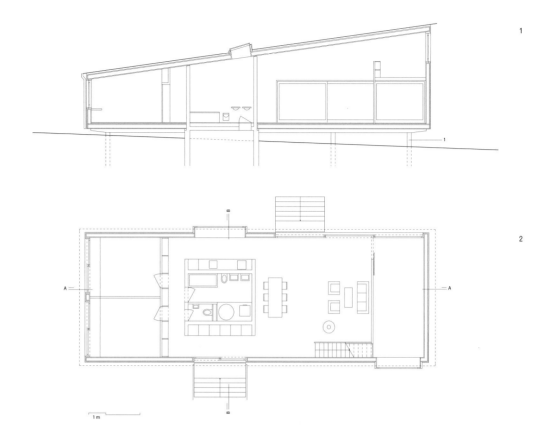

1

2

STROHHAUS

According to the Helmholtz Centre for Environmental Research, about 30 million tons of straw go to waste in Germany alone every year.[3] This vast resource, unattractive for bacteria and fungi because of its high silicate content level – especially when pressed into panels – can be activated easily for the construction sector. The German company Stropoly has recognized this potential and offers a wide range of compressed straw panel products for various applications according to the specific level of densification of the material. Performance in terms of compression strength and bending increases with the degree of compression of the material.

For a single-family house in Switzerland, two different kinds of such panels were used to construct all exterior and interior walls as well as the roofing structure. Two 40-mm highly compressed straw-fibre slabs, with a lightweight insulation slab sandwiched in-between, form a load-bearing system for the building. In this way, straw was used not only as a structural but also as an insulating material with stunning

thermal capacities. All straw slab elements were prefabricated and the entire house was constructed within four months. In order to protect the straw slabs from any humidity that could harm the material, the house was encapsulated with a corrugated glass-fibre panel system on all vertical surfaces and a metal sheet roof on top. The structure is almost completely raised from the ground, the only element touching soil being a concrete core that contains all wet spaces in the house as well as a small cellar. Even the floor panels are made of a combination of timber elements and straw, to be consistent with the overall construction concept.

While the specific company that produced the straw slabs for this single-family home went out of business soon after completion of the building, several other suppliers entered the market in recent years, some of which are presented in this publication. Importantly, alternative materials such as hemp, flax, or rice straw can potentially be used to press construction panels with similar properties.

1 The longitudinal section shows the core and wall elements and their different materialization strategies.

2 The floor plan is organized around a concrete core containing all wet rooms, which is the only element touching the ground.

3 Highly compressed straw boards are the basic building material for this single-family house in Switzerland. The performance of the panels is determined by the densification of the raw material.

4 Two 40-mm highly compressed straw-fibre slabs, with a lightweight panel sandwiched in between, form a load-bearing as well as insulating system.

3

4

PROJECT DATA

RESOURCE
Straw waste

MANUFACTURER
Stropoly, Güstrow,
Germany

DESIGNER
Felix Jerusalem,
Zurich, Switzerland

PRODUCT DIRECTORY
Load-bearing, page 177;
Insulating, page 181

PRODUCT DATA

STANDARD SIZE
< 6,000 mm × 2,500 mm

STANDARD THICKNESS
12–200 mm

DENSITY
300–600 kg/m^3

THERMAL CONDUCTIVITY
0.2 W/m^{2}K

FIRE RATING
Fire-retardant B2
(DIN EN 13501)

5

5 All straw slab elements were prefabricated, which allowed the house to be constructed in four months only.

6 Lifting the structure from the ground achieved a better protection of the straw panels.

6

STRAWJET

Strawjet is able to utilize most natural fibres to produce a building material through a purely mechanical densification process. Cereal grain stalks, such as wheat and rice straw, are the most evident substances to use; however, other commercial stalks such as tobacco, hemp, sunflower, and Jerusalem artichoke work equally well, next to naturally occurring stalks such as bamboo, palm fronds, river reeds, and wild grasses.

In the USA, 200 million tons of waste straw are produced every year. Every one million tons of straw burned releases 56,000 tons of CO_2, according to the *California Agricultural Magazine*.[4] As early as 1991, realizing that annual straw burning alone produces more CO_2 and particulate matter than all electric power plants combined, the State of California issued the Straw Burning Reduction Act to gradually reduce the amount of burned stalk. Following this example, China banned the burning of waste straw on the fields in 2011.

The Strawjet machine compresses the feedstock into a highly compacted and extruded strand, called cable, with a diameter of 5 cm. Fed by conveyor belts, compression rollers compact the straw before it is tightly bound by a rotating annulus with strings, at a speed of 40 m per minute. Various kinds of materials can be processed, from natural strings such as hemp, jute, or cotton to photodegradable nylon strings or synthetics such as Kevlar or polyester.

The cable can be cut to various desired lengths and wrapped into columns of either four strands (Quads) or seven strands (Hex) to be used in construction. No glues, resins, or chemicals are applied in the production of the material, making it an environmentally friendly, non-toxic, and durable building component. Quad columns consist of four 5-cm-diameter cables wrapped together with a specially designed machine to form a 10 cm × 10 cm column, comparable to a typical timber beam with the same dimensions. A Quad made of rigid materials, such as hemp or sunflower stalks, will not bend or deform. A Quad made of rice or wheat straw, by contrast, is flexible and can be formed as desired. Quads can be cut to any length with ease but commonly come in 3-m lengths and are stackable for easy storage and transportation. During construction, electrical wiring and light plumbing can be fit through a conduit that can be integrated simply by fitting it through the centre of the straw tube.

Consisting of seven cables formed in a hexagonal shape, the Hex column is ideal for interlocking tongue-and-groove assemblies. The system locks perpendicular Hex columns together, allowing for rapid assembly of walls and barriers. These can be plastered in any number of commercially available coverings, whether they are synthetic or all natural.

As a first prototype, the company built tobacco-drying sheds in Malawi, Africa, which traditionally were constructed from wood and resulted in heavy deforestation of the densely populated country. Strawjet utilized the waste stalk from the tobacco leaf production to erect these roofing structures in a load-bearing column-beam typology using Quad cables. Since powering the necessary machines on site proved to be a problem, the company developed a second version, which can be pedal-operated. All equipment is trailer-fit to reach construction sites and waste products directly where they occur.

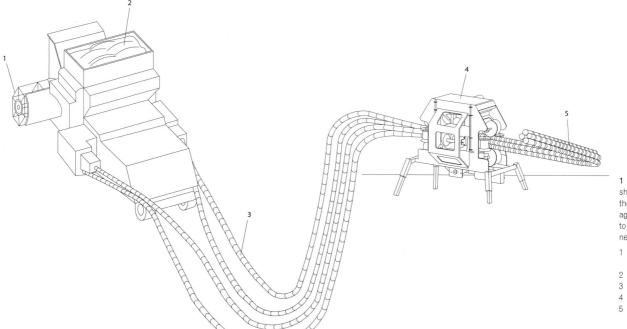

1 Process diagram showing the steps from the harvesting of the agricultural product to the emergence of a new building material.

1 modified combine harvester
2 grain
3 straw cables
4 multi-wrapper
5 Quad column

1

2

3

PROJECT DATA

RESOURCE
Straw waste

MANUFACTURER
Strawjet Inc.,
Talent, OR, USA

PRODUCT DIRECTORY
Load-bearing, page 176;
Insulating, page 183

PRODUCT DATA

STANDARD DIAMETER
50 mm

STANDARD LENGTH
Custom

FIRE RATING
No information

2 Strawjet cables are compressed out of agricultural waste stalk and can be used as a load-bearing construction material.

3 The Strawjet machine first compresses the straw into cables, which are then intertwined to form columns or beams.

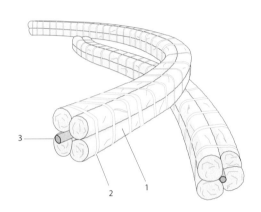

4

4 Quad columns consist of four intertwined 5-cm-diameter cables to form a 10 cm × 10 cm column, comparable in dimension to a typical timber beam. In the middle, a conduit can be placed for electrical installation.

1 straw cable
2 string
3 possible conduit

5 Stacked on top of each other, the cable walls can be finished with plaster or other protective layers.

5

055

1

SUSTAINABLE EMERGING CITY UNIT (SECU)

Usually only the seeds are seen as the valuable and desirable part of grain production. The grain straw, which constitutes the majority of the plant, is considered waste. The Sustainable Emerging City Unit (SECU) capitalizes on this rich resource and opens up the possibility of building double-story housing structures, using this widely available building material for large-scale housing projects in emerging urban settlements in Ethiopia, where straw is usually burned on the fields after harvesting. The project responds to the difficult availability of construction materials in rural areas of developing territories and incorporates waste products in the design and construction process.

Following this design strategy, a complete housing structure was made out of structurally active compressed straw board panels, supplied by the company Strawtec. Through heat exposure, the starch in wheat straw is activated and functions as a natural glue, without requiring other chemical additions, enabling the production of panels that are easy to handle on construction sites. The flat boards used in this project are 60 mm thick and clad on each side with recycled cardboard. The strawboard walls are self-supporting and do not require any kind of studwork. The material's excellent physical properties include high soundproofing and fire-protection ratings, due to a double-layer system with a thickness of 120 mm. The panels can be drilled, screwed, and even glued together to form larger units and systems. In addition, the material is 100% recyclable and biodegradable, with an excellent CO_2 footprint and a manufacturing process that uses only 10% of the energy needed to manufacture a comparable standard drywall system.

In most projects implemented as of the time of writing, straw panels are used mainly as non-load-bearing elements, such as partition walls, or as interior cladding material in renovation projects. SECU implemented methods for load-bearing applications. Questions of durability and maintenance were addressed and solutions tested in order to fully understand the material properties. Floor plans and sections were designed that react to the material's characteristics, for example the limited bending capacities, resulting in rather small spans of the ceiling and roof structures. Specific regional requirements were also taken into consideration, for example the Ethiopian way of living that asks mostly for covered, but otherwise open spaces. The resulting layout of functions arranges the elements to form simple boxes, whereby closed and open spaces alternate in regular sequences.

Special attention was given to the waterproofing of the material by using large roof overhangs and cladding materials that can be recycled and transformed, for example from the inner tubes of old car tires.

1 SECU construction during a two-week student workshop in Addis Ababa. The site was covered during construction to protect the straw material from rain.

2 Densified straw panels with recycled paper cladding. The starch in the wheat haulm is activated through pressure and heat and acts as a natural glue.

3 Ground floor layout. The arrangement is a direct consequence of the limited bending capacities of the straw panels used as a load-bearing system.

1 closed spaces
2 open spaces
3 floor board
4 recycled tire tube façade
5 foundation anchors
6 cement screed

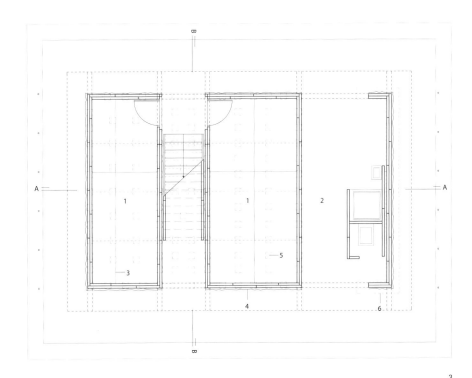

3

1 m

2

PROJECT DATA

RESOURCE
Straw waste

MANUFACTURER
Strawtec Building Solutions,
Berlin, Germany

DESIGNER
Ethiopian Institute of
Architecture, Building
Construction and City
Development, EiABC,
Addis Ababa, Ethiopia;
ETH Zurich/FCL Singapore;
Bauhaus University
Weimar, Germany

PRODUCT DIRECTORY
Load-bearing, page 177;
Insulating, page 181

PRODUCT DATA

STANDARD SIZE
1250–3,200 mm ×
1,200 mm

STANDARD THICKNESS
58 mm

DENSITY
380 kg/m³

SOUND INSULATION
58 mm = 32 dB

FIRE RATING
Fire-retardant B2
(DIN EN 13501)

CONSTRUCTION AREA
4 sheets = 4.0 m × 2.4 m
= 9.6 m²

4 Prefabricated elements form the floor slab between the two levels of the SECU housing unit. In these components, vertical ribs between two horizontal boards increase the structural capacity.

5 Easy-to-handle wall elements act as load-bearing components.

6 The SECU building introduces various recycled waterproofing materials.

5

6

4

7 Cross section showing the special design for the staircase built out of straw panels.

8 Longitudinal section. The spatial arrangement is based on the material properties.

1 closed spaces
2 open spaces
3 floorboard panels
4 recycled tyre tube façade
5 foundation anchors
6 cement screed
7 bracing
8 wall panel
9 stairs
10 awning
11 lintel
12 wooden support member

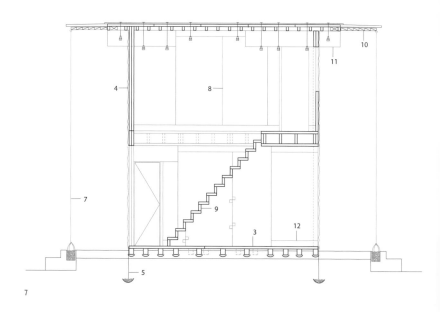

7

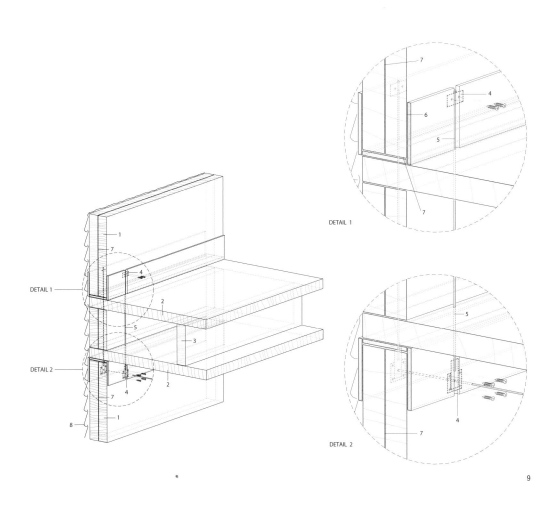

DETAIL 1

DETAIL 2

DETAIL 1

DETAIL 2

9

9 Connection detail between ceiling and wall. The ceiling construction required an increase in structural height, achieved by vertical spacers (ribs) made out of straw panels.

1 2 × 60 mm straw panel wall element
2 1 × 60 mm straw panel slab
3 vertical straw panel ceiling connector
4 metal plate
5 threaded rod
6 wooden support member
7 cottage cheese glue
8 recycled tire tube façade

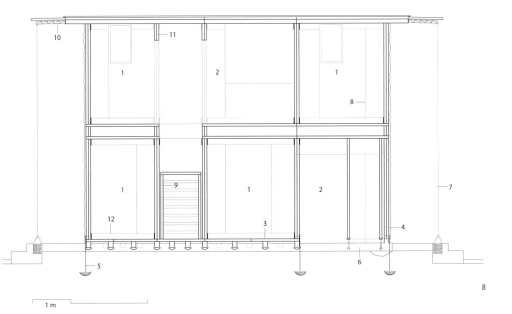

8

1 m

1

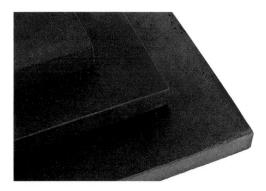

2

1 Decafe Tiles are a composite product made of disposed coffee grounds.

2 The designers are keen to retain the original coffee colour and aroma in the tiles to maintain the emotional appeal of this waste material.

3 The tiles can be applied with common tiling techniques.

4 The material is intended to be used indoors as a finishing material.

5 Experiments with different processes and shapes led the designer Raul Lauri to create Decafe Tiles.

DECAFE TILES

Decafe Tiles are produced from disposed coffee grounds and a natural binding agent. According to the Food and Agricultural Organization of the United Nations,[5] the world production of coffee beans per year reaches about 7.8 million tons. It is the secondmost traded commodity in the world. Once ground, brewed, and consumed, however, coffee grounds are usually declared organic waste and shipped to landfill sites for decomposition. Spanish designer Raul Lauri has been using this resource for furniture designs in recent years and is now applying the gained knowledge to building materials.

After mixture, the two components of disposed coffee grounds and a natural binding agent are pressed under heat into the desired shapes, using preformed moulds. Depending on the coffee grinding process, different densities and surface characteristics can be achieved, starting from a coarsely granular down to a fine-grained structure. While the exact formula is not disclosed by the designer, the selected binding agent clearly defines the properties and aesthetics of the final product. An important aspect in the products of Raul Lauri Design Lab is the fact that coffee is seen as an "experience-bearer, as we cannot ignore the fact that thousands of stories and events normally take place around a cup of coffee". Hence the designer is keen to retain the original coffee colour and aroma to be experienced in the products.

The designs are supposed to be used indoors as finishing materials, as they are not waterproof, on feature walls, ceilings, front counters, etc. As a natural organic material, slight colour variations occur, adding to the desired characteristics of a unique building material containing more than just physical substances.

3

4

5

PROJECT DATA

RESOURCE
Discarded coffee grounds

MANUFACTURER
AND DESIGNER
Raul Lauri Design Lab,
Alicante, Spain

PRODUCT DIRECTORY
Finishing, page 190

PRODUCT DATA

STANDARD SIZE
300 mm × 300 mm

STANDARD THICKNESS
20 mm

FIRE RATING
Fireproof, non-combustible

SPECIAL PROPERTY
Non-conductive

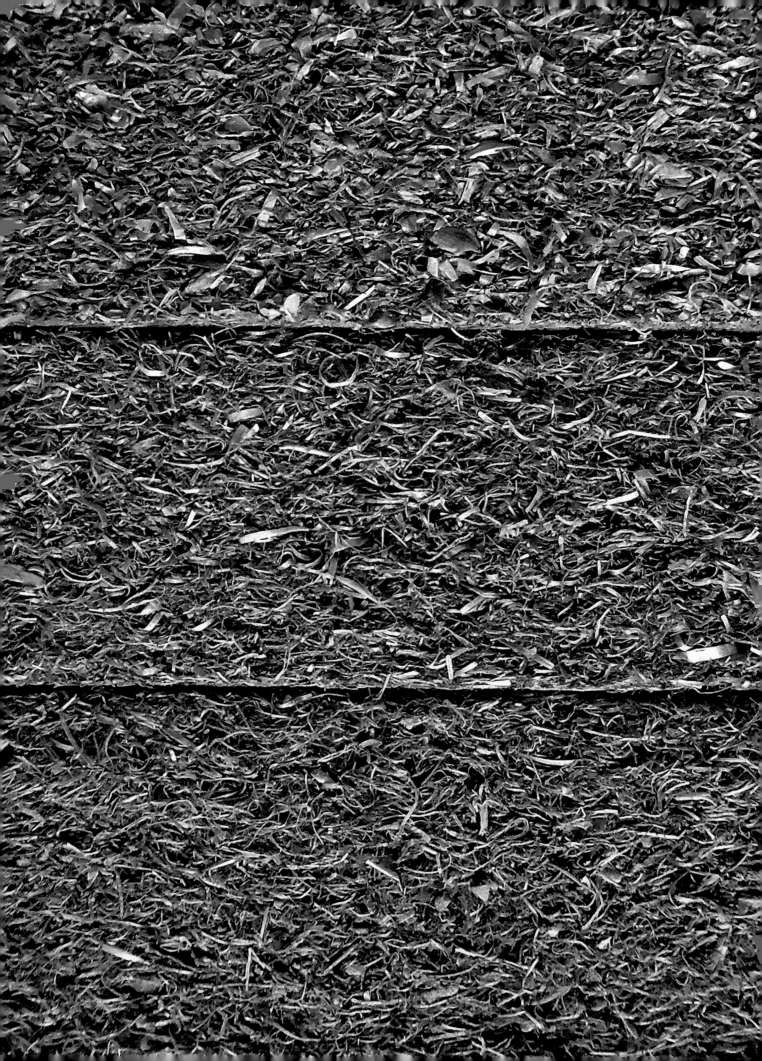

RECONFIGURED WASTE MATERIALS

CASE STUDIES

Tuff Roof p. 66
Plasphalt p. 70
Artek Pavilion p. 72
Paper Tile Vault p. 76
Agricultural Waste Panels p. 80
ReMaterials Roof Panels p. 82
Ecor p. 84
Natura 2 p. 86
Wine Cork Tiles p. 88
UltraTouch Denim Insulation p. 90
Vault201 p. 92

A configuration describes the arrangement of elements in a particular form, figure, or combination in order to perform a certain function. Reconfigured waste materials, in our definition, thus comprise all products where the components of raw waste have been rearranged before being processed into a new construction element. Shredding, breaking, sawing, or grinding are some of the forms of applied mechanical force used to change the original configuration of the waste material. The resulting pellets, chips, strands, fibres, etc. are then processed further, usually by mixing them with other components such as organic, inorganic, or mineral adhesives and pressing them into moulds of any form and size.

Even though reconfigured waste materials depend on similar processes as densified waste materials, the reconfiguration and rearrangement activates additional product characteristics and it implies the possibility to change form. Depending on the intended functionality of the construction elements to be conceived, the method allows to manipulate and control their density, weight, alignment, or even aesthetic qualities. While smaller pieces correlate with a greater surface area, thereby engendering more interaction and friction with the resins or adjacent materials, crushing to microelements may destroy some of the qualities of the original waste material.

This is especially relevant for products for load-bearing applications that are required to absorb external forces. Lumber waste materials, for example, can either be reconfigured in chips to function as open-strand board elements with high mechanical performance due to their directional fibre arrangement within the chip; or they can be used as sawdust with rather limited capacities.

Mixtures of different materials – waste or non-waste – are a common method of creating new products. Careful engineering allows waste materials to become part of an up-cycling process. The combined matter might have a higher performance in terms of material property, quality, or financial as well as environmental value than each individual component by itself. This process of up-cycling has become more and more widespread in the building industry and other markets, due to the "green" marketability of the resulting product and the savings in resources coming from the waste stream. In any case the process has to be carefully evaluated, since marketing sometimes seems more important than the actual scientific proof.

This chapter introduces waste particles as a basic material for product development. When Tetra Pak, a trademark of the food packaging industry, was invented in Sweden and marketed for the first time in 1951, the square and light packaging for liquids was celebrated as the new glass. Developed in an era of seemingly unlimited resources, the required layering of aluminium foil, cardboard, and plastic eventually destined for the landfill did not raise any questions. Over the decades, experiencing difficulties to recycle this compound, attempts were made to either change the material composition of the packaging system or invent new ways of separating cardboard and aluminium foil. Seen as a resource for the construction sector, however, even un-separated Tetra Pak cartons have interesting potentials

for designing a variety of products such as corrugated roofing sheets. Here, the combination of paper and aluminium, shredded in small pieces and arranged into sheets, offers an advantage over existing corrugated iron or fibre cement sheets, due to their non-corrosiveness, lightness, and low production costs.

A similar symbiosis between a consumer product and the construction industry is UltraTouch Denim Insulation. Jean fabric was originally invented in Genoa, Italy, and used by sailors to protect their goods on dock

from environmental or mechanical impact. In 1873, Levi Strauss and Jacob Davis became aware of the incredible properties of the material and developed the jeans as work pants for miners in the USA. Given the material properties, it is no surprise that trousers tailored out of jean fabric are now probably the most worn piece of casual clothing worldwide. This success story, on the other hand, produces a great amount of used and thrown-out jeans waste. It is only logical to search for a new function of this fantastic material. UltraTouch Denim Insulation is a heat and sound insulation product for buildings. For production, jeans are broken down into fibres and processed into non-woven mats that feature the same superior properties as the original fabric, thus closing the loop reaching from the protection of goods in the 19th century to the insulation of our homes today. Here, an inverted process of densification is happening, whereby the material is reconfigured in a loose state, allowing for air pockets to form, which are necessary to achieve the insulation properties.

A second major group of products in this chapter is based on cellulose waste, such as paper or wood. Chopped into pieces and pressed into bricks or panels, these elements can even be used in load-bearing applications. Recently, papier-maché bricks have been developed by the BLOCK Research

1 Layers of aluminium, paper, and plastic provide the resource for alternative roofing sheets made out of discarded Tetra Pak cartons.

In most reconfigured waste products, the raw garbage substance has been processed into new shapes, so that these products cannot be restored to their original use or life cycle without great effort. Once a plastic bottle, for example, has been chopped into pieces, these would need to be cleaned, sorted, melted down, and formed back into the original shape – if a bottle once again is the desired use of the resource. Economically and environmentally, this would be a costly process. As an alternative, in most cases a direct reprocessing into another construction element is achievable, or a number of other uses can be found within the family of reconfigured or even transformed waste materials.

Available production processes range from low to high-tech methods. Their application depends on the local availability of waste. This, and the many possible refuse resources usable for production, account for the wide variety of products here. The range of their uses, however, is even more astonishing, reaching from structural load-bearing applications to waterproofing, insulation, and finishing surfaces. In this perspective, reconfigured waste materials may be the most versatile type of waste construction elements for now.

Group of ETH Zurich for a Catalan vaulting structure for exhibition purposes. As a unique characteristic, such robust and self-supporting tile arch systems are charged in compression mode only, due to their curved formation and resulting force deflection. The load-bearing capacity required of the individual construction element is rather low, as long as it is functioning in a perfect load-distributing system.

Alternative structural systems are being designed from a wide range of waste materials, starting from paper via used coffee powder to even sludge. Chopped into pieces, ground to powder, and compressed into bricks, some of the resulting tiles seem to be brittle and unstable when they are held in hand. But when carefully installed in a structural system, for instance in a vault, they facilitate wide spans without any additional support. This is an example for the interaction and interdependence of the development of new materials with adequate structural concepts, detailing, and construction processes to fully activate the potential of waste as a construction material.

2 Laminated paper scraps can be a high-quality resource for the construction sector.

1 Tuff Roof is a corrugated roofing material made out of reclaimed Tetra Pak cartons.

2 The sheets are similar in size and shape to products made from metal or fibre cement.

3 Tuff Roof can be installed with standard fixtures as used for other corrugated roofing sheets. The sheets also need to overlap for waterproofing.

1

TUFF ROOF

In 1951, Ruben Rausing and Erik Åkerlund developed a new beverage container system that became known all over the world as Tetra Pak. The aim of the Swedish entrepreneurs was to provide food packaging that was safe, cheap, and very efficiently to be transported. The design principle was to minimize material consumption, making the product competitive with the sales price of loose milk or other liquids. The designers realized early that pre-packaging was the future of an emerging food and retailing industry, as they had experienced first hand as young men during their studies in the USA.

The final design of the Tetra Pak consists of several different layers of plastic films and aluminium in addition to raw paper. Therefore, the containers cannot be recycled as regular paper, metal, or plastic waste, but the waste need to be separated in special recycling apparatuses, which makes the process difficult and expensive. For the longest time, recycling of the beverage containers has been a huge challenge. Nevertheless, in 2010, 30 billion (milliards) of used Tetra Pak carton packages were recycled,[1] a doubling since 2002, following a trend that has continued since. This effort is due to the high value of the separated materials, mostly aluminium and pure paraffin, which can be reused in many industry applications.

Daman Ganga Paper Mill in India recognized the value of this highly engineered product. Since the necessary machines for recycling are expensive and usually not found in the developing world, they invented an alternative way to make best use of the resource. Waterproofing sheets, called Tuff Roof, are created from the composite of paper, polyethylene, and aluminium without requiring any other material in the production process. Shredded to very small pieces, the Tetra Pak carton remains are placed into a mould and heated to activate the inherent plastics, paraffin, and glues to function as the new adhesive mass. Under pressure, corrugated sheets are produced with a shape similar to that known from the competing metal product.

The roofing panels are waterproof, fireproof, flexible, corrosion-free, and extremely light. And the combination of paper and aluminium offers another huge advantage over existing corrugated iron or cement sheets: they are a potent reflector for heat radiation and protect the spaces underneath from overheating – a problem that occurs often with sheet iron roofing systems. Easy to produce, this roofing material actually profits from the existing distribution network of Tetra Pak cartons in most countries of the world, and ironically at the same time from the absence of appropriate recycling units. In India, the raw material is widely available but mostly ends up on landfills. Sadly enough, the missing collection system actually leads to waste imports into India to keep the Tuff Roof production running – a very negative side effect of a very good idea.

2

PROJECT DATA

RESOURCE
Discarded Tetra Pak cartons

MANUFACTURER
AND DESIGNER
Daman Ganga Paper Mill,
Gujarat, India

PRODUCT DIRECTORY
Waterproofing, page 184

PRODUCT DATA

STANDARD SIZE
2,250 mm × 950 mm

STANDARD THICKNESS
4 mm / corrugation: 45 mm

DENSITY
148 kg/m³

FIRE RATING
Fire-retardant
(DIN EN 13501)

FLEXION RESISTANCE
7,630 kPa

HEAT EVOLUTION
FACTOR (Q)
> 38.3 / < 55.9

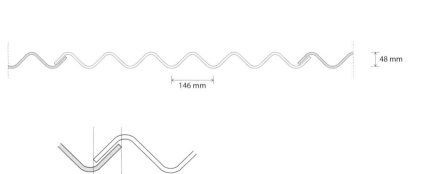

3

48 mm

146 mm

40 mm

4 The collected, unsorted Tetra Pak cartons are delivered to the factory in bales.

5 The material is fed onto a conveyor belt for shredding and processing.

6 Tuff Roof sheets are fire-retardant and offer a heat transition value inferior to commonly used metal sheets.

7 The non-corrosive material can be installed the same way as corrugated metal sheets.

8 Tuff Roof has been used in several buildings in India and Africa.

7

8

1

PLASPHALT

In the USA, 4,000 plants produce 500 to 550 million tons of asphalt pavement material per year,[2] 85% of which is used to pave the 3.2 million km of roads in the country.[3] Paving materials are a mixture of inexpensive, readily available elements. In asphalt concrete, or "blacktop", these elements are sand, gravel (95%), and an asphalt emulsion binder that together form the paved surface.

Plasphalt utilizes all types of unsorted plastic waste to produce an alternative to mineral aggregates such as sand and gravel in asphalt cement road pavement. The plastic material, a granulate of 6 mm or less in diameter, replaces about 1–2% by weight or 5–7% by volume of sand and gravel in the final mix. Asphalt plants only need minor adjustments to incorporate the alternative aggregates into the process. Temperatures, delivery, placement, and finishing of the enhanced mix on site are identical to regular asphalt cement application.

To produce one km of Plasphalt of a standard width, about 40 tons of unsorted plastic wastes are transformed into aggregates. The most important step in the production of the plastic substance is the excitation of the molecules on the surface of the aggregates. The individual grains are exposed to an ion-rich plasma field in order to bind additional free electrons to the plastic particles. In such an excited state, a molecule such as hydrocarbon asphalt oil binds more readily to the surface of the plastic, lending Plasphalt a new and strong matrix. This additional atomic bond creates a more durable road surface material and also reduces the negative effects from the degradation of the plastic components, by encapsulating them into the asphalt matrix.

Over the course of five years, the performance of the new pavement material was verified on several test sites in the USA. The concerned road segments showed a significant reduction in rutting, shoving, ravelling, and general surface wear compared to conventional asphalt cement. Also, the volume required to produce the driving surface was reduced by about 7%.

1 Plasphalt uses all types of unsorted plastic waste to produce a plastic aggregate that is apt to partially replace sand and gravel in asphalt cement pavement.

2 Due to its molecule structure, hydrocarbon asphalt oil binds more easily to the plastic than to sand or gravel, creating a new and strong matrix.

1 TRPA particles
2 mineral aggregate
3 bitumen

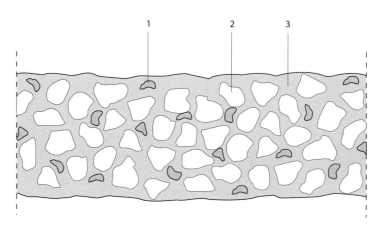

2

3

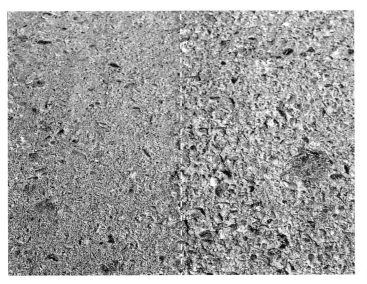

4

PROJECT DATA

RESOURCE
Discarded plastics

MANUFACTURER
AND DESIGNER
TEWA Technology
Corporation,
Albuquerque, NM, USA

PRODUCT DIRECTORY
Load-bearing, page 173

PRODUCT DATA

STANDARD SIZE
OF AGGREGATE
< 6.35 mm

MOLECULAR STATE
OF AGGREGATE
Radical ion

DENSITY
< 2,469 kg/m³

FIRE RATING
No information

TENSILE STRENGTH
4.52 MPa at -10°C

THERMAL CONTRACTION
2.95×10^{-5} °C

SHEAR
Permanent shear strain
at 5,000 cycles: 2.2%

3–4 Road segments that use the new material have shown a significant reduction in rutting, shoving, ravelling, and general surface wear compared to conventional asphalt cement pavements.

Left: New Plasphalt
Right: Standard asphalt

5 During production, the grains are exposed to an ion-rich environment, in this case a plasma field, in order to bind additional free electrons to the particles.

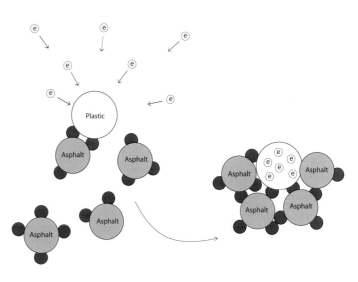

5

ARTEK PAVILION

In search of a material to build a showroom for the Artek furniture company at the 2007 Milan Furniture Fair, the commissioned architect Shigeru Ban selected a new wood-plastic composite created from label printing waste.

In the United Kingdom, an estimated 180,000 tons of waste is produced by self-adhesive label printing machines every year.[4] This plastic-based residue includes matrix coming from make-ready, set-up, misprints, or the remains of trimming and punching. Label printers are becoming more and more efficient, but they still create a vast amount of waste that usually cannot be recycled because various materials are bonded together: unsorted plastics, glues, papers, and printing ink. To separate these is very difficult or nearly impossible and for long the industry has looked for alternative solutions.

UPM, a Finnish forest industry company and producer of self-adhesive label materials and biocomposites, has developed a way to reuse the waste paper trimmings containing cellulose fibres and plastic polymers, which are an excess in the firm's self-adhesive label manufacture and processing. The proportion of raw materials in these labels is 60% cellulose and 40% plastics. Shredded and shaped under heat, the resulting flakes form a strong wood-plastic composite

without requiring any additional additives, combining the best properties of plastic and wood. Next to the structural robustness and strength, the new material shows very low moisture absorption rates, so that no additional surface treatment is required even for outdoor use. The absence of lignin, the natural wood binder, prevents the material from turning grey when exposed to UV light. Products can be manufactured by extrusion and injection moulding and handled with conventional tools.

For the Furniture Fair showroom, extruded L-shaped profiles were tested extensively for their structural and physical properties. Based on the findings, the architecture team developed a unique design, using only L-shaped profile types and combining them into columns and beams in areas where more strength was needed. The result is a 40-m-long building constructed out of a glue-laminated paper waste material. Due to their properties and versatile shapes, the L-profiles could also be used as a waterproofing roof and façade system, by overlaying the profiles shaping a corrugated surface. The building is easy to set up and dismantle, allowing the pavilion to move from its original location in Milan to several other fairs and exhibitions in Helsinki and Miami. In 2008, the pavilion was sold at Sotheby's sale of "Important 20th Century Design Objects".

1–2 The principle resource for the structural members are self-adhesive label scraps composed of paper and plastic.

3

3 Designed for the Milan Furniture Fair in 2007, the Artek Pavilion was subsequently re-erected in many parts of the world, including Helsinki and Miami.

4 Eventually, the pavilion was sold at Sotheby's as an "Important 20th Century Design Object" in 2008.

5 Translucent corrugation of the roof allows for natural lighting of the interior.

4

5

PROJECT DATA

RESOURCE
Label printer waste

MANUFACTURER
UPM Biocomposites,
Lahti, Finland

DESIGNER
Shigeru Ban, Shigeru Ban
Architects, Paris, France

PRODUCT DIRECTORY
Load-bearing, page 174;
Waterproofing, page 186

PRODUCT DATA

STANDARD SIZE
60 mm × 60 mm × custom

STANDARD THICKNESS
8 mm

DENSITY
1,200 kg/m³

BENDING STRENGTH
12 MPa (EN 310)

FIRE RATING
Class E (EN ISO 11925–2)

WATER ABSORPTION (24 H)
< 2.5% (CEN/TS 15534)

6

7

8

6 Biocomposites by UPM
are extruded in a variety
of different shapes and
properties.

7 The L-shaped profiles
went through a period of
structural tests to optimize
their design.

8 The pavilion structure
uses exclusively L-shaped
profiles for structural,
cladding, and finishing
applications.

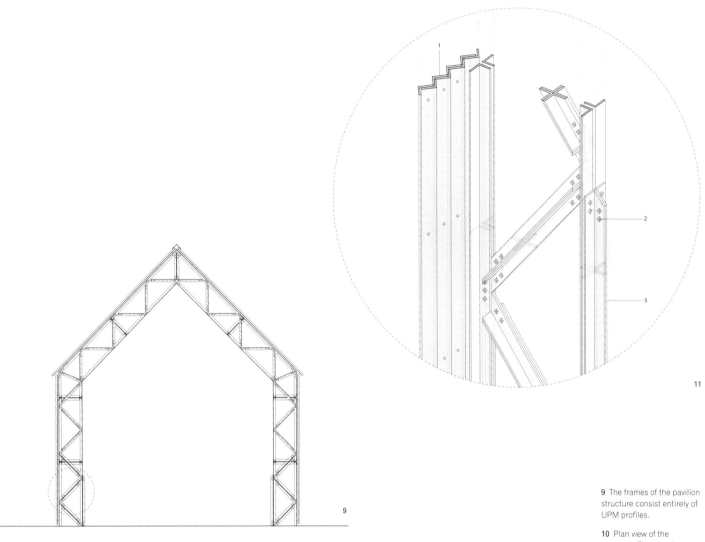

11

1 m

9

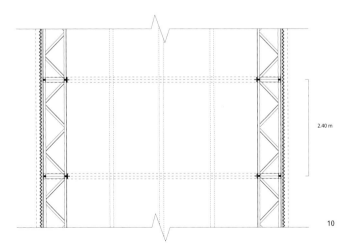

2.40 m

10

9 The frames of the pavilion structure consist entirely of UPM profiles.

10 Plan view of the structure. The 40-m-long, open-ended pavilion is based on a repetitive 2-m-long module.

11 The L-profiles are bolted together to form load-bearing T or X-shaped elements.

1 exterior cladding out of L-shaped profiles
2 connection bolt
3 T and X-shaped structural elements

PAPER TILE VAULT

According to the US Environmental Protection Agency, 27% of all municipal solid waste is classified as paper, more than any other discarded material in the USA.[5] Designed as a temporary structure for New York City, Paper Tile Vault taps into this huge resource and investigates the possibility of reusing paper as a cheap and easily available construction material.

When used paper and cardboard are re-pulped by adding water, the fibres and starch are dissolved and become a formable mass that can be pressed into virtually any shape desired. The composite material is widely known as papier-mâché. By pressing the pulp into cuboid moulds and letting the mix dry, paper building bricks can be produced in a very low-tech manner. Material testing for this project established that adding an organic wheat starch paste to the pulp before pressing, significantly increases the product's compressive strength. Since the drying time of the bricks highly depends on their thickness, thin tiles turn out to be more efficient than standard format stones in terms of the production process.

Using RhinoVAULT, a structural form-finding tool developed by the BLOCK Research Group, a thin-tile paper vault was designed by using the technique of Catalan vaulting. For the design loading, the structural form is optimized to transfer exclusively axial compressive forces, so that the vault does not have to resist bending stresses. This allows spanning wide spaces without a vast accumulation of material. More importantly, a compression-dominant solution is a prerequisite for using the bending-weak paper tiles. The dried tiles are bricked up into ribs and vaulted panels, either on site or in prefabrication on reusable, adaptable formwork.

The brick's texture and colour are mostly defined by the paper used for the pulp. Local context can be emphasized by not completely shredding the paper, leaving some frazzles large enough to still be legible. Furthermore, various imprints such as names, logos, or patterns, obtained by simply inserting cut-out forms into the press, emboss the still formable brick while pressing the water out. This creates a huge spectrum of possible aesthetic and tactile qualities.

Dismantling is another focus of this project. Since the vault was designed for a temporary installation, reuse or recycling had to be planned in order to leave a minimal footprint. By using nothing but paper, organic paste, and natural glue, the ingredients allow the entire process to be reversible. At the end of the pavilion's life span, all material can be brought back into a regular paper-recycling loop.

1 In the production process, the shredded paper is pulped by adding water to dissolve it into the original cellulose.

2 Shredded paper soaked in water is pressed into building bricks. Small portions of the initial print can remain legible to create a unique texture for the elements.

PROJECT DATA

RESOURCE
Paper waste

MANUFACTURER
AND DESIGNER
BLOCK Research Group,
ETH Zurich, Switzerland

PRODUCT DIRECTORY
Load-bearing, page 175

PRODUCT DATA

STANDARD SIZE
300 mm × 150 mm

STANDARD THICKNESS
25 mm

DENSITY
250–450 kg/m³

COMPRESSION STRENGTH
1.2–1.4 MPa

FIRE RATING
Fireproofing through
additional ingredients
or layers, e.g. borates

WATERPROOFING
through additional
ingredients or layers,
e.g. varnish

3 The bricks are arranged
next to each other and
glued together with a
fast-setting mortar.

4 Proposal for the
prefabricated vault system
made out of lightweight
paper bricks.

3

4

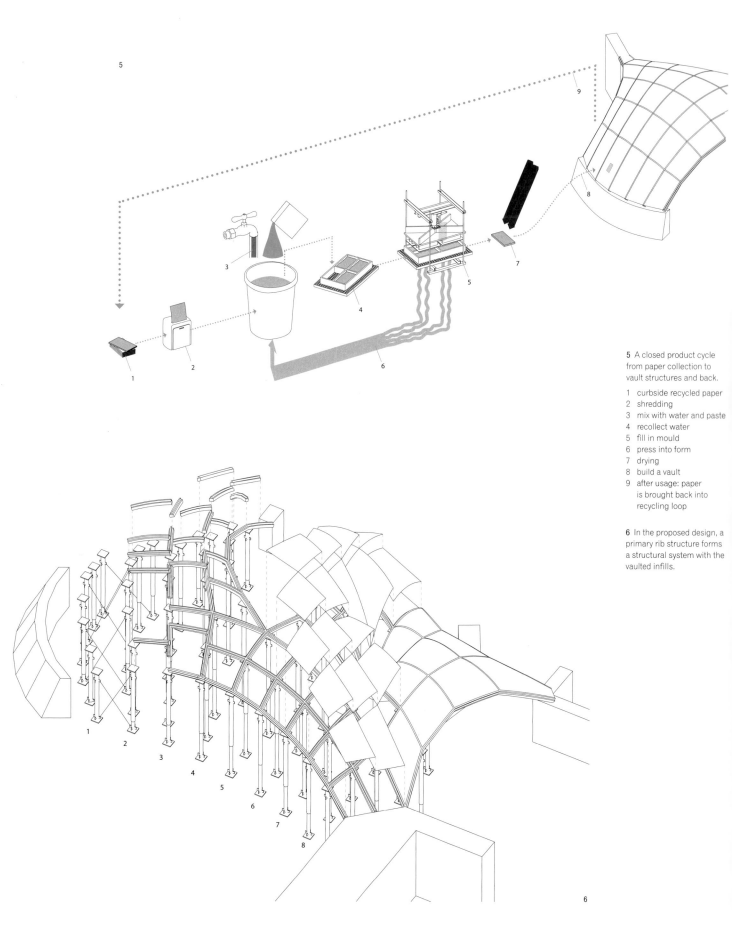

5 A closed product cycle from paper collection to vault structures and back.

1 curbside recycled paper
2 shredding
3 mix with water and paste
4 recollect water
5 fill in mould
6 press into form
7 drying
8 build a vault
9 after usage: paper is brought back into recycling loop

6 In the proposed design, a primary rib structure forms a structural system with the vaulted infills.

7

7 Depending on the paper waste used, a variety of colours can be achieved.

8 Cut-outs inserted during the pressing may be used to emboss the bricks' faces to individualize the product.

8

1

1 Various agricultural waste products can be used in the process: corn stalks, corn cobs, wheat husks, or barley husks.

2 The organic substances are pressed into panels by adding tannin for glueing.

AGRICULTURAL WASTE PANELS

Agricultural residues such as rice husks, ground nut shells, wheat husks, barley husks, corn stalks, corn cobs, or corn husks are a natural annual resource of lignocellulose. They can be employed in the fabrication of composite panels for varying applications. Depending on the country and its agriculture, these raw materials represent an available, sustainable, and cheap resource for new materials for building and furniture industries, providing a cascade of economic, environmental, and socio-cultural advantages for the producing country.

Whether destined for construction, insulation, or furniture, the panels can be manufactured with a low or high-tech approach, corresponding to the needs and capabilities of the host country and the available materials. In a low-tech approach, the raw material is left in its natural state and size after harvesting. A more advanced technology involves a hacker, flaker, or hammer mill to reduce sizes needed for the manufacturing of particle boards. This technology, of course, requires more energy to break down the natural resource into fibres.

The standard method of manufacturing requires the mixing of the raw materials with an adhesive. In a second step, this composite is laid out on a mould and hot-pressed into a panel. While formaldehyde-free synthetic adhesive can be used for manufacturing such boards, a much promising natural-based adhesive has been developed recently on the basis of tannin from tree barks and has been used successfully for the production of Agricultural Waste Panels.

The products can be employed in various fields, for instance as construction boards for affordable social housing applications. As such, in developed countries, insulation or fibre boards made from agricultural residues can provide a solution to stop deforestation as practiced momentarily in most of these territories.

2

3

4

PROJECT DATA

RESOURCE
Agricultural waste

MANUFACTURER
Berne University of Applied
Sciences, Biel, Switzerland

DESIGNER
Berne University of Applied
Sciences, Biel, Switzerland;
University of Nigeria,
Enugu Campus, Nigeria;
Ahmadu Bello University,
Zahia, Nigeria

PRODUCT DIRECTORY
Load-bearing, page 177;
Insulating, page 182

PRODUCT DATA

STANDARD SIZE
Research panel,
700 mm × 500 mm

STANDARD THICKNESS
5–40 mm

DENSITY
150–1,000 kg/m³

FIRE RATING
No information

THERMAL CONDUCTIVITY
0.044–0.051 W/m²K

INTERNAL BOND
0.05–2 N/mm²

3 A low-tech mixer blends
the agricultural waste
material with the tannin
binder.

4 Prior to processing,
the materials are
hammer-milled.

5 Insulation boards are
one of many possible
applications.

5

2

1

1 ReMaterials Roof Panels are a light and waterproof alternative to corrugated iron or fibre cement roofing sheats.

2 Cardboard and organic fibres are placed into moulds and compressed to extract excess water, reconfiguring the mixture into a hard panel.

REMATERIALS ROOF PANELS

Concerned with the housing situation in India's slums, Hasit Ganatra and Swad Komanduri have developed a roofing panel to solve two problems at a time: the amount of waste accumulating in the streets and the severe difficulties of house builders to provide a roof over their heads. The current market offers two solutions: very inexpensive corrugated metal sheets and expensive concrete slabs. While the first provides only poor insulation from heat and corrodes quickly, the second is unfortunately not affordable to many. Gathered by the local trash collectors, packaging materials such as cardboard and organic wastes like coconut fibres could provide a cheap and widely available resource to develop an alternative roofing system.

The process is fairly simple: cardboard is shredded and blended together with water into pulp, then organic fibres are added as a reinforcement material. The resulting paste is poured into moulds and compressed cold to get rid of excess water and reconfigure the mixture into a hard panel. Clammed between metal sheets to prevent bending, the panels are heated to reduce any moisture left in the composite. Finally, the boards are coated with a specially developed waterproofing paint.

The panels interlock in a modular fashion, making it easy to ship, install, and maintain the roof. In a first full-scale application, the company has successfully installed a roof in a slum community in Ahmedabad, India. The designers are now working on a way to implement solar cells into the panels to provide sufficient energy with eight panels to charge a 20-V battery in one day.

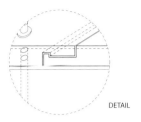

DETAIL

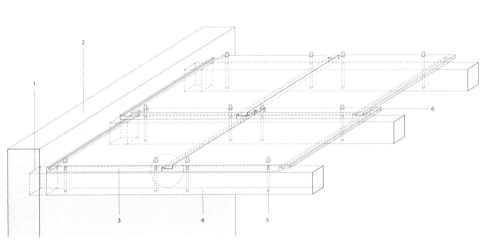

3

PROJECT DATA

RESOURCE
Packaging and
agricultural waste

MANUFACTURER
AND DESIGNER
Hasit Ganatra and Swad
Komanduri, ReMaterials,
Ahmedabad, India

PRODUCT DIRECTORY
Waterproofing, page 185

PRODUCT DATA

STANDARD SIZE
610 mm × 610 mm

STANDARD THICKNESS
25 mm

BENDING STRENGTH
6.58 kPa

FIRE RATING
No information

4

3 The panels interlock in a
modular fashion, making
the roof easy to install and
maintain.

1 bearing wall
2 roof panels
3 wooden substructure
4 bolt
5 overlap of roof panels

4 ReMaterials Roof Panels
aim to solve two problems
at a time: the amount of
waste accumulating in
the streets and the severe
difficulties of house builders
to provide a roof over their
heads.

2

3

ECOR

According to the Environmental Protection Agency, plastics make up 12.4% of the overall municipal solid waste in the USA; wood accounts for 6.3%, paper for 27.4%, and food scraps for 14.5%.[6] All of these waste products have one thing in common: they contain highly valuable fibres in one form or another that can be activated as a building material component.

Following this logic, ECOR was developed as a high-strength moulded fibre composite panel. It uses waste materials with high fibre contents, typically gathered from urban, farm, and forest sources. Examples include recycled office paper, corrugated cardboard, kenaf fibres, sawdust from mills, and even rotted wood from the forest floor. The process also incorporates waste streams coming from dehydrated food scraps, recycled denim and other mixed fabrics, as well as recycled beverage containers. The fibres contained in all of those materials are separated and mechanically cleaned before used in the process.

The production of the panels is rather simple: the fibre, or blend of fibres, is mixed with water, the resulting pulp then flows into a mould of the desired shape (flat, corrugated, etc.) whereby the majority of the water is removed. This mass is subjected to heat and pressure, producing a fully formed high-density panel. The manufacturing process allows an endless variety of different shapes and thicknesses according to application characteristics and needs. Aesthetic appearances and surface structures can also be modified.

The result is a strong, light, and impact-resisting product that does not contain any toxic additives or non-recycled contents. Neither is its production limited in raw material sourcing options, since the waste being used is available everywhere on our planet. In addition, properties such as waterproofing and fire resistance can be controlled by applying additional functional material layers.

1 A blend of fibres is mixed with water and subjected to heat and pressure to manufacture the high-density ECOR panels.

2 Aesthetic effects and surface structures can be modified by selecting different resource materials. Functionality such as waterproofing and fire resistance can be controlled by adding layers of other materials.

3 Sandwiched between cover sheets, a corrugated version made of the same material can improve the mechanical properties of the product.

1

4

4 The manufacturing process allows for an infinite variety of shapes and thicknesses.

5 One of the produced designs is WavCOR, a corrugated shape used for decorative applications and structural panel elements.

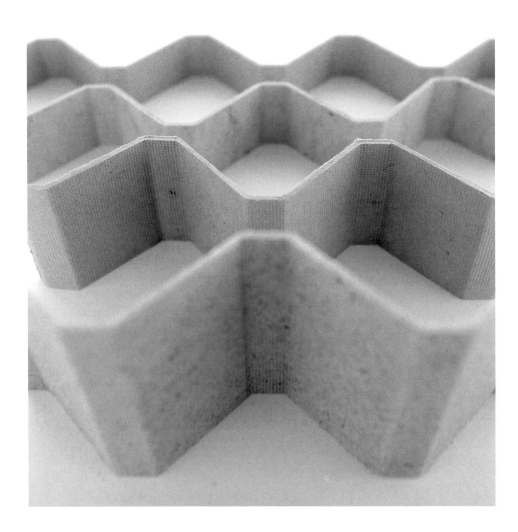

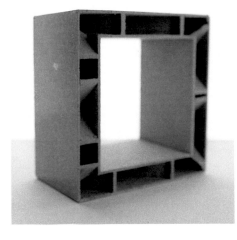

PROJECT DATA	PRODUCT DATA
RESOURCE Waste materials with high fibre contents	**STANDARD SIZE** < 610 mm × 2,440 mm
MANUFACTURER AND DESIGNER Robert Noble of Noble Environmental Technologies, San Diego, CA, USA	**STANDARD THICKNESS** 2.5 mm
	DENSITY 940 kg/m³
	SOUND INSULATION Custom
PRODUCT DIRECTORY Self-supporting, page 179; Finishing, page 191	**FIRE RATING** Untreated ASTM Class B; treated ASTM Class A (EN 13501–1 B-s1, d0)

NATURA 2

Natura 2 is a wall covering material made from recovered wasted water hyacinth plants. Water hyacinths constitute one of the biggest biological masses in sweetwater reservoirs in the Philippines. Here, the fast-growing plant with dark-green, circular leaves attached to a spongy, inflated petiole is one of the main reasons for repeated severe floods. Dislodged from its natural habitat by heavy rain or other external influences, the plant moves downstream, clogging bridges and turns with its dangling roots of up to 3 m length and soil in tow. Since 2001, the Department of Environmental and Natural Resources of the Philippines has approved the harvesting of water hyacinth to eliminate river and lake clogging, resulting in some 200 km² of cut-down water hyacinths per year, which represents approximately 14 million tons of biological dried mass.[7]

Next to being a superb source for biomass fuel production, this huge amount of wasted organic substance can be used for the building sector to produce affordable and easy-to-apply finishing products. To obtain a flat stalk from the collected and dried material, it needs to be de-fibered first. Using a water-based adhesive, it is then glued atop a paperboard for stability. Once dried properly, the die-cutting machine trims the stalks into strips of regular size. Using a handloom, these strips are then connected into standard rolls by manual weaving. Depending on the colour of the stalks and the desired final appearance, different shades of polyester thread can be used in the loom. A final water-based coating protects Natura 2 wall covers from external impact and influences.

Due to the properties of this organic waste resource, the material's application possibilities are limited to areas with direct sunlight or high moisture content, such as kitchens and bathrooms.

1 Natura 2 is a decorative wall covering material for internal applications made from organic residues of the water hyacinth plant.

1

2 The Department of Environmental and Natural Resources of the Philippines has approved the harvesting of water hyacinths to eliminate clogging of rivers and lakes.

3 The stalk of the water hyacinth is collected and dried as a resource.

4

2

3

5

4 Natura 2 products are available in a variety of shades.

5 Strips of the material are connected by manual weaving to form standard rolls.

PROJECT DATA

RESOURCE
Eradicated water hyacinth

MANUFACTURER
AND DESIGNER
La Casa Deco, Manila,
Philippines

PRODUCT DIRECTORY
Finishing, page 190

PRODUCT DATA

STANDARD SIZE
910 mm × 10,980 mm

STANDARD THICKNESS
2 mm

FIRE RATING
Non-combustible
(in-house test)

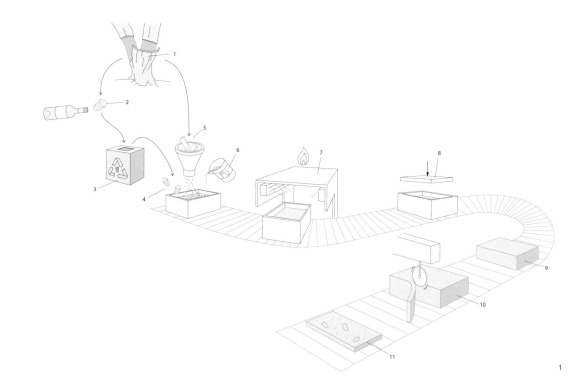

1 Production process
of Wine Cork Tiles.

1   cork oak tree bark
2   wine cork stoppers
3   collection for recycling
4   whole recycled stoppers
5   granulated cork waste
6   food-grade polyurethane
    binder
7   curing oven
8   press
9   cork block
10 cutting of sheets
    and veneer
11 wine cork tile

WINE CORK TILES

About 31.7 billion bottles of wine are consumed worldwide each year.[8] After a decline in the use of wine cork stoppers in the first decade of the new century due to a shift towards cheaper synthetic alternatives and screwing caps, they have come back and currently represent approximately 60% of the wine stopper market. This results in 19.2 billion wasted cork stoppers per year, usually thrown out with the household garbage and consequently burned or deposited on landfills.

Cork is a natural product from the bark of the cork oak tree (*Quercus suber*), a medium-sized evergreen and broadleaf plant that grows to heights of 20 m. The cork oak forms a bark that over time develops a thickness of up to 15 cm, suitable for producing wine bottle stoppers. The bark is removed from the tree by hand every nine to 12 years. Limited supply and manual labour render cork an expensive, high-quality organic material.

The trouble with recycling wine corks is that they tend to get overlooked by municipal recycling programmes due to low volume: in spite of the big quantities, wine corks are small and not every family or business generates them. For the

production of Wine Cork Tiles, the manufacturers depend on people and businesses to take the initiative and send in their corks for recycling.

Contamination in post-consumer cork, as in the overall post-consumer waste stream, is another major factor when transforming waste into a useful commodity. While metal, glass, and plastics are melted and the impurities are either burned off or screened out, this cannot be done with cork if the stoppers are to remain intact in the final product. Regardless of the method used to decontaminate post-consumer cork, the cost of this step is a significant factor in the overall process.

In order to represent the origin of the material in the product, the designers decided to use whole cork stoppers in their tiles, filling the voids in between with recycled granulated cork, a by-product of cork production. This mixture is then combined with a food-grade polyurethane binder, heated and pressed into blocks, and finally cut into sheets for veneer. For cost reasons, this thin layer is usually applied to a 3.6-mm base of cork granules. The result is a cork floor and wall tile made out of a very unique recycled material.

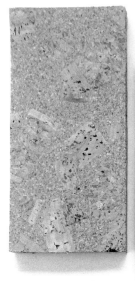

4

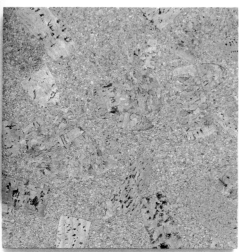

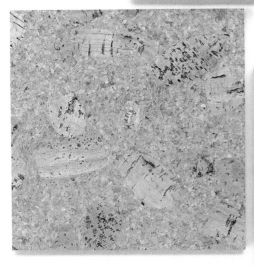

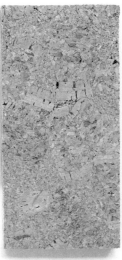

PROJECT DATA

RESOURCE
Discarded wine cork
stoppers

MANUFACTURER
AND DESIGNER
Yemm & Hart Green
Materials, Marquand,
MO, USA

PRODUCT DIRECTORY
Finishing, page 190

PRODUCT DATA

STANDARD SIZE
300 mm × 300 mm,
up to 600 mm × 900 mm

STANDARD THICKNESS
4.8 mm (veneer) or
6–152 mm (sheet)

DENSITY
320 kg/m³

COMPRESSIBILITY
AT 689 KPA
15–30% (F36)

FIRE RATING
Fire-resistant (E136)

VOC
E1, 100% formaldehyde-
free (F148)

2 About 19.2 billion cork
stoppers are wasted worldwide per year.

3 Thin layers cut from
bigger blocks preserve
the original shape of the
resource material.

4 The manufactured large
blocks contain the original
cork stoppers, the voids
between them filled with
recycled granulated cork.

5 Wine Cork Tiles are a
natural product of recycled
wine cork stoppers for
interior flooring or wall
applications.

5

1 UltraTouch Denim Insulation uses post-consumer recycled textiles as a source of natural cotton fibres.

2 The material comes in standard sizes ready for assembly between the interior and exterior walls and the ceiling structures.

3 A perforation allows easy customization for use in corners or unconventional applications.

4 The fibres of UltraTouch are not harmful to the human organism, they contain no chemical irritants and are easy to handle.

ULTRATOUCH DENIM INSULATION

Jeans and denim are known as a very robust and almost impossible-to-destroy fabric, which makes the material very popular in the textile industry. These superb properties can be extended to a second life cycle as a high-quality building material, showing that waste is a viable resource for future building applications.

The global jeans and denim market is about 1.9 billion units, with an average consumption of 0.28 units per person per year.[9] In the USA, with a yearly market of about 450 million produced units, consumption numbers are even higher. Although denim is a valuable material made from organic cotton twill textile and coloured with a synthetic indigo dye, it is mostly recycled in Do-It-Yourself projects or second-hand shops. On an industrial scale, Bonded Logic produces the insulation material UltraTouch Denim from the natural cotton fibres of post-consumer recycled textiles. Their inherent qualities are the basis for the effective sound absorption and thermal performance of the new products. The fibres of UltraTouch are not harmful to the human organism, cause no chemical annoyances, do not irritate the skin, and are easy to handle and work with.

In the production process, the denim is first separated from any other fabric as well as the zippers, buttons, and hardware, similar to removing staples from paper before processing. Large shredders hack the denim into pieces before a second processor un-weaves the strips, returning the textile to its original fibre state. This raw material is treated with a borate solution to make the insulation fire-resistant and repel mould and mildew. Mixed with other natural fibres (80% denim, 20% new material), the blend is baked together in a large oven. Finally, the material is pressed into a variety of different thicknesses in a continuous rolling process and cut to its shipping size.

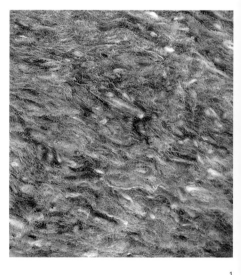

1

2

4

3

PROJECT DATA

RESOURCE
Discarded jeans and
denim fabrics

MANUFACTURER
AND DESIGNER
Bonded Logic Inc.,
Chandler, AZ, USA

PRODUCT DIRECTORY
Insulating, page 182

PRODUCT DATA

STANDARD SIZE
381 / 584 mm × 1,220 /
2,320 / 9,750 mm

STANDARD THICKNESS
51 / 89 / 140 / 203 mm

DENSITY
15.83–21.32 kg/m³

FIRE RATING
Non-combustible, Class A,
Class 1 (ASTM E-84 /
E-119 / UL-263)

NOISE REDUCTION
COEFFICIENT (NRC)
R13–R19 (ASTM E90–02)

THERMAL CONDUCTIVITY
0.125–0.03 W/m²K
(ASTM C-518 at 24°C)

1 The masonry construction method used for Vault201 was inspired by techniques used by Rafael Guastavino in the late 19th century.

2 Guastavino-type constructions use quick-setting mortar to glue the tiles in place.

3 The form of the Catalan vault follows the line of momentum, so that the bricks need to absorb only compression forces.

1 guiding formwork
2 Green Leaf Brick

VAULT201

New York City produces approximately 1,200 tons of bio-solids from its 14 wastewater treatment plants per day.[10] Ocean disposal of bio-solids was banned in 1988 and the city was required to find an alternative land-based use for this material. Today most of the bio-solids in the USA are recycled to fertilize crops and improve soil conditions for plant growth. Innovative companies, such as Green Leaf Brick, propose tapping into regional bio-solid waste streams to create materials for the building industry. Specifically, they produce bricks made from 100% pre- and post-consumer waste.

Vault201 is a thin-shell masonry construction that showcases bricks made from this waste resource and demonstrates an engineering technique that minimizes material use through structurally efficient design. The brick is composed of 30% processed sewage waste, contents from industrial dust filtration, and the by-products of open-pit mining operations, such as recycled iron oxides, recycled glass, mineral tailings, and virgin ceramic scrap. Even though processed sewage is one of the main ingredients, the bricks are odourless, as they are fired above 1,030°C. Most of the materials used are collected from waste streams within a 160-km radius of the manufacturing plant in North Carolina, USA. Their dimensions and structural performance qualities allow the bricks to be competitive with conventional building elements.

The masonry construction method for Vault201 was inspired by techniques used by Rafael Guastavino in the late 19th century. Quick-setting mortar minimizes the amount of formwork required and thereby reduces construction waste. Also known as tile vaulting, or Catalan vaulting, the geometry is derived from a series of catenary arches. All forces are carried in axial compression so that internal stresses in the vault are low and the structure has considerable stability under both dead and live loadings. As a result, the vault can be constructed with a thinness proportional to that of an eggshell.

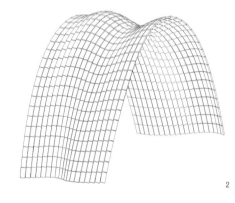

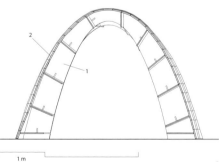

1 m

4 The brick vault is built onto a formwork, which is removed after the mortar has set.

1 guiding formwork
2 Green Leaf Brick

5 Vault201 bricks are manufactured using pre- and post-consumer recycled materials including 30% sewage waste.

6 Also known as tile vaulting, or Catalan vaulting, the geometry of the vault is derived from a series of catenary arches and allows for minimal thickness, proportional to that of an eggshell.

7 Once the vault is closed and the mortar is set, the formwork can be removed from underneath.

5

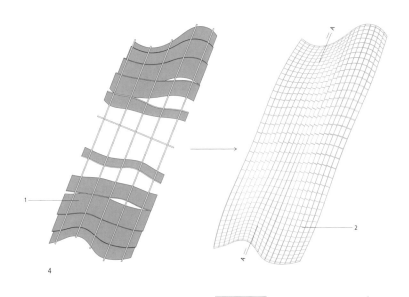

4

1 m

6

7

PROJECT DATA

RESOURCE
Sewage waste and scrap materials

MANUFACTURER
Green Leaf Brick, Charlotte, NC, USA

DESIGNER
Masonry Research Group, Massachusetts Institute of Technology, Cambridge, MA, USA

PRODUCT DIRECTORY
Load-bearing, page 176

PRODUCT DATA

STANDARD SIZE
194 mm × 92 mm

STANDARD THICKNESS
25 mm

DENSITY
2,380 kg/m³

COMPRESSION STRENGTH
112 MPa

FIRE RATING
Non-combustible up to 1,093°C

TRANSFORMED WASTE MATERIALS

CASE STUDIES

StoneCycling p. 98
Alusion p. 102
CRT Glass Tiles p. 104
FOAMGLAS T4+ p. 106
Olzweg p. 110
Byfusion Bricks p. 114
GR Green Slate p. 116
Nappy Roofing p. 118
Recy Blocks p. 120
Tire Veneer Tiles p. 122
Blood Brick p. 124

Next to densification and mechanical processing of waste, there is a third method used in the production of construction elements from refuse: through transformation of the molecular state of waste. This process enacts the conversion of garbage into a new state of existence in different form, composition, shape, and function through the complete loss of the existing organizational structure of the material.

Transformation is an alteration of the material state by direct intake or incorporation of other materials or forms of energy from the surroundings – these are typically man-made and come in the shape of mixing chambers or pressure moulds. On the extreme end of the spectrum, vitrification – the transformation of a substance into a glass-like condition under very high temperatures – could be a future technology to transform even problematic waste into building materials. The key benefit of this method is that hazardous substances can be converted to a new material state without facing any risks for health and environment.

Similar to the densification process, transforming waste requires the addition of energy to the system in order to achieve another state of the material, resulting in altered forms or properties of the final product. Typically the first step in the process is grinding the material into a sand- or powder-like aggregate. After mixing it with other components, the crush is then usually heated to its melting point or beyond, put into a mould, and formed into any desired shape. Additional steps of cutting or milling may be applied. We are fully aware that the involved additional input of energy to most of the processes described here may be considered a waste production in itself, depending on the source of energy. Only by applying corresponding processes in the energy sector a full-fledged and convincing circular waste-to-product system can be achieved.

The chapter "Transformed Waste Materials" addresses the most extreme form of waste treatment: high-tech procedures that involve liquefying or gasification of the original material in order to create a new element with specific properties and resulting functional purposes. A well-known example from another field is the transformation of organic waste into bioethanol, a form of renewable energy that is used as a replacement for regular gasoline. While this transformation approach is well established in the field of energy production from wasted agricultural goods, so far little has been done in the area of building construction and materials.

One example described here comes from the Netherlands, where Tom van Soest has developed a method to transform one of the biggest waste resources of our urban habitat:

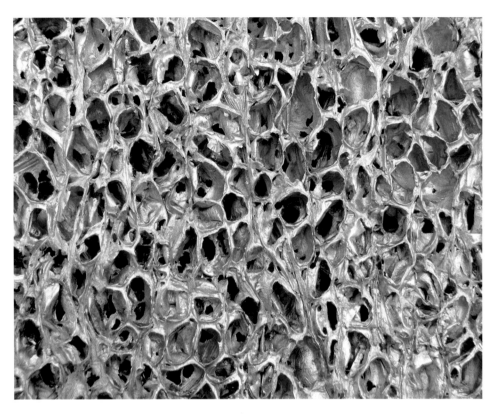

building rubble. In the process, discarded building materials such as concrete, stone, glass, or ceramics are pulverized in a grinder, mixed, and baked into new stone-like products without addition of artificial binders or any other no-waste substances. The resulting elements can be used again as construction and building units, re-entering the same environment they originally came from – a perfect metabolic scenario. This concept stands in the context of a wider discussion that may lead us to actually start to mine our cities for resources instead of continuing to carve them out of the earth crust, wasting time, water, and energy. For centuries, our cities have accumulated natural resources. This project shows one possible way of how to recover them for future generations.

The product Nappy Roofing deals with a very distinct waste material resource, so-called absorbent hygiene articles. Here, the invention is twofold: how to extract the valuable material from the unwanted human waste, and how to process the plastics, fibres, and polymers into a new substance. The company Knowaste in the UK has managed to develop such a production line and compose a material that next to other applications can be used in the concrete industry as an aggregate. In an interesting move, the recyclers have teamed up with the company Light Weight Tiles to manufacture also roofing tiles out of their transformed material. And even though nothing can be seen or otherwise sensed of the product's origins, the thought of having a nappy roof casts a new and innovative light on a consumer good that is usually associated with mixed feelings and perceptions when disposing it.

Next to buildings, also big infrastructural elements can be constructed from waste. Besides the already common aggregate fly ash, a waste by-product from the steel industry and lately even from waste incineration plants, other substitutes for natural aggregates have become available recently. Plasphalt is such a substitute, made out of 100% recycled plastics and already used in road construction in California today. When poured, the plastic synthesizes with the other aggregates in the asphalt mix and forms a strong matrix. The result is a longer-lasting, more durable version of asphalt, which is at

1 Panels made out of recycled aluminium can be used in various construction applications.

the same time lighter, cheaper, and easier to pour.

Other synthesized plastic products appeared on the market in recent years, mostly panels and boards, for many different indoor and outdoor applications. Such transformed waste materials on an industrial scale require high-tech production processes and, while they are present mainly on the US and European markets for the time being, recycled plastic materials are also becoming available within entirely different markets and clienteles. Three-dimensional printing is currently revolutionizing our understanding of product design and transportation. Anyone, anywhere can potentially shape plastic or metal based on a digital file that travels around the world in seconds anytime. In the near future, replacement parts might no longer need to be shipped to customers. And also new designs based on individual demands can be realized easier and cheaper than before. In his 2013 State of the Union address, US President Obama mentioned 3D printing as a future technology to revolutionize the American industry in coming years. The question, however, will remain about what resources should be used to feed the printers.

At the time of writing, 3D printers use mostly cartridges with specially produced, clean, and new plastics. Recently, the first proto-typical home-use plastic grinders claimed to be able to utilize any kind of discarded plastic to produce the granulate necessary for off-the-shelf 3D printers. This could change the way plastic waste is perceived in the future. An empty water bottle suddenly offers endless possibilities when seen as potential "ink" for your 3D printer – only limited by the ability to use the required software when creating new objects. Do-It-Yourself 3D printing, in combination with the almost endless resource that is waste, might revolutionize our built environment.

Transformed waste materials, at the end of their specific life cycle, can be recycled again to a product of the reconstructed waste materials type. Within the conceptual framework of waste underlying this publication, there will always be another product that can utilize any transformed construction element as a "raw" material for further production.

2 Scrap material from 3D printing to be turned into new filament.

1 StoneCycling tiles can be used for roofing, façade construction, and finishing applications with a variety of colours and shapes.

2 A wide range of different building elements can be produced from construction rubble.

3 First prototypes of tiles.

STONECYCLING

Demolition waste will remain a renewable resource as long as our civilization continues to constantly build and re-build its habitat. Many materials in the resulting demolition waste are already being recycled, from reinforcement steel via concrete aggregates and reused timber to bricks. Recycling schemes, however, are usually downcycling processes, whereby the quality of the new product is reduced with every life cycle.

The amount of construction and demolition waste produced in the Netherlands every year is estimated at 15 million tons, while the demand for new raw construction materials is ten times higher.[1] Although some of the demolition waste is used to build foundations for highways and roads, the rest usually ends up in landfills and land reclamation areas. The idea behind StoneCycling is, by contrast, to increase the value of the new product by transforming the waste and applying the product within different functions and properties. Tom van Soest has developed a

method that pulverizes glass, concrete, bricks, and even complete ceramic washbasins into powder, using a special blender.

The chain of reproduction starts already at the demolition site, where materials are collected that are specifically suitable for this process of transformation, similar to the separation of municipal solid waste at the household level. Through mixing and baking the powders coming from building waste materials in various compositions, Tom van Soest manufactures new stone-like products without adding any artificial binders or no-waste additives. The first experimental series of "trial baked goods" showcases the enormous variety and potentials concerning shapes, colours, and textures.

Application possibilities are very wide, starting from roofing, bathroom, or kitchen tiles to floor or wall covering elements, window sills, or kitchen counters.

1

2

3

PROJECT DATA	PRODUCT DATA
RESOURCE Demolition waste	STANDARD SIZE 600 mm × 600 mm
MANUFACTURER AND DESIGNER Tom van Soest, Eindhoven, The Netherlands	STANDARD THICKNESS 8 mm
	FIRE RATING Fireproof, non-combustible (DIN EN 13501)
PRODUCT DIRECTORY Waterproofing, page 184; Finishing, page 191	

4 Demolition waste is widely available and a renewable resource of its own right.

1 stones/tiles
2 application
3 demolition
4 StoneCycling grinder
5 powder

5 Different colours reflect the varying original resources of the mix.

6 Tom van Soest has developed a method to pulverize recycled building materials from demolition sites and create new products out of them.

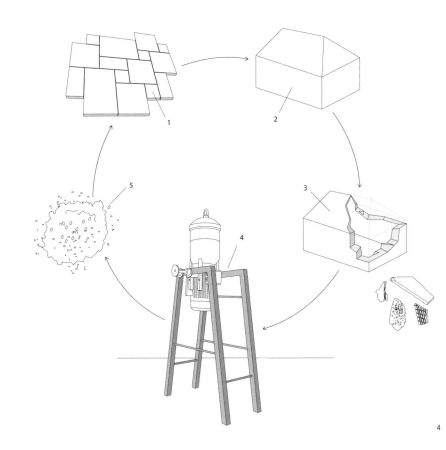

4

5

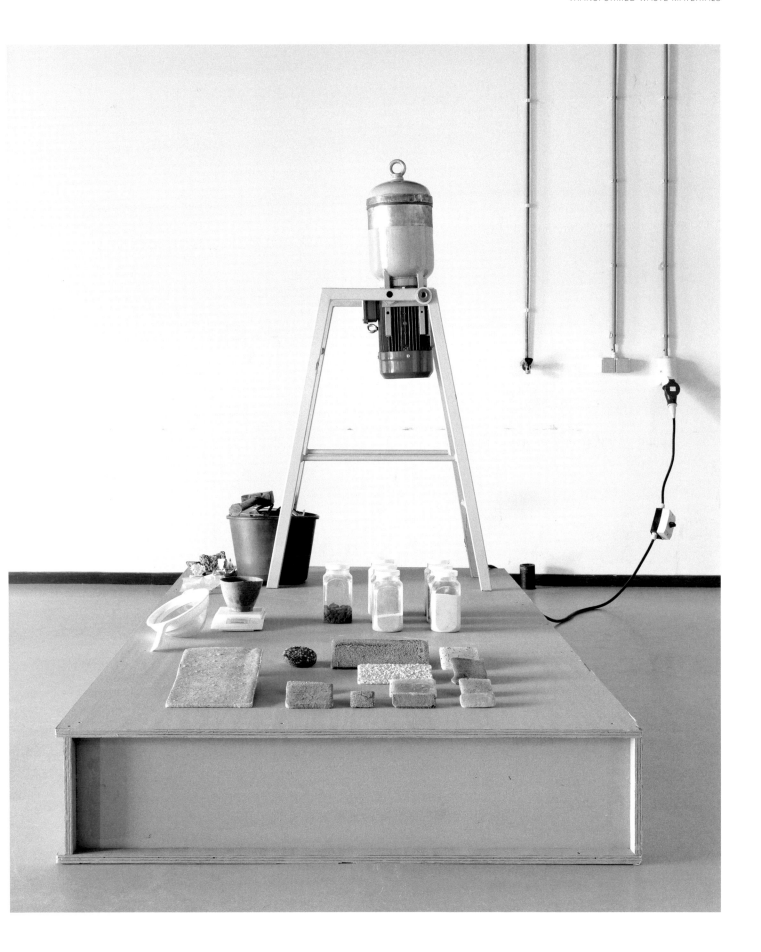

1 Alusion Stabilized Aluminium Foam is produced by injecting air into molten aluminium.

1

ALUSION – STABILIZED ALUMINIUM FOAM PANELS

Aluminium recycling is a simple process that involves re-melting the metal, requiring only 5% of the energy used in creating new aluminium through the electrolysis of aluminium oxide. Sources for used aluminium include old aircrafts, cars, bikes, electrical boards, cooking pots, cables and wires, and many other products that ask for a strong lightweight material, or a material with high thermal conductivity. As recycling does not transmute the element as long as it is not contaminated with other substances or lower-grade aluminium, the material can be recycled indefinitely. In fact, three quarters of the estimated 900 million tons of aluminium produced since 1880 is still in productive use today: 30% is located within transport applications, 30% in electrical cables and machinery, and around 35% in buildings.[2] Recycling the metal currently stored in use would equal up to 17 years worth of annual primary aluminium production.

Cymat's Aluminium Foam Alusion extends the regular recycling process with an additional loop. With the use of up to 100% scrap aluminium and in combination with virgin material, this process creates a versatile substance for many architectural, automotive, and other design applications.

The production process requires a lot of technical know-how. The material is heated beyond the melting point and is then poured into a casting apparatus, where air is injected into the molten aluminium. The resulting bubbles rise and allow the material to continuously foam out of the casting apparatus and onto a production line, where it is cooled and solidifies into a flat panel. The resulting lightweight panels are similar in appearance to a metallic sponge and can be cut into desired forms and lengths. No compounds are added to the material during the casting process,

thus maintaining an acceptable melt quality for recasting. As such, the material is 100% recyclable within the process.

The surface of the new material is either left in its solid form, as cast, or undergoes surface treatment that provides many different appearances, from a solid-surface "shimmering" look to a translucent "cellular web" look. As the thickness increases, the density decreases, giving each thickness a distinct expression. Small-cell materials are typically used when applications require increased mechanical strength, while a large-cell structure is extremely lightweight and often used in combination with lighting effects or for wall construction. Besides its unique appearance, the product has good energy, sound-absorbing, and thermal insulation properties, and is flame-resistant.

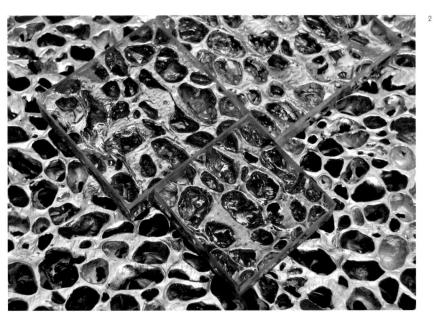

2

PROJECT DATA	PRODUCT DATA
RESOURCE	STANDARD SIZE
Discarded aluminium	2,440 mm × 1,220 mm
MANUFACTURER	STANDARD THICKNESS
AND DESIGNER	12.7 / 25.4 / 43.2 mm
Cymat Technologies Ltd.,	
Mississauga, ON, Canada	DENSITY
	110–550 kg/m³
PRODUCT DIRECTORY	
Insulating, page 183;	TENSILE STRENGTH
Finishing, page 187	414 MPa (ASTM B557)
	FIRE RATING
	Non-combustible (E136)
	SOUND ABSORPTION
	Class B (ISO 111654)

3

4

2 The surface of the new material is either left in its solid form, as cast, or undergoes surface preparations that provide many different appearances, from a solid-surface "shimmering" look to a translucent "cellular web" look.

3 The higher the density, the smaller the cell size, the heavier and more robust the material.

4 Exterior wall cladding applied on a church building in Barcelona, Spain.

CRT GLASS TILES

Cathode ray tube glass was developed to create a way for projecting images onto a screen. The technology required that the glass was exceptionally thick and shatter-resistant, which makes it one of the hardest types of electronic waste to recycle. Tube glass could be recycled into more tube glass, but with rapid technological change and declining costs for LCD screens and plasma displays there is no longer a viable use for cathode ray tubes. In fact, almost no such tubes are used in today's electronics, while at the same time TV sets and computer monitors constitute 43% of all e-waste products in the USA. Some 20 million outdated units are stored each year in recycling centres and landfills,[3] partially constituting even hazardous waste due to the approximately 5–6 g of lead in a screen.

CRT Glass Tiles are intended for indoor or outdoor residential applications, while engineered for the rigours of a commercial job site. The production firm cooperates with a local electronics waste recycling company, which first runs the glass through a saw to separate the front, middle, and back sections. Performing chemical analysis of the glass to guarantee that it is safe to use, Fireclay Tile uses only the front of the screen, about 2 cm thick. In a second step, the chunks of the front parts of the screens are crushed to demagnetize the material at the start of a multi-step crushing process that ultimately produces glass particles small enough to melt when exposed to heat. After the glass is sorted, the tiles are cast into moulds, adding white colour pigment to lighten the original tube glass and achieve a light grey colour named "phosphor". The tube glass tiles are available in different rectangular sizes as well as a round mosaic variation.

1 CRT Glass Tiles are produced out of materials gained from the screens of reclaimed cathode ray tubes.

2 CRT Glass Tiles are available in different shapes and sizes.

3 White colour pigments are added to the crushed glass, brightening up the natural CRT glass look into a light grey appearance.

4

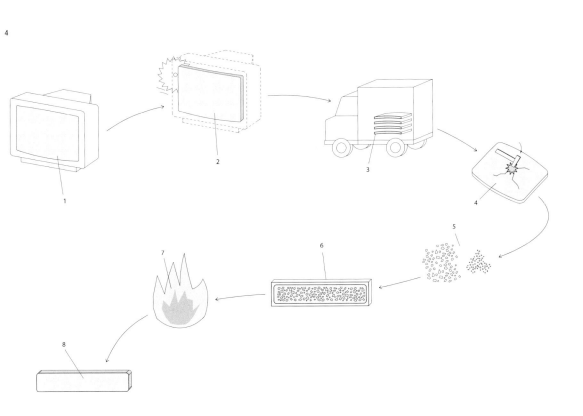

1 cathode ray tube
2 recovery of screens
3 delivery to factory
4 crushing into fine
 particles
5 adding pigment
6 placing mix into moulds
7 melting of glass
8 CRT Glass Tiles

5 Cathode ray tube glass is
considered one of the most
difficult types of electronic
waste to be recycled.

5

PROJECT DATA

RESOURCE
Discarded cathode
ray tubes

MANUFACTURER
AND DESIGNER
Fireclay Tile,
San Francisco, CA, USA

PRODUCT DIRECTORY
Finishing, page 187;
Waterproofing, page 186

PRODUCT DATA

STANDARD SIZE
50 mm × 100 / 200 mm
or ø 20 mm

STANDARD THICKNESS
9.5 mm

DENSITY
6,500 kg/m³

COMPRESSION STRENGTH
900 MPa

BREAKING STRENGTH
2.94 MPa

FIRE RATING
Fire-resistant
(DIN EN 13501)

FOAMGLAS T4+

FOAMGLAS T4+ cellular glass belongs to the large group of products made out of recycled glass. It is a resilient insulating building material composed of hermetically sealed glass cells, each in itself an insulating element. This inorganic, all-glass, closed-cell structure provides an unmatched combination of physical properties ideal for the overall building envelope. The product comes from Belgium, the number three glass recycler in Europe with a recycling rate of 94%, which is well above the European average of 70%,[4] according to the European Container Glass Federation. Glass can be recycled without a loss of quality and offers a wide range of application possibilities and forms, rendering it attractive for the building sector.

The insulation material is manufactured primarily from recycled glass and additional natural raw materials such as sand, dolomite, lime, and iron oxide, making for an almost unlimited resource. The glass waste is mostly obtained from defective automobile windscreens and windows. The glass product with its precisely defined properties is obtained from the fusion of these specific materials. The glass mass is ground down, mixed with a small amount of carbon and put into high-grade steel moulds. These pass through a furnace where the glass foam powder is expanded like dough for bread. Thin glass air cells emerge from this process, which are retained in a controlled cooling process.

Due to the cell structure consisting of millions of the smallest possible hermetically sealed glass cells, this material boasts extraordinary compressive strength, waterproofness, and highest insulation values. It does not contain any ozone-depleting propellants, flame retardants, or binding agents, because the raw materials used for manufacturing are exclusively mineral and ecologically safe. It can be applied to protect bearing walls and foundation rafts, or as façade and roof insulation elements. Terraces, parking decks, and interior insulation for walls, floors, and soffits – even under harsh humidity conditions – are also among the many areas of application for this rigid insulation material.

The service life span of FOAMGLAS T4+ matches the one of the building. At the end of its life span, cellular glass can be reused best as crushed stone – for example as bedding in road constructions – or as a filler for acoustic protection walls.

1 FOAMGLAS T4+ consists of hermetically sealed glass cells.

2 The resources used in the production are inherently mineral, with more than 60% recycled glass.

1

2

3

3 Blocks are cut to size. Scrap material is re-introduced into the production process.

PROJECT DATA

RESOURCE
Discarded glass

MANUFACTURER
AND DESIGNER
Pittsburgh Corning
Europe NV, Tessenderlo,
Belgium

PRODUCT DIRECTORY
Load-bearing, page 177;
Insulating, page 180

PRODUCT DATA

STANDARD SIZE
450 mm × 600 mm

STANDARD THICKNESS
30–180 mm

DENSITY
117 kg/m^3

COMPRESSION STRENGTH
600 KPa

FIRE RATING
Non-combustible
(A1 cf. EN 13501/
ASTM-E 136)

THERMAL CONDUCTIVITY:
at 24°C: 0.043 W/m^{2}K
(at 10°C: 0.041 W/m^{2}K)

4 Stainless steel moulds filled with fine powder pass through a foaming furnace, "baking" the insulation blocks homogeneously.

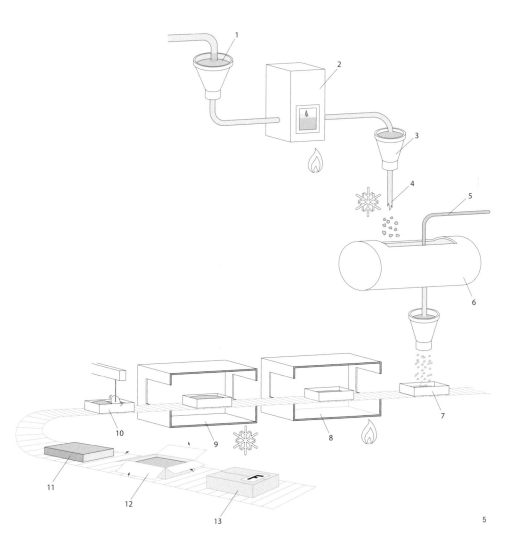

5 The manufacturing process starts from the recovered glass.

1 raw material mix
2 furnace at 1,250°C
3 molten glass
4 cooled glass pieces
5 production waste
6 ball mill; addition of "carbon black"
7 stainless steel moulds filled with fine powder
8 cellulating oven at 850°C
9 annealing oven for controlled cooling
10 cutting of blocks
11 sorting
12 packing, labelling, palletizing
13 FOAMGLAS T4+ insulation

6 The insulation material can be glued easily to any substructure.

7 The insulation can be used on top of a bed of fine gravel.

8 Parking deck built with FOAMGLAS T4+.

6

7

8

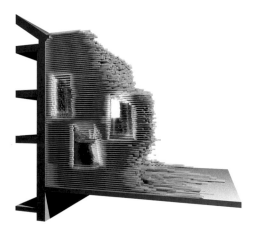 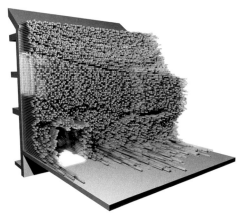

1

OLZWEG

The Olzweg project – an allusion to the philosopher Martin Heidegger's term "Holzweg", meaning wrong track – suggests to use discarded glass as the main construction substance for a building component. The project was developed for a competition to transform a former military building conglomerate in the conurbation of the city of Orléans, France, into the Regional Contemporary Art Fund FRAC.

The project idea is rather simple: discarded bottles – 10,000 tons of glass are discarded every year as waste in the immediate regional neighbourhood of the project – are transformed into rectangular-shaped, massive glass bar elements. These glass bars would then be positioned by a specially installed robotic arm into an inhabitable building layer in front of the existing structures, extending their spatial presence into the courtyard. The massive glass bars all have the same length and are stapled on top of each other, some of them shifted by 90° to form a stable structural system. The robotic arm is able to pull and push them into position in such a way that spatial pockets in the

ensuing glass conglomerate can be created. The glass bars can also be rearranged periodically, reacting to shifting needs and functional requirements or even intuitive responses of the visitors. Thus the proposed architectural extension can be seen as a negotiation platform between the existing buildings and its users. In the project's logic of using only glass waste from the neighbourhood, it would take up to 30 years to finish the proposed design. This long stretch of time would allow users to identify with the project and assume an important role in the building process.

Although the project was winning the architectural competition, it has not been commissioned to be built by FRAC under the authority of the French Ministry of Culture, which argued that it was too "avant-garde" in the sense of never reaching a final configuration. Nevertheless, the experimental design strategy opens up a perspective to see waste not only as an alternative building material, but even reprogramme the very act of producing and using waste from a negative perception into a creative and innovative one.

1 The Olzweg project proposes to use recycled glass bar elements as the main building material for the Regional Contemporary Art Fund FRAC in Orléans, France.

PROJECT DATA

RESOURCE
Discarded glass

DESIGNER
New-territories / R&Sie(n),
Paris, France

PRODUCT DIRECTORY
Load-bearing, page 172

PRODUCT DATA

STANDARD SECTION
Custom

STANDARD LENGTH
Custom

DENSITY
2,500 kg/m³

COMPRESSION STRENGTH
1,000 MPa

FIRE RATING
Fireproof, non-combustible
(DIN EN 13501)

CONSTRUCTION TIME
30 years

2 Discarded glass bottles
are transformed into
rectangular-shaped,
massive glass bars that
are placed into position
by a specially designed
robotic arm to create a
building extension.

2

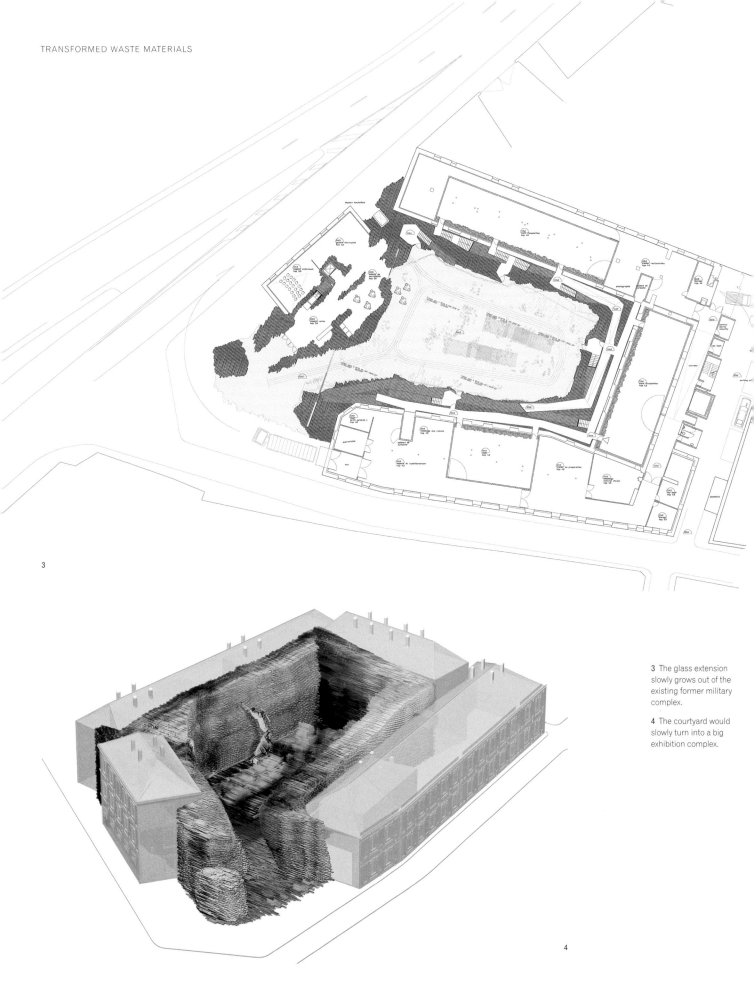

3

4

3 The glass extension slowly grows out of the existing former military complex.

4 The courtyard would slowly turn into a big exhibition complex.

5 The spatial pockets in the glass extension are circulation and exhibition spaces in one.

6 The robotic arm can pull and push the elements into different positions, reacting to shifting needs or intuitive statements of the visitors.

5

6

BYFUSION BRICKS

Unsorted consumer plastic waste mostly ends up in landfills; in the USA, only 7% of all plastic waste is being recovered.[5] With a technology called Byfusion, a company from New Zealand found a solution to reuse 100% mixed domestic post-consumer plastic waste and transform it into building materials such as bricks or panels.

In the production process, the mixed, unsorted plastics are shredded into thin strips and cleaned in a rotary washer tumble, then dried by hot air and compressed into a batch mould, which is afterwards capped and moved into a fusion chamber. Using heat and pressure, the plastic is fused into a solid mass in predefined shapes and cooled down to about 25°C before leaving the compartment. When fully established, the process can run 24 hours, seven days a week and produce from 250 to 10,000 units per day or even more, depending on the size of the production plant and the available plastic intake.

In a first application, Byfusion started producing building blocks. Designed as an interlocking system similar to toy bricks, the blocks do not require additional mortar or glue to hold together. In practice, however, vertical steel guides are added to ease construction and increase the coherence between the units. By placing a plate on top of the finished wall and binding it back to the foundation, a structural system can be created that withstands high lateral forces of the kind that occur in earthquakes. The blocks can be shop-coated in any colour, or finished on site with common plaster techniques. The bricks have high thermal and acoustic insulation values.

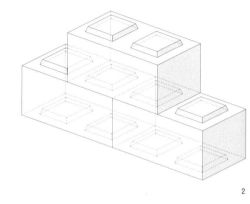

2

1 A standard Byfusion brick.

2 Due to an interlocking system similar to toy bricks, these blocks do not require mortar or glue to hold together.

1

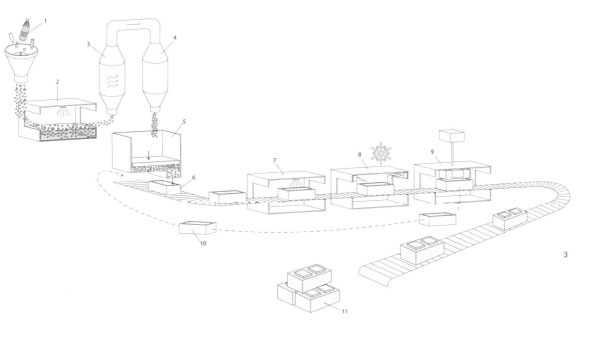

3 The process comprises the shredding, washing, and drying of the plastic before it is compressed into a batch mould, which is then capped and moved into a fusion chamber. Using heat and pressure, the plastic is fused into a solid mass in the predefined shape.

1 plastic waste shredder
2 washer
3 dryer
4 silo
5 batch press
6 conveyor belt
7 fusion chamber
8 cooling cycle
9 de-lidding
10 mould recovery
11 Byfusion Brick

3

PROJECT DATA

RESOURCE
Discarded plastics

MANUFACTURER
AND DESIGNER
Byfusion Limited,
Wellington, New Zealand

PRODUCT DIRECTORY
Load-bearing, page 174;
Insulating, page 183

PRODUCT DATA

STANDARD SIZE
400 mm × 200 mm

STANDARD HEIGHT
200 mm

DENSITY
375–625 kg/m³

COMPRESSION STRENGTH
950–1,002 kPa

FIRE RATING
No information

YOUNG'S MODULUS
2.1–4.5 MPa

4

4 The Byfusion production machine fits into a standard 40-foot container.

5 The blocks can be pressed into different sizes and shapes.

6 Building blocks are the first application that Byfusion started producing.

5

6

115

GR GREEN SLATE, GR GREEN CEDAR

GR Green Building Products has developed a technology that can turn discarded Polyethylene milk bottles, plastic bags, and limestone waste materials into roofing tiles and siding products for the construction industry. Milk bottles are made from High-Density Polyethylene (HDPE), a thermo-plastic made from petroleum, with a global market volume of more than 30 million tons. Products manufactured through blow moulding, like milk or water bottles, are the most important application of this plastic material, accounting for more than eight million tons or nearly one third of worldwide polyethylene production.[6] Although these jugs are recyclable and could be melted down and turned into new bottles, in the USA no milk containers are actually made from recycled material, due to safety concerns over bacterial and chemical contamination and strict federal guidelines for the manufacturing of food packaging from second-hand sources. Altogether, only one third of milk containers are recycled into new products; the rest may spend hundreds of years decomposing in landfills, be

incinerated, or end up as plastic debris floating in the oceans.

A typical GR Green Slate roof recycles about 4,400 milk bottles and 44,000 plastic bags in a zero waste process that uses 20% polyethylene and 80% limestone waste materials. Excess trim from the construction site can be returned to the plant for reprocessing, minimizing landfill waste and reducing costs by eliminating dumping fees. Ultimately, all GR Green products can be recycled into new products at the end of their first life cycle, without a loss of quality or value.

GR Green products have an appearance similar to real slate or natural cedar and come with a 50-year warranty. GR Green roofing products require a minimum slope of 18° to achieve the required runoff, up to a maximum slope of 63°. They are installed with regular mounting fixtures, while siding products utilize a proprietary system. All GR Green products are fire and wind-resistant, water-repellent and maintenance-free.

1 GR Green Slate products imitate the look of natural slate tiles.

2 The tiles can be nailed for easy installation and are maintenance-free.

1 roofing nails (2 per tile)
2 roofing felt underlayment
3 metal drip edge
4 starters

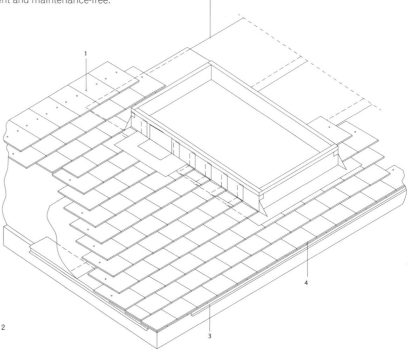

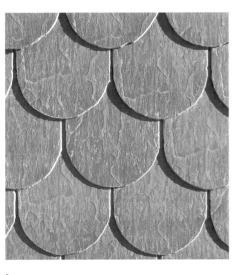

3

4

3 Different tile shapes and colour variations are available.

4 GR Green Cedar resembles natural cedar finishing tiles.

PROJECT DATA	PRODUCT DATA (ROOFING TILE)
RESOURCE	STANDARD SIZE
Discarded milk bottles, plastic bags, and limestone waste	457 mm × 254 mm
	STANDARD THICKNESS
	6 mm
MANUFACTURER AND DESIGNER	DENSITY
GR Green Building Products Inc., Vancouver, BC, Canada	182 kg/m³
	FLEXURAL STRENGTH
	> 5.2 MPa (ASTM D790–07)
PRODUCT DIRECTORY	FIRE RATING
Waterproofing, page 185; Finishing, page 191	Fire-resistant (E163)
	WATER ABSORPTION
	< 0.4% (CMCC 6.4.2)

5

5 The roof needs a minimum slope of 18° to achieve the required runoff, with a maximum slope of 63°.

6 A typical roof cover recycles about 4,400 milk bottles and 44,000 plastic bags in a zero waste process.

6

1

1 Knowaste reclaims fibres and plastic pellets from absorbent hygiene products.

2, 3 At the plant, the collected hygiene products are conveyed into the machine for processing.

4 The plastics are granulated and washed before being pelletized for further processing into consumer products.

1 collected absorbent hygiene waste
2 conveyed to an autoclave, opened, and sterilized
3 brown water treatment
4 shredding and material separation
5 reclaimed fibers
6 reclaimed plastic granulate
7 washing process
8 plastic pellets
9 Nappy Roof Tiles

2

NAPPY ROOFING

Absorbent hygiene products contain plastic materials, fibres, and super-absorbent polymers. This waste, containing disposable baby diapers, adult incontinence, and feminine hygiene products, is a very valuable resource, since all products use the same plastics substances, resulting in highly sorted recycling material. More than one million tons of absorbent hygiene product waste is generated in the UK every year. The company Knowaste is specialized in processing this unique waste resource and can handle 36,000 tons in one plant annually, while such highly developed and specialized products would need decades if not centuries to decay in landfills.

In the recycling plant, the waste is conveyed to an autoclave to be sterilized and then shredded and separated. The super-absorbent polymers need to be collapsed in order to release the captured organic residue, which is disposed into the sewage system. The fibres are reclaimed first;

they can be used for industrial cardboard tubing and other fibre-based construction materials. The plastics continue through granulation and multiple washing stages before being bagged for shipment in pelletized form. The pellets can be used as an ingredient for injection moulding to produce new composite materials.

An application that seems most promising to enter the market are roofing tiles. The company Light Weight Tiles teamed up with the recycling plant to create a three-part roofing system, aiming at houses and garden structures including carports and log cabins. Products comprise roofing sheets, ridge tiles, and side flashings, all available in various colours and surface structures. Compared to a conventional clay tile, they are extremely light-weight, UV-resistant, and non-corrosive. In addition, the material is easy to install and shows good thermal insulation and sound absorption qualities.

3

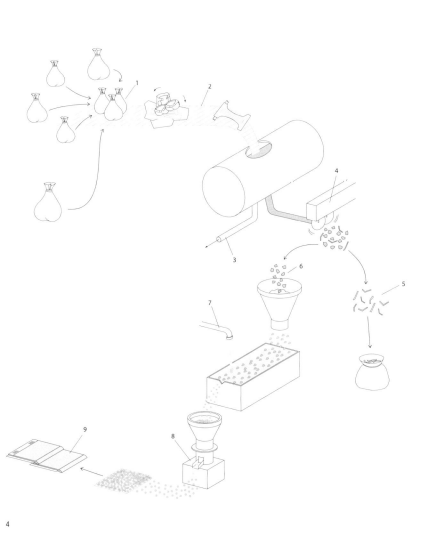

4

5 Knowaste is specialized in processing this unique waste resource and can handle 36,000 tons in one plant per year.

6 Absorbent hygiene products also contain plastic materials, fibres, and super-absorbent polymers.

7 Light Weight Tiles have created a three-part roofing system out of reclaimed pellets.

PROJECT DATA

RESOURCE
Discarded absorbent hygiene products

MANUFACTURER AND DESIGNER
Knowaste with Light Weight Tiles Ltd., Bromsgrove and Lydney, United Kingdom

PRODUCT DIRECTORY
Waterproofing, page 185

PRODUCT DATA

STANDARD SIZE
Approx. 1,100 mm × 320 mm

STANDARD THICKNESS
Approx. 6 mm

DENSITY
Approx. 750 kg/m^3

FIRE RATING
No information

1 Recy Blocks are made out of plastic wrapping materials and can vary in transparency and texture, depending on resources used.

2 Recy Blocks are waterproof, which allows for both interior and exterior applications.

1

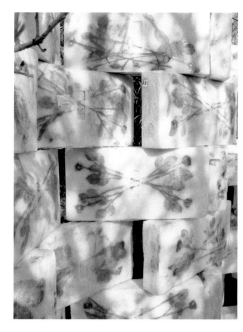

RECY BLOCKS

Recy Blocks use discarded plastic bags and other waste products with similar material properties to form new building bricks. Even in Europe, traditionally the top recycling continent, recycling rates of plastic bags amount to only 6%;[7] worldwide every minute more than one million plastic bags are used, according to the Worldwatch Institute, adding up to approximately 500 billion to 1 trillion plastic bags used every year.[8]

Recy Blocks combine structural capacities with a highly artistic approach. Aiming for products for division walls, furniture, or lighting objects, the process requires the selection of appropriate plastics to produce the semi-transparent and colourful building elements. They can be additionally decorated with motifs from other recycled synthetic substances. The basic Recy Blocks resource is wasted polyethylene, which can be found in plastic bags or food packaging products. The recycled material is placed in a mould, where

it is heated and compressed in order to form a solid building element.

Due to their rectangular shape, Recy Blocks can be easily assembled to construct walls or other architectural elements. An interconnection system using holes and metal tubes secures the elements from shifting and connects them into a structurally active building system. The tubes allow for slight alterations and turns of single elements, giving enough freedom to open or close the wall for light and view. The massiveness and materiality of the blocks allow indoor as well as outdoor applications.

Another product manufactured with the same material – Recy Screen – is a much thinner alternative to the block, to be used for finishing works and elements where a translucent material character is required. 4–10 mm thick, the tiles are usually attached to a frame or other substructure for support.

2

3

PROJECT DATA	PRODUCT DATA
RESOURCE Discarded plastics	STANDARD SIZE 600 mm × 300 mm
MANUFACTURER AND DESIGNER Gert de Mulder, Hertogenbosch, The Netherlands	STANDARD THICKNESS 100–150 mm DENSITY 167 kg/m³
PRODUCT DIRECTORY Finishing, page 191; Self-supporting, page 178	FIRE RATING No information PRODUCTION TIME 40 min

4

5

3 The interlocking block system is based on holes and tubes.

4 Pillow-shaped bricks are manufactured under heat and pressure in specially designed moulds.

5 Recy Blocks can be decorated with motifs from other recycled synthetic materials.

TIRE VENEER TILES

Rubber tires are among the largest and most problematic sources of waste. Each year approximately 300 million units are discarded in the USA alone. Their life cycle can be extended by a process called re-treading, which preserves about 90% of the original material and adds a new layer on top.[9] In this process, the old tread is first removed by grinding, before a new layer of rubber is applied and profiled. The dust of the grinding process can be the source for a whole new set of building materials.

In the production of Tire Veneer Tiles, the grinder dust is mixed with a polyurethane binder and placed into a mould. Heat and pressure are applied to create a solid block of a refurbished rubber, which is sliced or veneered into thin material sheets. This 4-mm layer can be cut in any desired pieces or shapes, creating for example an interlocking tile system. Aesthetic appeal is given by adding colourful non-recycled rubber granules. A typical homogenized mixture contains approximately 80% black rubber and 20% coloured rubber, with the percentage of black rubber indicating the post-consumer content.

The product can be applied bonded or unbonded to any flat, clean, hard, and dry surface and will not shrink, buckle, warp, or crack. It is available in several thicknesses, in tiles or rolls, and in many colour patterns. It is often used as a resilient interior and exterior flooring material that reduces noise emissions and functions as a soft protection layer for instance for playgrounds. It is also applied in a variety of other functions such as vibration dampeners and furniture surfaces. It is easy to clean and maintain when a finish is applied. The material will resist stains, chemicals, weather, impact, and punctures and is also non-corrosive.

1 A typical homogenized mixture of Tire Veneer Tiles contains approximately 80% post-consumer black rubber and 20% coloured rubber.

1

2

PROJECT DATA

RESOURCE
Re-treaded automobile
and truck tires

MANUFACTURER
AND DESIGNER
Yemm & Hart Ltd.,
Marquand, MO, USA

PRODUCT DIRECTORY
Finishing, page 191

PRODUCT DATA

STANDARD ROLL SIZE
Approx. 1.22 m × 176 m

STANDARD THICKNESS
Approx. 4 mm

DENSITY
Approx. 1,041.2 kg/m³

TENSILE STRENGTH
1,378 kPa

FIRE RATING
Fire-retardant,
Class C (E-84)

VOC EMISSION
0.5 mg/m³

2 Colourful non-recycled
rubber granules add
aesthetic appeal to the
recovered material.

3 In the process, big blocks
of the material are pressed
and later cut into veneer.

1 rubber dust from tire
 retreatment
2 colourful non-recycled
 rubber granulate
3 polyurethane binder
4 curing oven
5 press
6 rubber block
7 cutting of sheets
 and veneer
8 Tire Veneer Tiles

3

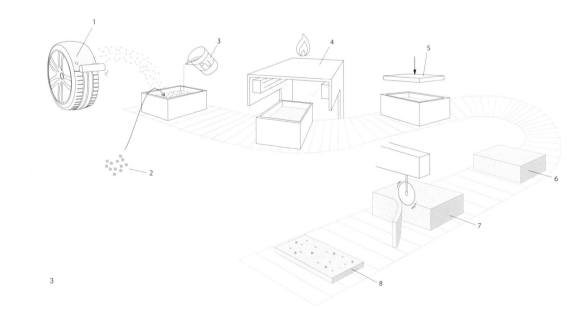

1

2

BLOOD BRICK

Bio-adhesives have been used by humans throughout our existence, from the most basic forms of dried gelatine or dissolved flour to the more complex forms of alkali-denatured proteins. Animal blood is known to produce one of the strongest available bio-adhesives, due to its high concentration of the protein Albumen, which forms an extremely strong binding agent. At the same time, animal blood is an abundant waste product in those societies worldwide that have no industrialized food production system. For example, a slaughtered cow delivers around 40 l of blood. Until the Second World War, blood glue was the most widely used adhesive in many industries, such as plywood lamination, due to its relative water resistance by comparison to Casein and other bio-adhesives.

Waste animal blood is a valuable resource for construction. The method described here produces one of the most simple blood glues for use in remote and poor communities, without expensive, inaccessible chemicals or complex formulae that involve denaturing alkalis. For the production of Blood Bricks, the discharged blood residues are mixed with a preservative and an anticoagulant immediately after collection to allow short-term storage; alternatively, the blood can be freeze-dried to obtain a powder for long-term storage. The blood is then mixed with sand at a ratio of about 1:4 to create a thick paste, which forms the base for production. The paste is either poured over a sand dune, using the crest pouring technique developed for this project, or cast as bricks. In order to become a solid structural material it must be heated sufficiently to coagulate the blood and drive off excess water. This can be achieved simply by leaving it exposed to the sun, or by using solar ovens.

1 Blood bricks are manufactured from waste animal blood and sand.

2 Blood bricks can be produced in different kinds of moulds.

3 The bricks can be handled and used as any other regular masonry element.

4 Discharged blood residues are mixed with a preservative and an anticoagulant immediately after collection to allow short-term storage.

5 The blood is mixed with sand at a ratio of roughly 1:4 to create a thick paste.

4

5

3

PROJECT DATA

RESOURCE
Discarded animal blood and sand

DESIGNER
Jack Munro, Arthur Mamou-Mani, Toby Burgess, University of Westminster, London, United Kingdom

PRODUCT DIRECTORY
Load-bearing, page 176

PRODUCT DATA

STANDARD SIZE
500 mm × 120 mm

STANDARD THICKNESS
40 mm

DENSITY
1,300 kg/m^3

COMPRESSION STRENGTH
115.42 KPa

FIRE RATING
No information

DESIGNED
WASTE
MATERIALS

CASE STUDIES

World Bottle (WOBO) p. 130
Jiilkeen Cube p. 134
POLLI-Brick p. 136
UNITED BOTTLE p. 140
WaterBrick p. 144

This chapter deals with the ongoing, still futuristic idea of specially designed goods that potentially never go to waste: they spend their material lifetime in a constant state of reuse, readaption, and recycling, without having to be densified, reconfigured, or transformed. Throughout their life cycle they are meant to keep their original form, properties, and material composition while their functions may change dramatically. Once such products have been used in the way and at the location for which they were originally destined, their particular character allows for yet another – second, third, even fourth – life cycle with different functions. They might also be combined (without being mixed) with other materials into a heterogeneous condition of being, maintaining their ability to change their state again when required.

Despite a growing environmental awareness, we are still strongly attached to a linear kind of thinking when it comes to waste handling, a "take-make-waste" mentality. Concepts for future cities call for architects and designers to think, work, and create in a more holistic manner, envisaging future life cycles of their products already while modelling the initial one. Design *per se* should actually be a sustainable process, since it anticipates the future. And yet the imagination of creators often stops at the point when artefacts are produced or buildings constructed and handed over to the clients. Objects and buildings are not yet seen as the resource for something completely different, even though this could be a dream becoming true for creative workers: one design effort generates several projects.

This approach questions the common recycling strategy as implemented so far in our society – which is, in fact, a down-cycling concept, meaning that the quality of a material diminishes when combined with other similar products. A good example for this phenomenon is the steel industry. Despite the fact that steel can easily be melted again, reshaped, and reformed, this process usually goes along with a loss of value and quality. The design of steel products very often includes paint, plastics, copper for electrical wiring components, and other materials that are impossible to separate with the current mass-applied technologies of the waste industry, as required prior to melting as part of the established recycling process. Plastics, copper, and paint lower the steel quality of the recycled product to a point that the concerned charge of metal cannot be used to produce the same product again. Each repetition of this cycle more and more reduces the original material quality. Most recycled products that we as educated consumers approve of follow this down-cycling strategy; this is true even for many of the products shown in this book. Pressing

problems occur in cases where newly recycled products threaten to be harmful for our environment and health. McDonough and Braungart, in their book *Cradle to Cradle: Remaking the Way We Make Things*,[1] describe these phenomena as a real dilemma: "The creative use of down-cycled materials for new products can be misguided, despite good intentions. For example, people may feel they are making an ecologically sound choice by buying and wearing clothing made of fibres from recycled plastic bottles. But the fibres from plastic bottles contain toxins such as antimony, catalytic residues, ultraviolet stabilizers, plasticizers, and

antioxidants, which were never designed to lie next to human skin."

The question of design therefore becomes a core issue when discussing alternative concepts of building from waste. McDonough and Braungart developed an argument where the quality of waste is the most important factor in considering recycling strategies. This is a complete reversal of a concept of mere waste reduction or avoidance. In fact, they claim that we should produce even more waste – but in a quality that allows for a complete closed-circle approach. Developing a secondary

material, as represented in this book in many examples, would then mean to continuously redesign the original product so as to avoid diminishing qualities. Any individual material in a given product must be easily retractable in order to avoid an irresolvable mixing with others. Yet a different approach is conceivable: that a design would allow for a second use without change. This could be called a smart design approach, which takes the question of sustainability seriously in the sense of looking far ahead instead of satisfying only the immediate need or demand.

For this re-design or better: pre-design strategy, commonplace consumer goods seem to be a good case in point, as long as they are made in large quantities and easy to manufacture. Surprisingly at first sight, all projects presented in this chapter deal with beverage containers in one or the other form. We seem to have a deep and intimate relationship to bottles; size, weight, and tactility seem to be so familiar that when thinking of an alternative brick system made out of a pre-designed waste product it is bottles that come up first in our minds. Manufactured usually through a thoroughly established blow-moulding technology, the change of shape of plastic or glass bottles seems rather simple to perform, with the intention that, once emptied, the containers could be used as a building element immediately. And yet in all cases the question arose how the sales

1 The World Bottle of the Heineken brewery was designed to be used as a construction brick in its second life cycle.

2 The UNITED BOTTLE represents a pre-designed waste product, as it can function as a building brick once emptied.

departments of those big companies reacted when a change of a well-established product was proposed. Is the confirmed benefit of a sustainable use enough to make up for a certain risk of a loss of customers?

"Designed Waste Materials" addresses the possibility of a positive answer to this question. The design ideas presented here have started to take shape already in the mid-20th century by various entrepreneurs and eco-actors. In 1963, Alfred Henry Heineken, owner of the Heineken beer brewery, together with architect John Habraken envisioned a possible solution for recycling Heineken beer bottles by activating them as a building element to solve housing shortage in the Caribbean, a major market for the bottles' primary use. Time and again, Heineken had noticed empty bottles being washed on shore, in many places around the islands but also in other Latin American countries and in Africa. He must also have been aware of the type of glass houses built in the American West during the construction of the first transcontinental train line, with such telling names as "The House of the Thousand Headaches". Being the only potential construction material constantly shipped into the worker camps, beer and whisky bottles constituted an ideal and cheap building material. So Heineken and Habraken started to design square bottles with a "goosebump" surface for a better friction between the

bottles and the mortar, and in two different sizes. The idea was to stack them horizontally and lay them out similar to traditional brick structures, with one bottleneck fitting into the hollowed bottom of the adjacent bottle. The project never passed the research stage, due to concerns of the marketing department about the change of the characteristic bottle shape. Nevertheless, the initiative left a significant stamp in the field of product design.

The UNITED BOTTLE project can also be seen in this line, embracing the fact that empty PET bottles are one of the biggest waste resources worldwide and rethinking their shape in order to elevate them from a mere garbage product into a building element that can be filled with earth, feathers, or other substances to manipulate the material properties when used in construction. Pre-designing waste materials can actually increase the value of a product and thereby provide another rationale to avoid early disposal. This thinking is especially important for materials such as plastics, which are considered as cheap and of no value today, with the well-known disastrous consequences.

Numerous emerging projects illustrate the shift towards a second life cycle, or closed-loop ideology, to prevent such scenarios. In the construction sector, as of the time of

writing, most projects are theoretical and rarely reach beyond the research stage. But we believe that the selected projects and materials have the potential to influence future designers and entrepreneurs, reach mass production, and change the quality of future waste through intelligent design strategies.

1

WORLD BOTTLE (WOBO)

In 1960, Alfred Henry Heineken, at the time owner of the major Amsterdam Heineken brewery, noticed large amounts of discarded beer bottles during his visit to the island of Curaçao of the Dutch Antilles. Like on many other Caribbean islands, remains of the industrialized world were used here in the garbage house structures of the *bidonvilles* (shanty towns), since the vegetation of the islands did not allow for the use of timber or any other natural building material. Empty oil drums, the only good coming in regularly from the mainland, had their tops and bases removed and were flattened into thin sheets to serve as construction elements. The natives saw the oil drums not as waste, but as available and free building material.

At that time, it was the strategy of the Heineken company to brew all beer, including for worldwide export, in the Netherlands, where quality could be strictly controlled. Here, empty bottles were collected, cleaned, and sterilized in order to be refilled, but those sent overseas were not returned. Becoming aware of the effects of this one-way situation, Heineken decided to produce a beer bottle that could serve as a building brick when empty, thereby responding to the need for shelter on the Caribbean Islands and elsewhere.

In 1963, Heineken commissioned architect John Habraken to rethink the bottle shapes, also taking into consideration the technical aspects of the application as a building material. Habraken started to study the glass manufacturing process, understanding the properties and characteristics of the material as a prerequisite to dealing with formal design. A first approach looked at using the bottle in a vertical interlocking system with the bottleneck as connector, profiting from the considerable compression strength in this direction. Yet Habraken searched for a more simple solution to use the bottle horizontally while still gaining the required compression strength. The final design with the two flattened sides was called the World Bottle, WOBO.

It came in two sizes, 330 ml and 500 ml, and was based on the idea to bond the bottles with a layer of mortar, hence the roughened surfaces with a surface structure that looks like goose bumps. The bottles were laid horizontally, like regular bricks, with the neck fitting into the hollowed bottom of the adjacent bottle. As a bottle could not be cut like a brick, a system had to be devised to make a wall opening or turn a corner without the need for half-bottles, while maintaining the shifting of the joints from one layer to the next to form the

bond and ensure the necessary interlocking. The solution was found in alternating directions of the bottles from layer to layer, combined with using the bigger bottle size at the corners and the smaller one at the centre of the wall.

Some 60,000 units of the World Bottle were produced by the Royal Glass Works in Leerdam, the manufacturer of the Heineken glass bottles, in 1963. Heineken had a small experimental house built on the grounds of his villa at Noordwijk, near Amsterdam, based on the ideas and sketches of Habraken and with walls constructed entirely using the World Bottle. Over the following years, Heineken and his research team monitored the behaviour of this new building material. Although the results were promising in that no cracks or de-bonding occurred between the bottles and the mortar, not a single World Bottle was ever filled with beer. Marketing was convinced that this design would ruin the image of the brand and there was also the concern that the countries to which the World Bottle would be sent might consider the initiative paternalistic and demeaning. Today, the only remains of this remarkable concept can be seen in the Heineken Museum in Amsterdam. The structure in the garden of Heineken's villa disappeared long before he died.

1 The final design of the World Bottle was produced only in a small test charge. The product was never implemented into the market.

2 The special design allowed the World Bottle to be used as a building block.

3 The section of the bottle shows the fitting system at the bottom and the specific surface texture designed to increase mechanical friction in the mortar bed.

2

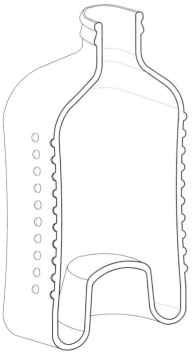

3

PROJECT DATA

RESOURCE
Glass bottles (green-coloured silicate glass)

MANUFACTURER
Heineken International
(Breweries company),
Amsterdam,
The Netherlands

DESIGNER
John Habraken,
Amsterdam,
The Netherlands

PRODUCT DIRECTORY
Load-bearing, page 173;
Waterproofing, page 186

PRODUCT DATA

STANDARD FILLING
CAPACITY
330 ml and 500 ml

STANDARD BASE
DIMENSION
80 mm × 60 mm

STANDARD HEIGHT
140 mm or 220 mm

STANDARD WEIGHT
Approx. 220 g and 330 g

CONSTRUCTION AREA
1000 bottles = approx.
3 m × 3 m = 9 m²

4

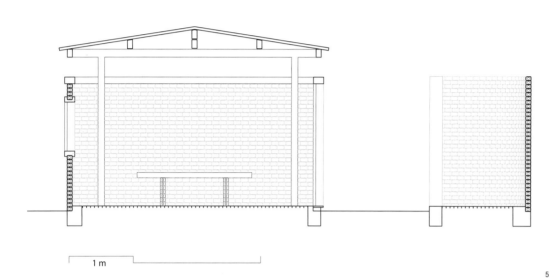

1 m

5

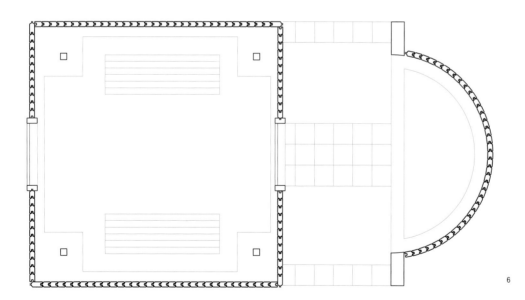

6

4 The WOBO test structure
was built on the grounds of
Alfred Heineken's Noordwijk
villa next to Amsterdam in
1965. It disappeared long
before he died.

5 John Habraken's design
of 1964 for a WOBO House
to be marketed in the
developing countries. The
section of the WOBO House
reveals the idea of natural
ventilation to control the
heat gain in the interior
engendered by the glass
material.

6 The plan shows the four
columns that carry the roof
and an uncovered vestibule
at the entry area.

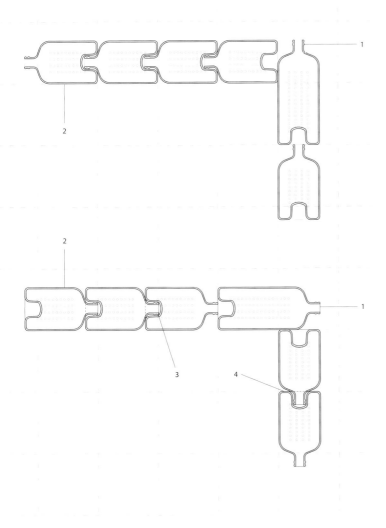

7 The corner solution required bottles in two lengths to accommodate the shift in direction.

1 rule: a big bottle finishes the row pointing towards the corner
2 direction of bottles changes with each layer; bottles are straight on top of each other to ensure smooth ending for doors or windows
3 top at grid line
4 bottom at grid line

8 The bonding system of the test structure used mortar with a silicone additive.

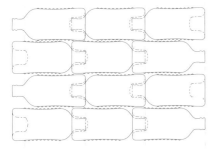

7

8

133

JIILKEEN CUBE

Looking at the effectiveness of spatial use, round bottles have the disadvantage of generating free and therefore wasted space when placed next to each other for storage or transport. All else being equal, bottles with a cubic shape would save up to 50% of space when stacked. The usual round shape of bottles is a reminiscence of early-day manual glass production and has shown several advantages in industrialized processes: during the filling process, round-shaped bottles standing on a conveyer belt are easy to be singled out. The round form also resembles a strong structural system, ideal for a fully automated process, while rectangular bottles usually show higher rates of breakage, especially on parts that stick out.

The avoid this effect, the design of the Jiilkeen Cube proposes a perfectly cubic-shaped body by pushing the bottleneck inside these limits as well. The resulting form, beyond its advantage for packaging and transport purposes, makes the cube also a very interesting waste product

for the building sector. Here once again, the bottle design carries the ability for reuse in a completely different function subsequent to the original use.

Through their ability to be placed in a very compact way, the glass cubes can be handled like any other brick. Different from the World Bottle or the UNITED BOTTLE described in this publication, the glass cube does not make any demands in terms of orientation or order of application. Its form allows for an intuitive approach, whereby bigger building elements can be formed out of this small particle. As the design does not provide a self-interlocking system, it requires a second material functioning as mortar. Bottle houses that were built during the times of the gold rush and the transcontinental train line project in the USA in Nevada or California[2] and still exist today, demonstrate impressively that the lack of a self-interlocking system is not necessarily a disadvantage.

1 The design of a Jiilkeen Cube beer bottle is based on modularity. The neck of the bottle recedes into its cubical shape, which allows placing the glass cube on any of its six sides.

2 The design process leading from a round bottle to the square cube.

3 The simple square shape allows for an intuitive approach in construction design by forming larger building elements out of the basic unit.

1

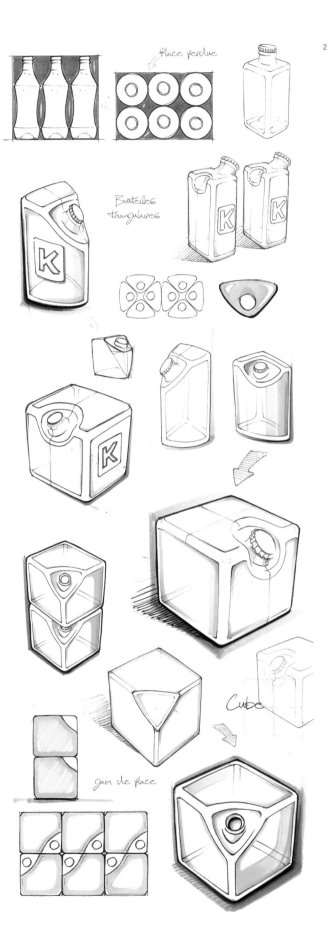

2

3

PROJECT DATA	PRODUCT DATA
RESOURCE Glass bottles (green-coloured silicate glass)	STANDARD FILLING CAPACITY 500 ml
DESIGNER Petit Romain, Lyon, France	STANDARD BASE DIMENSION Approx. 100 mm
PRODUCT DIRECTORY Load-bearing, page 173; Waterproofing, page 186	STANDARD HEIGHT Approx. 100 mm
	STANDARD WEIGHT Approx. 350 g
	CONSTRUCTION AREA 1,000 bottles = approx. 3.1 m × 3.2 m = 10 m²

1 The shape of the POLLI-Brick enables the construction of modular structures.

2 POLLI-Brick elements fit tightly due to their honeycomb design concept.

1

POLLI-BRICK

Specially designed and engineered bottles made of post-consumer Polyethylene Terephthalate (PET) can be a resource for a translucent, insulating, light, and mechanically recyclable building material. The POLLI-Brick is a multi-functional product made from 100% recycled PET and can be used as a building material after its first use as a drinking bottle. The designers changed the usual round shape to a modular three-dimensional honeycomb form that makes the bottle extremely strong as a beverage container, but also suitable for the construction sector. A system constituted by a multitude of bottles can form a structural component, but

since it is missing an interlocking feature it needs a frame structure to support it.

The iconic EcoARK building of the 2010 International Flora Exposition in Taipei, Taiwan, used the POLLI-Brick to create an unusual façade. Placed inside a metal frame structure, the bottles form an infill that is reinforced by an additional plastic panel system controlling UV light emission and wind as well as water seepage. In this project, the bottle is used as an additional aesthetic infill element, while the structural capacities of the bottle would indeed allow for small load-bearing applications, for instance as shelter constructions.

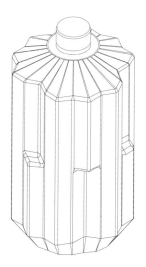

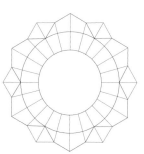

2

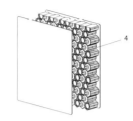

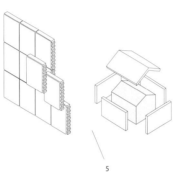

3 The life cycle concept of POLLI-Brick.

1 recycle
2 remould
3 assemble
4 modularize
5 build

4 The POLLI-Brick is produced out of 100% post-consumer PET material.

PROJECT DATA

RESOURCE
PET bottles

MANUFACTURER
Far Eastern Group and
MINIWIZ, Taipei, Taiwan

DESIGNER
MINIWIZ, Taipei, Taiwan

PRODUCT DIRECTORY
Load-bearing, page 177;
Insulating, page 180

PRODUCT DATA

STANDARD FILLING
CAPACITY
6000 / 690 / 400 ml

STANDARD BASE DIAMETER
160 mm

STANDARD HEIGHT
308 /180 / 118 mm

STANDARD WEIGHT
Approx. 48 g

CONSTRUCTION AREA
130 bottles = approx.
1.624 m × 1.76 m =
2.85 m²

FIREPROOF PERFORMANCE
OPTIONS
Self-extinguishing; fire-
retardant to specification
(translucency may vary)

5 The bottles can be integrated in a frame structure and clad with a plastic sheet to form POLLI-Brick modular façade elements.

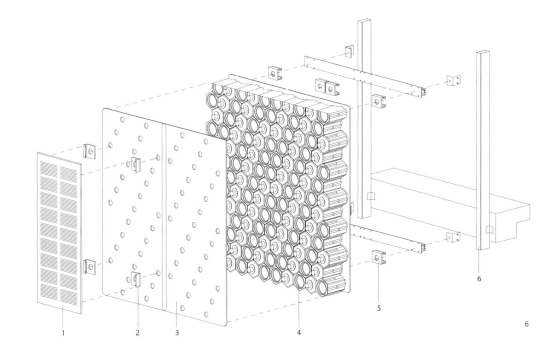

6 POLLI-Brick curtain wall standard module.

1   solar PV module
2   solar PV clipping joint
3   nano-treated
    PC hard coat
4   prefabricated POLLI-
    Brick assembly
5   fastening joints
6   structural sub-frame

7 The EcoARK project was built for the 2010 Taipei International Flora Exposition. The façade of the nine-story structure consists of 1.5 million plastic bottles, produced out of recycled material.

UNITED BOTTLE

50 billions one-litre plastic bottles are currently sold in Europe alone every year.[3] Since a compulsory bottle deposit was introduced in most European countries in the last two decades, the recycling rates on the continent increased dramatically, while numbers worldwide are still disappointing. Overall, the majority of bottles seen on a global scale are not returned to the recycling process – especially in developing territories – and usually end up as waste material since recycling mechanisms are not in place.

UNITED BOTTLE suggests to introduce a new design strategy that allows a regular plastic bottle also to be used as a building element and thereby avoid having to discard containers made of Polyethylene Terephthalate (PET) or Polypropylene (PP). The design prepares the bottle for its secondary use without diminishing the functionality of the first. It is equipped with two inward and two outward-oriented tucks, fitting into each other perfectly. With this added element, each bottle can be connected to four other bottles surrounding it, by sliding one tuck into a corresponding tuck of its neighbour. In principle, this system allows endless wall constructions, without using any mortar or gluing device. Once connected, the bottles form a horizontally as well as vertically linked structural system, similar to a regular masonry wall.

Additionally, the bottles can be equipped with locally available substances in order to increase their physical properties. Sand, earth, or any kind of liquids can be filled in to stabilize specific areas of a UNITED BOTTLE structure. This process adds weight to the bottles, which even allows for the formation of foundation elements. Also materials such as hair, wool, plastic films and bags, paper, textiles, or feathers can be stuffed into the empty containers. This will increase their thermal, acoustic, or aesthetic properties.

Ideally, the UNITED BOTTLE would become the standard in local sales and thus be instantly available whenever the need for an easily applicable building system arises. In order to achieve the required market penetration, the bottle is designed in such a way that regular PET preforms and machines can be used for manufacturing. The only addition is a pushing mechanism for the blow mould, since the tuck-in system of the bottle prevents an automatic drop when the production mould is opened.

So far, the UNITED BOTTLE is only available in small charges, mostly being shown in museums around the world. Marketing experts of large companies are concerned about the unusual look of the bottle. Yet this project shows that a simple PET bottle could be literally a container for the awareness that each and every consumer product is facing a future life as a waste substance. The question remains if the potential value of this waste can be activated through sustainable design strategies.

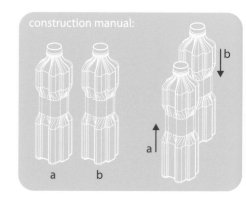

1

1 The special design concept of the UNITED BOTTLE allows a second life cycle of this everyday product as a building component and to construct elements without using any mortar or glue.

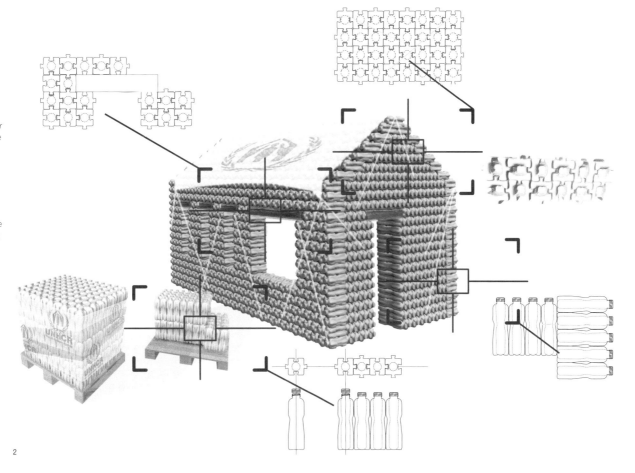

2 Removed from the regular recycling process, the bottle can instantly function as a building brick. Filled with other materials such as earth or feathers, it can serve different purposes.

3 Any consumer product has the potential for a future life in a completely different function without being changed.

2

3

PROJECT DATA

RESOURCE
PET bottles

DESIGNER
UNITED BOTTLE Group,
Zurich and Basel,
Switzerland

PRODUCT DIRECTORY
Load-bearing, page 174;
Insulating, page 183

PRODUCT DATA

STANDARD FILLING
CAPACITY
1,500 ml

STANDARD BASE
DIMENSION
89 mm × 89 mm

STANDARD HEIGHT
350 mm

STANDARD WEIGHT
Approx. 40 g
(PET without cap)

CONSTRUCTION AREA
1,000 bottles = 2.45 m ×
2.45 m = 6 m²

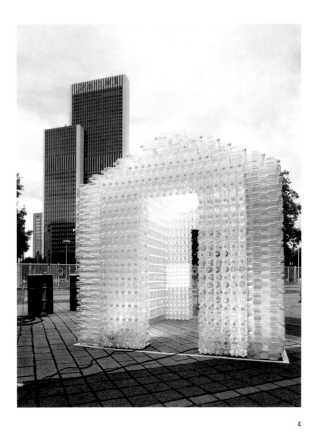

4

6 The additional life cycle does not stop the first one, it extends the functionality in an added value process.

7 The bottles can be filled with locally available materials to vary its properties as a building element.

4 The UNITED BOTTLE project was given several awards and showcased at many locations around the world, here at The Design Annual fair in Frankfurt in 2007.

5 Each unit can be connected to four others by sliding the tucks into each other.

1   screw-on bottleneck
2   outer tusk
3   hand grip
4   inner tusk

Each bottle is equipped with two inward and two outward-oriented tucks, smoothly fitting into each other.

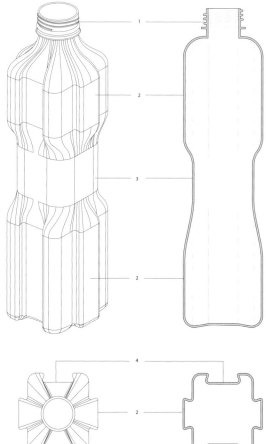

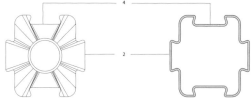

5

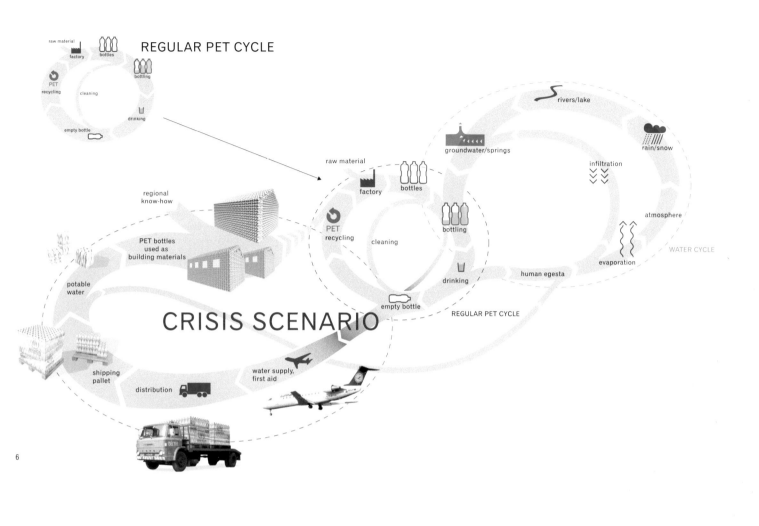

REGULAR PET CYCLE

raw material
factory
bottles
bottling
PET recycling
cleaning
drinking
empty bottle

regional know-how

PET bottles used as building materials

potable water

shipping pallet

distribution

water supply, first aid

CRISIS SCENARIO

raw material
factory
bottles
PET recycling
cleaning
bottling
drinking
empty bottle

REGULAR PET CYCLE

rivers/lake
groundwater/springs
rain/snow
infiltration
atmosphere
evaporation
human egesta
WATER CYCLE

6

7

WATERBRICK

To live in a remote area is either a condition of no choice or a conscious decision to leave one's own comfort zone. In both cases, one is cut off from regular supply chains. Waste then no longer exists – due to the fundamental shortage of resources. This awareness is the essential principle of the design of the WaterBrick water and food container. Produced out of recycled High Density Polyethylene (HDPE) from discarded milk bottles, this storage element is meant to provide a very durable and long-lasting packing unit. Due to its shape, the element can be stacked very efficiently and lends itself as a functional equipment piece for outdoor activities, such as camping, in remote zones.

The original design idea is that the containers can be activated in a second life cycle as a building element for transitional housing projects. Here, the first definition of remoteness plays the key role. With their unique capacity to be very

efficiently transported, the WaterBrick elements can be used to deliver water and food to people in need. They can be palletized, shrink-wrapped, and airdropped anywhere.

Once emptied of their original contents, WaterBrick elements can enter a second life cycle as basic building blocks. Their design does not require any mortar to be applied; they can be combined almost like toy bricks. Each unit shows a top-side with at least one positive lug and a lower side with a corresponding cavity. This system allows the units to be layered and form a robust interlocking structure, while the regular opening, lid, and handle, placed on the side, do not interfere with this feature. In addition, each WaterBrick element has one or two central voids, so that when in place the system can be reinforced by threading vertical PVC pipes through the layers. The result is a strong load-bearing structure.

The WaterBrick unit comes in two different sizes, one exactly at half the size of the other. Layers can be constructed as an interlocking system, whereby the vertical joints shift by half a brick at every stratum, forming a stable bond structure as known from masonry systems. Interlocking and thereby structurally active corner details can be achieved with the same layout and this also applies to openings allowing for doors and windows. Filled with sand or earth or even empty, WaterBrick elements can also function as foundation stones. Due to their design, they can be used even in two directions, shifting by layer, so that for instance thicker base sections can be built, while the walls on top can taper back to a single thinner system.

Considerations of secondary use strategies informed the design of the WaterBrick element. It contains not only water or food, but a promise to be a multifunctional product that never has to be turned into waste after its production.

1 With additional reinforcement, WaterBrick can be used to construct load-bearing wall elements, also allowing for efficient corner solutions.

1 screw-on cap
2 hole for connection rod
3 groove-and-tongue
   system
4 connection rod

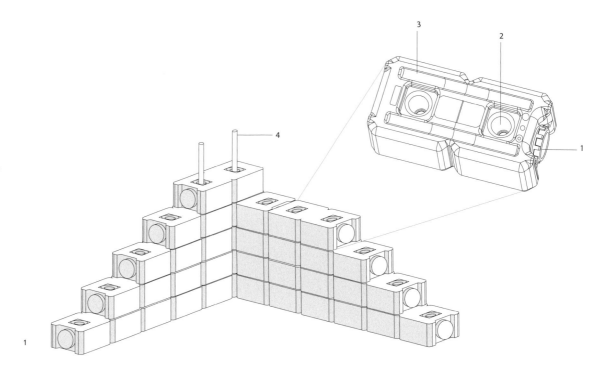

2

PROJECT DATA

RESOURCE
High Density Polyethylene
(HDPE) water container

MANUFACTURER
AND DESIGNER
Wendell Adams, WaterBrick
International, Winter
Garden, FL, USA

PRODUCT DIRECTORY
Load-bearing, page 174;
Waterproofing, page 186

PRODUCT DATA

STANDARD FILLING
CAPACITY
13.25 l and 6.05 l

STANDARD BASE
DIMENSIONS
229 mm × 229 mm and
229 mm × 458 mm

STANDARD HEIGHT
152 mm

STANDARD WEIGHT
Approx. 1,025 g and 530 g

CONSTRUCTION AREA
1,000 large containers =
approx. 14.2 m × 4.86 m
= 69 m²

2 WaterBrick is a container
and building component
that can be stacked
very efficiently, a quality
important for transport and
construction alike.

3 In its first life cycle,
WaterBrick is a food and
liquid container made out of
recycled HDPE milk jugs.

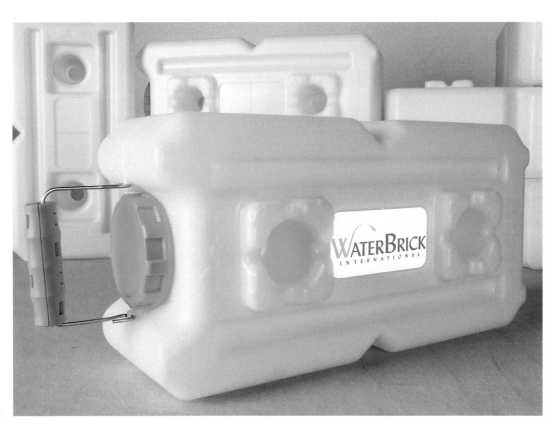

3

ORGANIC WASTE DESIGN
A NEW CULTURE OF DESIGNED WASTE PRODUCTS

Sascha Peters

Earth Overshoot Day was reached as early as August 20th in 2013, two days earlier than in 2012. This is the approximate date, according to the calculations of the Global Footprint Network, after which the resource consumption for a given year exceeds the planet's ability to replenish these resources or absorb the produced greenhouse gases. Human societies have been living beyond nature's capacity for at least 30 years. WWF Germany has estimated that, in 2013, about 150% of the yearly available worldwide resources were consumed. The Western industrialized nations as well as some of the oil-producing countries of the Arab world are the greatest ecological debtors. The *Living Planet Report 2012* estimates that, based on today's standards and with consideration of the population growth, resource consumption will double by 2050.

In addition to the worldwide problem of resource availability, diminishing oil reserves for energy production are becoming an ever greater concern, especially for the industrialized nations. Not least as a reaction to the Fukushima disaster, the German government decided to opt out of the nuclear energy programme and by doing so proclaimed the new age of renewable energy. This sparked a flood of innovations, the positive effects of which will only become clear over the next few years. Many social groups have already recognized the need for a radical change in our living habits and our construction and product cultures. Among them is the younger generation of product and industrial designers, who aspire to a new awareness in the use of materials that takes into account a product's entire life span. The new creative professionals try, through numerous projects, to utilize waste and by-product material in the development of new products in order to conserve energy and resources. They are continuously discovering residual materials that have so far been neglected, and subsequently increase their value by using them in a new context. The BIQ, a bio-intelligent building with a biomass-producing algae façade; the research into the biotechnological use of termites for the production of hydrogen; or the development of biohybrid solar cells based on spinach proteins are only a few examples of the many attempts to put organic raw materials to good use.

One of the great dreams inspiring designers is to develop a prototype based on natural resources that will degrade biologically at the end of its life.

Ex-presso by Julian Lechner
The Berlin designer Julian Lechner succeeded in realizing that dream to a great extent in 2010. He was one of the first to see coffee grinds not just as a resource for natural fertilizers but also as a potential base material for product design. In his Ex-presso project, which he carried out at the Free University of Bozen, he collected the organic waste material from the surrounding cafés and pressed them into the shape of cups, using caramelized sugar as bonding material. What is more, during use, the coffee in an Ex-presso cup ended up dissolving it to some extent, thereby adding a new aroma to the drink! In a similar approach, Raul Lauri Design Lab presses coffee grind into interior design objects and, recently, also building materials. (See Decafe Tiles, p. 60 in this book)

1 Ex-presso

Mushroom Surfboard by Ecovative Design

The developers at Ecovative Design in New York were aware as early as 2007 of the fact that coffee grinds, when recycled, were most often used as an energy-efficient medium for cultivating mushrooms. They founded a start-up company for the industrial production of mushroom foam as a replacement for polystyrene foam in the packaging sector. The special types of mushrooms used form a thread-shaped cellular network around organic residual materials, for example grain husks and seeds from agricultural waste. The energy-efficient growing process takes place in the dark and is stopped by drying out the material at a temperature of almost 43°C. Being one of many unconventional company formations originating from the realm of higher education, Ecovative Design seem to have blazed a trail into the marketplace,

judging from the fact that adaptive solutions utilizing the mushroom material are now being proposed in the construction and automobile industries. Among the latest design developments is a surfboard made of mushroom foam that was introduced in California at the end of 2013. In that object, the list of advantages of the organic growth process is impressive: the mushroom foam grows perfectly into the shape of a surfboard, its degree of hardness can be finetuned by means of the cultivation process, and when damaged the board does not release plastic into the ocean. Ecovative recently also started to utilize this mushroom for growing building elements, from insulation panels to load-bearing bricks. (See Tiny Mushroom House and Hy-Fi, p. 158 and 160 in this book)

Oki Naganode by Julia Lohmann

The cultivation of biomass does not, in itself, require any cultivable agricultural acreage. Biomass even absorbs a great deal of carbon dioxide during its growth. In this context,

algae have the potential to turn into an important resource. Algae grow three times as fast as annual plants and absorb three times as much carbon dioxide in the process. With these benefits in mind, the designer Julia Lohmann at the Royal College of Art and the Victoria & Albert Museum in London is exploring the possibilities of using algae fibres as biomass material for interior design and furniture construction. During her research, she discovered a way to conserve the mechanical and optical features of this aquatic plant, making it more than suitable for interior finishing materials.

Fish Scale Project by Erik de Laurens

The London designer Erik de Laurens made a further spectacular discovery in the field of oceanic organic residual materials while studying in South Africa. He was able to make a material out of fish scales that could be used to produce moulded parts, like goggle frames and drinking cups, by

2 Mushroom surfboard

3 Oki Naganode

4 Fish Scale Project

means of applying heat and pressure without requiring a binder. His discovery could play an important role in the transition from petro-based to bio-based chemistry: fish scales accrue in large amounts in the fishing industry and contain a component that, being a thermoplastic substance, enables fibres and particles to be joined to form a solid building component.

Zerbrechlich by Ulrike Böttcher

In her project Zerbrechlich (Fragile), the Berlin designer Ulrike Böttcher addressed a waste problem of which a large part of the public did not even know that it existed. The natural life cycle of eggshells has been disrupted by the practice of factory farming. The problem of disposal is particularly nettlesome for producers of pasta or liquid dairy products for use in commercial kitchens, since eggshells have been declared

hazardous waste. When improperly stored, they are a great medium for bacteria, which can then find their way into the water supply. Ulrike Böttcher developed a building material based on crushed eggshells that has a notably low negative energy balance. The material can be used as plaster in construction, for printing on paper and ceramic, and as a filler in plasterboards.

Maize Cob Board by Dr. Ulrich Müller

Created by Dr. Ulrich Müller from the Kompetenzzentrum Holz in Linz, Austria, Maize Cob Board is a wood composite whose middle layer is made of corncobs. The foam-like structure of the cob has a high degree of compressive strength in an axial direction, adding to the potential of the sandwich panel to be used for construction. Maize Cob Boards are 50% lighter that conventional wood panels and have good acoustic and thermal insulation qualities due to the large amount of air in the structure.

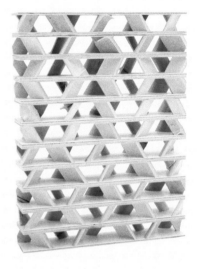

CONBOU High Heel Table by Wassilij Grod

Wassilij Grod is the designer of another successful product that activates high-strength organic by-products in a sandwich structure for the construction sector. Using diagonally cut pieces of bamboo cane for the middle layer of his CONBOU bamboo lightweight construction panel, he achieved an unusual degree of mechanical strength with a relatively small amount of material. The round bamboo sections can be placed next to each other at different densities and configurations, thereby reducing the waste to a bare minimum while at the same time allowing to adjust the firmness of the board

5 Zerbrechlich (Fragile)

6 Maize Cob Board

7 CONBOU high heel table

to different uses in furniture, trade shows, and stage constructions or in coachwork construction. Wassilij Grod won numerous awards for applications of the CONBOU sandwich panels in the furniture industry, then turned towards industrial production of this composite material for applications in logistic services and automobile construction.

Dye-sensitized Solar Cells Integrated into Concrete by Thorsten Klooster and Heike Klussmann

Architect Thorsten Klooster and artist Heike Klussmann created one of the truly spectacular examples of building materials using organic by-products. Within the framework of a research project at the University of Kassel, Germany, they developed a way to produce dye-sensitive solar cells integrated into concrete. The goal was to create a

special board material for the building trade by utilizing a principle discovered by Michael Gretzel in 1992, which concerns the transformation of solar energy into an electrical current by employing organic dyes derived from grape juice.

All these examples for product design on the basis of waste and by-product materials point to the beginning of a development that will only become more dynamic throughout the coming years. We are in need of a new understanding of production in the sense of a closed-circle economy. How better to close this loop than by activating the huge potential of waste in our cities as a resource for the construction industry? However, considering the many tests and standardizations that are necessary in the development of building materials to guarantee health and structural safety, product design constitutes a faster and less regulated domain to experiment with alternative resources. Proposed by designers in their function as society's seismographs and trend scouts, it will be very interesting to see how the type of products and materials described here will be applied in a larger framework to construct our cities in the near future.

8 Dye-sensitized solar cells
integrated into concrete

CULTIVATED WASTE MATERIALS

CASE STUDIES

Biorock p. 154
Bacteria-based Self-healing Concrete p. 156
Tiny Mushroom House p. 158
Hy-Fi p. 160
Mycoform p. 164
Mycotecture p. 166
Dustyrelief p. 168

A cutting-edge approach in the building sector might be summarized with a bold statement: "Grow your own house". The verb in this context refers to the change of volume, to a layering or multiplication of particles in an effort to form construction elements over time. The concept is based on the growth of microelements that until now were unappreciated or even considered hazardous: just waste. By contrast, in our understanding microelements belong to a rich resource of new building materials that are not to be categorized as renewable, but as self-growing – an important difference. Their value and potential has been discovered in the construction sector only recently, but research and also implementation is already underway with several products, as this chapter will show.

The advantages of such products are significant: following the concept of metabolic thinking, most of them can be composted after their original use. In their second phase of life, they become the fertile matrix for the next generation, or even generations of the material in a natural recycling process. These materials can easily be grown wherever they are needed, decreasing the need for long and energy-consuming transport. Last but not least, as most of them are organic materials that absorb carbon dioxide during their growth, they function as a CO_2 sink.

The production of these new building materials is rather simple: as a rule, the environment has to be kept moist and the temperature needs to be controlled for a certain time. In addition, the right nourishment for the organic creators of the materials has to be available   in some of the cases described here, the diet is actually based on another waste product. Most helpful can be the fact that the start of production of these materials can be remote-controlled by the environmental conditions. This is especially interesting for materials that are used to "heal" others. Only when the original building substance fails and, for example, allows water to penetrate, the inserted organisms start their magic work and through their material production rebuild the original. Another switch in the environmental conditions can deactivate the growing process at any desired point in time, for example by drying out the material or exposing it to special light conditions or different temperatures. All of this may sound too good to be true, but the projects presented here seem to pave the way for a whole new industry, even if there is still a long way to go.

Due to their structural patterns and spongy property, the substances described here offer a hybrid condition highly desired in the building industry: on the one side they are very light due to the encapsulated air pockets, which makes them ideal insulation

materials, and on the other side they show an amazing structural strength due to their rhizomatic growth pattern. Their physiognomy as a fibre structure lends these organic materials very high compressive strength capacities, opening up the option to be used for building blocks or sectional beams. We believe that such organically grown substances and the resulting products can become a real alternative for established materials in the building industry. Like many other products introduced in this book they still need to overcome their persisting stigma as being either hazardous or valueless – customers usually want to avoid having fungi or bacteria in their homes.

Considering the concept of "Cultivated Waste Materials" can lead to extremely surprising products and transdisciplinary

thinking. Little is known so far about the use of bacteria to our advantage when designing construction materials. But they could function as adhesives and binding aggregates in compact and resilient substances. Here, a huge field of research is emerging, with an incredible potential for the future. Biochemical processes could in fact replace oil and gas as the main resources for the chemical industry.

In this line, the biologist Henk M. Jonkers entered the field of the building industry addressing one of the biggest building problems of our time: damages in concrete structures. In the process of curing as well as during the life span of the buildings, concrete structures develop numerous micro- and nano-cracks, which might lead to a disastrous outcome if not taken care

of properly: water may reach the reinforcement system and cause its corrosion. Jonkers' invention is to add special bacteria, together with encapsulated nutrition, to the concrete mix before pouring it. The bacteria can survive for years, to wake up only when exposed to water and air through the cracking. Once activated, the bacteria produce calcium, which is able to seal the cracks.

Another unusual approach is exemplified by a project by the interdisciplinary architecture and design group New-territories, also known as R&Sie(n), called Dustyrelief. The authors turn smog, one of the biggest nuisances of urbanized areas, into a controversial yet impressive building element. Over time, layers and layers of micro-pollutants from the air are collected by an electrostatically charged metal structure, creating a condensed particle façade while simultaneously reducing air pollution. Here, the building material has a rather short life span, but nevertheless introduces a new way of thinking about the use of waste as a design strategy.

While some developments aim at intelligent and active materials, others seek to reduce the environmental impact of consumer products by replacing their conventional materials with organically grown resources. The Ecovative team started their business

1 Smog particles attracted by an electrostatic metal mesh form a cultivated façade element.

by producing packaging materials out of fungoid substances that they had developed in the context of their academic master's thesis. By scaling up this idea, one of their most recent projects – Tiny Mushroom House – opens up the perspective to future large-scale constructions built out of cultivated mushroom substances. Ecovative teamed up with the architects of The Living from New York to develop a first application of fungoid panel structures acting as a façade element. Both projects are described here in full detail.

"Cultivated Waste Materials" introduces a concept that is completely new to our most efficient building industry: growth time. Including the element of time into the design and construction of our buildings has the potential to change the way we perceive architecture. The design process of a building is not necessarily finished when it is handed over to the client; rather the building is alive as long as we want it to develop and may even heal itself when necessary. All of these perspectives are based on the existence or production of waste or other

unwanted or allegedly value-free substances. The concepts presented in this chapter may sound futuristic, yet the showcased projects and products are proof of their importance for the present and their capacity of linking back to existing knowledge. On some Indonesian islands, house owners traditionally grew new trees next to their homes as repair materials for the next generation. With mushrooms and bacteria, the same path could be taken, in a much shorter period and on a par with the technological means of our time.

2 Mushroom mycelium can be cultivated to grow into any desired form, here as specially shaped packaging material.

1 Biorock materials grown in the sea at Ihuru, North Malé Atoll, Maldives, around a 6-mm-diameter steel bar in approximately three years.

1

BIOROCK

For a long time, electrolysis in seawater has been used for galvanic protection of metals from corrosion, a method used today to protect ships, bridges, or other metal objects from rust. In principal, electrolysis for galvanic protection uses a difference in voltage potential between two different metals, the cathode and the anode. As long as the electrical current flows, the metal acting as the cathode is completely protected from corrosion, while the metal acting as the anode usually dissolves as the reaction proceeds, and needs to be periodically replaced in order to continue to prevent corrosion of the cathode.

In this process, increased currents accelerate reaction rates, which causes mineral growth of scale. But mineral growth reduces thermal conductivity and thereby heat transfer and conductivity. Therefore, most methods of cathode corrosion protection use the lowest possible voltages and currents; a minimum voltage of

1.23 V (at standard conditions, plus junction potentials) is needed to initiate electrolysis of water.

In 1976, Wolf Hilbertz realized that the accruing solid mineral precipitate could be a resource rather than a problem. Working on self-growing construction materials, the innovative architect experimented with electrolysis of seawater and discovered that, by varying the voltage and current applied, different minerals could be grown on the cathode, ranging from soft to hard. Extremely hard calcium carbonate limestone deposits could be grown under low electrical current conditions, made up of crystals of aragonite, the same compound mineral of which consist coral skeletons and the bulk of tropical white sand beaches.

Higher currents cause the growth of the mineral brucite, or magnesium hydroxide, which is soft and tends to break off easily. It is possible to grow

rock-hard limestone coatings of any preferred thickness on steel frames of any desired shape or size. The resulting material has a compressive strength about three times higher than standard concrete made from Portland cement. This innovative material grows faster and gets harder in warm tropical waters than in cold boreal waters. It could play a crucial part in maritime and even underwater architectures.

Today, what is now called Biorock is a more and more successful marine construction material that gets larger and stronger with age and is self-repairing, like biological materials. Although the metal used as cathode and anode in this process is at the same voltage potential, reduced or absent mineral coatings cause the increase in electrical current and the mass transfer to flow through the water. At the point when the newly grown material has become as resistive as the existing coating, the growth rate is self-limiting.

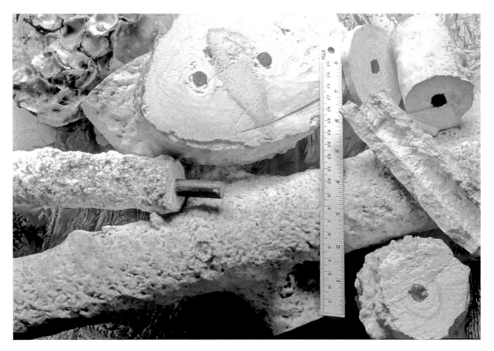

2 Brucite crystals (rosettes) and Aragonite crystals (elongated needles) are minerals grown by electrolysis. (Scanning electron micrograph by Noreen Buster, US Geological Survey.)

3 Biorock materials from various locations grown in a two-and-a-half-year period at Ihuru. Samples from that set tested at the University of Graz, Austria, had compressive strengths of 60–80 MPa, around three times the load-bearing strength of ordinary Portland cement concrete.

3

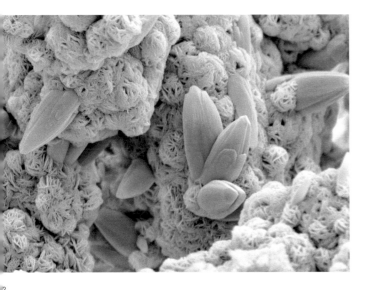

2

PROJECT DATA

RESOURCE
Mineral-saturated seawater

MANUFACTURER
AND DESIGNER
Wolf Hilbertz,
Dr. Thomas J. Goreau,
Biorock Inc., MA, USA

PRODUCT DIRECTORY
Load-bearing, page 172

PRODUCT DATA

PROCESS
Electrolysis

NOURISHMENT
Mineral calcite,
electrical current

EXPECTED LIFETIME
> 50 years

GROWTH TIME
1–2 cm/year in diameter

COMPRESSION STRENGTH
80 MPa

VOLTAGE
100% efficiency at 1.23 V

FIRE RATING
No information

1 Bacteria can act as a
self-healing device of
a concrete matrix.

BACTERIA-BASED SELF-HEALING CONCRETE

A typical durability-related phenomenon in many concrete constructions is crack formation. While larger cracks hamper structural integrity, smaller sub-millimetre-sized cracks may also result in durability problems, as connected cracks in particular increase matrix permeability. Corrosion of steel reinforcement systems in the concrete mix is today one of the main causes of building damages. Water ingress and chemicals cause premature matrix degradation and consequently oxidization of the embedded metal. As regular manual maintenance and repair of concrete constructions is costly and in some cases not possible, an autonomous self-healing repair mechanism would be highly beneficial as it could both reduce maintenance and increase material durability.

The research work of Henk M. Jonkers and his team investigates various bacteria-based additives to achieve a new generation of self-healing concretes. The bacteria act largely as a catalyst and transform a precursor compound into a suitable filler material. The biochemically mediated process is a metabolic conversion of calcium lactate to calcium carbonate. In other words, the waste product of the bacteria results in efficient sealing of sub-millimetre-sized cracks.

For effective self-healing, both the bacteria and the bio-cement precursor compound have to be integrated in the material matrix before pouring and must resist the production process and not die from the harsh environmental conditions in the concrete mix. Sitting idle in their position for years, they are activated at the moment when a crack appears and water and air enter the matrix. Such robust microorganisms exist in nature, and appear related to a specialized group of alkali-resistant bacteria. One of their interesting features is that they are able to form spores, which are specialized spherical thick-walled cells somewhat homologous to plant seeds. The spores, viable but dormant cells, can withstand mechanical and chemical stresses and remain viable in dry state for periods of over 50 years.

It is expected that further development of this new type of self-healing concrete will result in a more durable and sustainable concrete, especially suited for applications in wet environments, where reinforcement corrosion tends to impair the durability of traditional concrete constructions. In this way, a substance such as bacteria, which used to be considered as unwanted and of no value, could help develop a truly sustainable system.

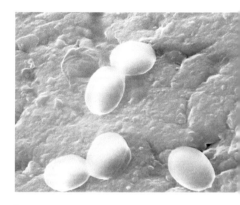

1

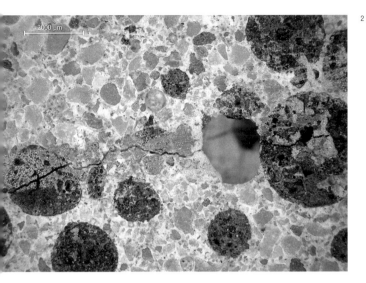

2

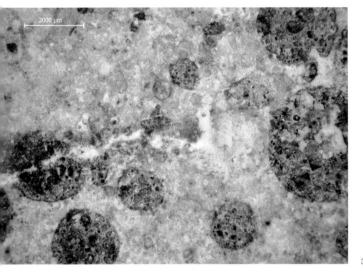

3

PROJECT DATA

RESOURCE
Bacteria

MANUFACTURER
AND DESIGNER
Henk M. Jonkers, Microlab,
Delft University of Techno-
logy, The Netherlands

PRODUCT DIRECTORY
Waterproofing, page 186

PRODUCT DATA

ORGANISM
Bacteria, alkali-resistant,
spore-forming

NOURISHMENT
Calcium lactate (bio-mineral
precursor compound)

EXPECTED LIFETIME
> 50 years

GROWTH TIME
60 days for sub-millimeter-
sized cracks with 100%
healing results

FIRE RATING
Fireproof, non-combustible
(E136)

2 The bacteria are activated when a crack lets water and air reach the precursor.

3 Through the production of calcium carbonate, bacteria have the ability to close cracks in the matrix and heal the concrete completely.

4 The first-aid emergency post in Galder, near Breda, The Netherlands, was built in 2009 using a protective layer of self-healing concrete. At the time of writing, the structure showed no cracking or other deficiencies, due to its built-in self-healing mechanism. (Architect: Frank Marcus, Leeuwen; constructor: Rob van Gestel, Eindhoven; special advisor: Henk M. Jonkers, TU Delft)

4

1 Mushroom mycelium can potentially be used to grow building materials with stunning properties.

TINY MUSHROOM HOUSE

In a cube of 10 cm side length of colonized organic matter – such as a decomposing tree trunk – the root network of fungi organisms, also called mycelium, can reach a length of about 170 km.[1] The New York City-based company Ecovative uses mycelium and agricultural by-products to grow building materials. Mycelium acts as natural, self-assembling glue, digesting crop waste to produce cost-competitive, environmentally responsible, and structurally active materials.

These kinds of mushroom-grown materials use plant-based farm waste as their nourishment. They are fully compostable. In the process, corn stalk and mycelium are mixed into a moist mass and poured into a mould of the desired shape. Left alone in a dark space, the mixture grows into the form in the course of days. Heating in an oven stops the growth process. The properties of the building element can be finetuned depending on the type of mushroom and agricultural nourishment. Today, Ecovative offers a variety of products and applications, from insulation to building bricks and automotive parts.

The initial research that eventually led to this development focused on rigid board building insulation material to replace plastic foams. The team grew test panels and installed them in walls behind glass in several buildings. These early prototypes still insulate well and look as good as ever today. Expanding their product range, Ecovative built their first production system focusing on mushroom-grown packaging elements, a sustainable alternative to ordinary plastic foam constituents.

Running a successful business based on these packaging products, Ecovative later returned to its roots and started to look deeper for a possible market share in the building materials sector. As a "lighthouse project", the company constructed the world's first mushroom house, with walls made of mushroom-grown insulation material. The mushroom-based insulation cultivates into wood forms over the course of a few days. After stopping the process, the material had to dry out over the next month (similar to the curing of concrete) to finally create a strong airtight wall with a high thermal performance, as the material builds one continuous insulated wall assembly. This method does not require any studs in the wall, since the mycelium develops high load-bearing capacities.

The Tiny Mushroom House with a size of 3.6 m × 2.1 m is mounted on a trailer and travels through the country, in reference to moving homes. At the time of writing, Ecovative is also developing insulated sheathing, structural insulating panels, and an engineered wood replacement called Myco Board for the building materials market.

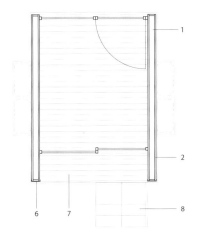

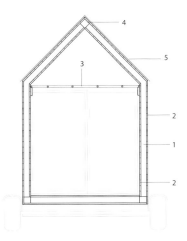

PROJECT DATA

RESOURCE
Mushroom mycelium,
agricultural waste

MANUFACTURER AND
DESIGNER
Ecovative, Green Island,
NY, USA

PRODUCT DIRECTORY
Load-bearing, page 177;
Insulating, page 183

PRODUCT DATA

ORGANISM
Fungi

NOURISHMENT
Corn stalk

EXPECTED LIFETIME
Unlimited if desired

GROWTH TIME
15 days

COMPRESSION STRENGTH
Variable

FIRE RATING
Class A (ASTM E84)

2 The Tiny Mushroom House is the first building with wall fillings grown out of mushroom mycelium material.

1 mushroom material
2 lost formwork cladding
3 mushroom panel ceiling
4 wooden beam
5 aluminium roof panels
6 aluminium cladding
7 floorboards
8 staircase

3 Grown between wooden planks within few days, the mycelium forms an airtight seal and rigid building element.

4 Ecovative's Tiny Mushroom House toured through the USA built on a trailer.

3

4

HY-FI

In 2014, the Museum of Modern Art in New York gave the award of its Young Architects Program to David Benjamin and his architectural firm The Living. Their Hy-Fi project is a collaboration with Ecovative and proposes a cluster of towers built out of bricks grown from mycelium at the PS1, MoMA's satellite venue in Long Island City. The architects claim this project to be the first sizable structure with a near-zero carbon footprint in its construction process and beyond.

The mycelium bricks, using corn stalk as their nourishment, grow in special daylighting mirror film formworks in the block's shape. In the construction process, the organic bricks are positioned at the bottom of the structure, while the reflective empty formworks themselves are placed at the top and bounce light down onto the towers and the ground. The moulds are meant to be shipped back to the producer for use in further research after the dismantling of the temporary building. The design of the towers is calibrated to create a cool microclimate in the city in the summer by drawing in cool air at the bottom and pushing out hot air at the top through a series of gaps in the walls.

Hy-Fi offers a familiar-yet-completely-new structure in the context of the glass towers of the New York City skyline. After deconstruction, the bricks are planned to be processed by the local company Build It Green Compost and distributed to local community gardens as compost and fertilizer. In this way, the building is completely cultivated and compostable throughout its life cycle.

1

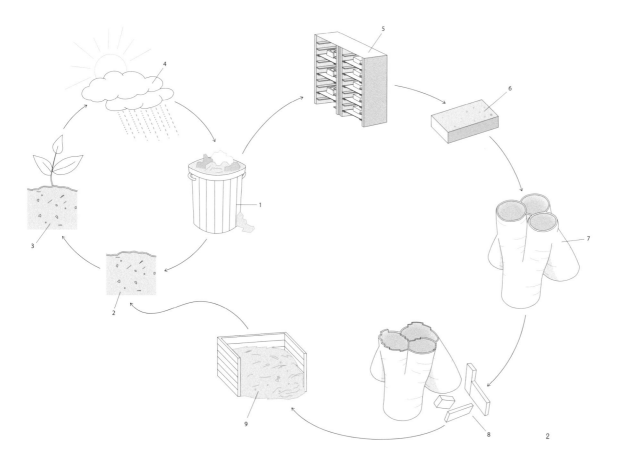

1 Specially designed mushroom bricks from Ecovative for the Hy-Fi building.

2 The bricks are grown using agricultural waste as nourishment. They can be reintroduced into the regular metabolic life cycle through composting.

1 organic waste
2 soil
3 plants
4 atmosphere
5 growth of bricks
6 mushroom brick
7 building construction
8 building deconstruction
9 brick composting

3 A collaboration of New
York-based architects The
Living and Ecovative, Hy-Fi
is a cluster of brick towers
grown from mushroom
mycelium at MoMA's
satellite venue PS1.

PROJECT DATA

RESOURCE
Mushroom mycelium,
agricultural waste

MANUFACTURER
Ecovative, Green Island,
NY, USA

DESIGNER
The Living, New York City,
NY, USA

PRODUCT DIRECTORY
Load-bearing, page 177;
Insulating, page 183

PRODUCT DATA

ORGANISM
Fungi

NOURISHMENT
Corn stalk

EXPECTED LIFETIME
Unlimited if desired

GROWTH TIME
15 days

COMPRESSION STRENGTH
Variable

FIRE RATING
Class A (ASTM E84)

3

4 Interior view of the Hy-Fi building.

5

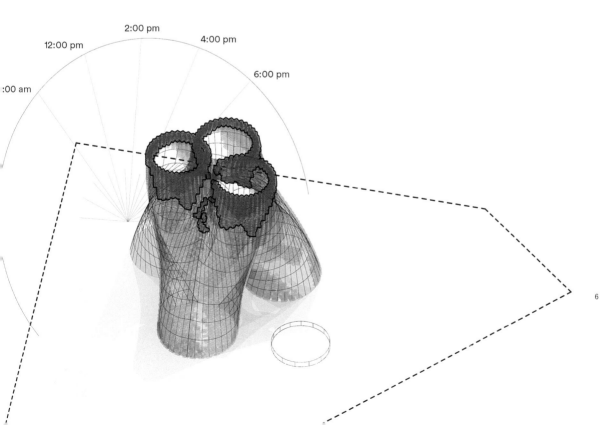

2:00 pm

12:00 pm

4:00 pm

:00 am

6:00 pm

6

5 The building uses biologically engineered bricks produced by Ecovative.

6 The architects claim their project to be the first sizable structure with a near-zero carbon footprint in its construction process and beyond. Study of shadows and reflections cast by the structure.

MYCOFORM – MYCELIA AMALGAMATION METHODS FOR URBAN GROWTH

Mycoform structures grow into a specific 3D-fabricated geometry using the strains of fungi. The main objective of Mycoform is to establish a smart, self-sufficient, perpetual-motion construction technology. By combining fungal mycelia with varying types of organic substrates and carefully controlling their expansion within prefabricated moulds, it is possible to generate the literal growth of structural materials.

Mycoform is grown from biological materials. The polypore fungal species *Ganoderma lucidum* (Reishi) possesses enzymes that readily digest a wide variety of cellulose-based organic by-products. The rapid growth of the branching mycelia results in a dense matrix with structural properties conducive for use as a construction material. The fungal substance is encased within a strong and durable outer-layer shield of compacted material, such as recycled aluminium.

The Mycoform building block production is a low-tech, low-energy process. Only few inexpensive and readily available tools, free refuse and agricultural by-products, 27°C and a high degree of humidity are required to compact and grow them. The process is pollution-free and has the potential to contain little embodied energy, as it is part of the local ecosystem. Computer simulations and computation can predict growth scenarios of Mycoform building blocks, and climate/time control allows regulating the growth.

The fungal building block concept is not only environmentally sound – it requires only readily available organic waste material and needs no extra energy – but it may also have the capacity to clean the environment. Fungi could break down even toxic organic materials into inert building substances. Additionally, the technology is easily transferable to the developing world, where otherwise building materials would need to be imported.

Advances in formwork and moulding methods also played a major role in reducing the ecological footprint of generating this material. Alternative low embodied energy mould-making processes involve either sand casting or Phase Change Materials such as paraffin and plant-based natural wax moulds. In these cases, the sand or wax is used and reused as the formwork for each mycelium component. These casting materials are much lower in cost and environmental impact when compared to aluminium tooling and plastics. They do not degrade profile qualities or characteristics.

The exemplary New Museum model was grown in a period of ten days in an incubator. For this prototype, Terreform One used a starting mixture containing oak pellet fuel, wheat bran, gypsum, and hydrogen peroxide, which resulted in a dense mycelium structure.

1 Close-up image of mycelia, the vegetative part of a fungus, which can be hardened into rigid forms and is potentially usable as a building material.

2 Cities of the future could be built from municipal solid waste, a resource that is available worldwide and in immense quantities.

3 The familiar form of the New Museum in New York City, designed by Kazuyo Sejima and Ryue Nishizawa/ SANAA, reimagined and built using mushroom blocks.

4 Different material stages during the growth process of the mycelium.

5 The Mycoform building block is made from the mycelia of Reishi mushrooms encased in recycled sheets of aluminium.

3

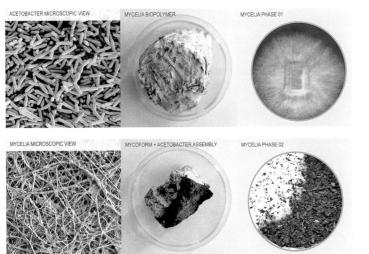

4

5

MYCELIUM

DISCARDED ALUMINIUM

PROJECT DATA

RESOURCE
Mushroom mycelium, paper waste, and discarded aluminium

DESIGNER
Mitchell Joachim, Maria Aiolova, Oliver Medvedik, Dylan Butman, Greg Mulholland, Terreform ONE, New York City, NY, USA

PRODUCT DIRECTORY
Load-bearing, page 177

PRODUCT DATA

ORGANISM
Ganoderma lucidum, *Ganodema tsugae*, and *Ganoderma sichuanense*

NOURISHMENT
Organic waste materials

EXPECTED LIFETIME
Unlimited

GROWTH TIME
10 days

COMPRESSION STRENGTH
2–46 kPa at 10% mycelium, 496–1,792 kPa at 50% mycelium (ASTM D695)

FIRE RATING
Class A (ASTM E84) (mycelium)

1

1 A cured fungal brick with antlers growing off its top, 2008.

2 During their growth process, the mushrooms used in the project digest cellulose and transform it into chitin. The image shows a close-up view of the resulting cultivated material.

3 The fungus bricks for Mycotectural Alpha were grown at the Far West Fungi farm in Monterey, CA, in 2008.

MYCOTECTURE

This test structure, Mycotectural Alpha, is part of a larger project in which artist Philip Ross intends to grow an entire building out of fungal material. The initial goal is to create a space that can shelter up to 20 people at a time. His basic research aims to prove the value of the Reishi mushroom as a sustainable building material. Mycelium, the root network of the *Ganoderma lucidum* fungus, has surprising properties when dried. It is non-toxic, fireproof, as well as water and mould-resistant. Mushrooms digest cellulose and transform it into chitin, the same hard material that insect shells are made from.

In order to produce the building bricks, sawdust is steam-cooked in airtight bags for several hours to produce pasteurized wood chips. When these have cooled down, small pieces of mushroom tissue are introduced into the bag. The mushroom eagerly devours the neutralized wood. As the fungus digests and transforms the contents of the bag, it solidifies into a mass of interlocking cells, gradually becoming denser. At this stage, the mixtures are transferred from the initial dark environment into the growing room. The tops of the bags are cut off and the fungus is left to grow in a high-humidity environment for a week.

The mushrooms can be cast into almost any shape. The ensuing bricks are dried out using fans, heaters, and dehumidifiers so as to stop the growing process. The bricks have the feel of a composite material with a core of spongy cross-grained pulp that becomes progressively denser towards the outer skin. The skin itself is very hard, shatter-resistant, and can handle large compression forces. The bricks can be shaped by common wood-working tools, even though considerable force is necessary to do so.

The approximately 400 bricks for Mycotectural Alpha were grown at the Far West Fungi mushroom farm in Monterey, California, and the structure was exhibited as part of the Eat Art exhibition at the Kunsthalle Düsseldorf in Germany in 2010. The constructed arch was assembled on site from three different pre-grown brick shapes. Placed on top of each other along a guiding support structure, the single bricks were stacked in segments and interlocked with small bamboo sticks for additional support. After a section of the arch was completed, the support structure was removed and another row assembled.

2

3

4

5

4 Mushrooms can grow in any shape or mould, as shown here in the interlocking 4Kab Polyominoe bricks, 2013.

5 Mushroom building bricks can be used in combination with common elements such as wooden beams.

PROJECT DATA

RESOURCE
Mushroom mycelium, sawdust

MANUFACTURER
AND DESIGNER
Philip Ross, MycoWorks, San Francisco, CA, USA

PRODUCT DIRECTORY
Load-bearing, page 177; Insulating, page 182

PRODUCT DATA

ORGANISM
Ganoderma lucidum

NOURISHMENT
Sawdust

EXPECTED LIFETIME
Unlimited

GROWTH TIME
14–30 days in sealed environment

FIRE RATING
No information

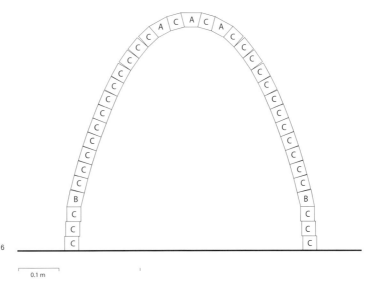

6

0.1 m

7

6 The arch of Mycotectural Alpha is loaded only in compression, activating the structural potential of the mushroom bricks.

7 Mycotectural Alpha was exhibited at the Kunsthalle Düsseldorf, Germany, in 2009.

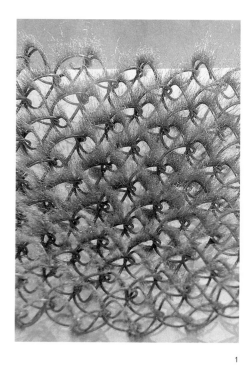

1

DUSTYRELIEF

Smog particles belong to one of the biggest groups of waste materials. Coming from industrial pollutions, combusted fossil energy carriers, volcanic eruptions, or simply lifted by weather, these small waste components are usually acknowledged as being a hazard for our health and environment, especially in the case of "smog": introduced in the early 20th century as a combination of the words "fog" and "smoke", today it refers mostly to vehicle emissions and their combustion engines. The remains of the burning process are very fine and light, and when they get into our atmosphere they stay until wind blows them away, or rain washes them out.

The project Dustyrelief capitalizes on smog as a resource by introducing a process of perception-transformation of this waste material. The building resembles a design for a new art gallery in the city of Bangkok. The capital of Thailand is known to be one of the heaviest air-polluted cities in the world, mostly due to a non-functional public transport system – and therefore (in the eyes of the architects) offers huge amounts of building material for free. While the building's inner spatial organization

follows a Euclidian system of stacked cubes, the external envelope is to be understood as a living organism. In order to harvest this rich resource, smog, the façade consists of a metal mesh that through an electrostatic mechanism attracts the dust particles from the surrounding air. This apparatus glues the small waste elements together, so to speak, forming a hairy fur that in its final stage would carpet the entire building structure. This procedure will repeat itself whenever the seasonal monsoon rain will wash down the particles, whereby they can be collected and recycled.

The envelope acts as a catalyst between the highly controlled environment of the art gallery and the sometimes hazardous outside conditions. It filters the smog waste particles, turns them into a building material for a limited time, and then releases them to be collected and treated. In this way, the building changes its appearance in accordance to natural as well as man-made climatic and environmental conditions. Even though the building was never realized, it establishes a strategy to see waste as a matter to be sculpted, manipulated, and controlled.

1 In order to harvest smog particles as a freely available resource, an electrostatically charged metal mesh is installed, covering the entire building.

2 The mesh "glues" the waste particles together, forming a hairy fur that in its final stage will carpet the entire structure.

PROJECT DATA

RESOURCE
Electrostatically charged
smog particles

MANUFACTURER
City of Bangkok

DESIGNER
New-territories / R&Sie(n),
Paris, France

PRODUCT DIRECTORY
Finishing, page 191

PRODUCT DATA

FLOOR AREA
5,000 m²

EXPECTED LIFETIME
Depending on air-
pollution rates

FIRE RATING
No information

2

3 The atmosphere of the
interior spaces changes
according to the density
and formal arrangement
of the living outer skin.

3

4

4 The façade acts as a catalyst between the highly controlled environment of the art gallery and the sometimes hazardous outside conditions.

5 While the spatial organization of the interior follows a Euclidian system of stacked cubes, the façade is conceived as a living organism.

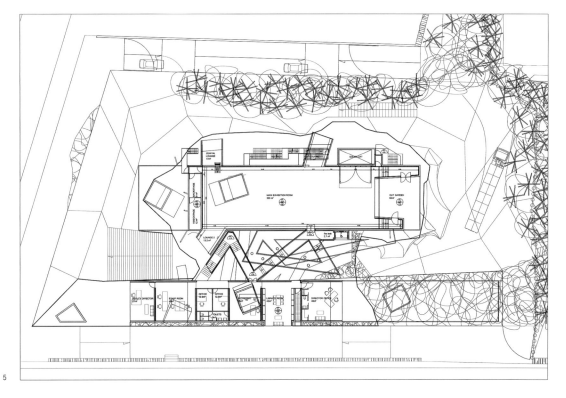

5

PRODUCT DIRECTORY

LOAD-BEARING PRODUCTS

Load-bearing Products p. 172
Self-supporting Products p. 178
Insulating Products p. 180
Waterproofing Products p. 184
Finishing Products p. 187

Biorock
Construction Beams

RESOURCE
Mineral-saturated seawater

TYPE
Cultivated

SIZES
Custom

MANUFACTURER AND DESIGNER
Wolf Hilbertz, Dr. Thomas J. Goreau,
Biorock Inc., MA, USA

PROJECT
Biorock, p. 154

Biorock grows rock-hard limestone
coatings of any preferred thickness
on steel frames of any desired
shape or size through electrolysis.
The resulting material has a
compression strength about three
times the strength of concrete made
from ordinary Portland cement.
A minimum voltage of 1.23 V (at
standard conditions, plus junction
potentials) is needed to initiate
electrolysis of water. This innovative
material grows faster and harder in
warm tropical waters than in cold
boreal waters and is envisioned to
play a crucial part in maritime and
even underwater architectures.

Olzweg
Construction Bricks

RESOURCE
Discarded glass

TYPE
Transformed

SIZES
Custom

DESIGNER
New-territories / R&Sie(n), Paris, France

PROJECT
Olzweg, p. 110

The designers propose to produce
glass bars, each from three recycled
green glass bottles, heated and
poured into an elongated mould.
The glass reaches a density of
2,500 kg/m^3 and an extremely high
compression strength of 1 GPa,
rendering it a highly valuable
building material, also considering
additional qualities such as
transparency and insulation. These
glass bars are non-combustible.

World Bottle (WOBO)
Building Bricks

RESOURCE
Glass bottles

TYPE
Designed

SIZES
Capacity 330 or 500 ml, dimensions
80 mm × 60 mm × 140 or 220 mm

MANUFACTURER
Heineken International (Breweries company),
Amsterdam, The Netherlands

DESIGNER
John Habraken, Amsterdam, The Netherlands

PROJECT
World Bottle (WOBO), p. 130

World Bottle introduces a new
recycling circuit for discarded glass
bottles, whereby the design of the
bottle allows for a second life cycle
as a building element. The neck of
one bottle slides into the bottom of
the next one, creating a continuous
horizontal masonry row. To increase
the vertical connection, the bottles
are equipped with friction nobs on
both sides. About 1,000 bottles are
required, each at a weight of about
220 or 330 g, to construct a 9 m^2
wall area.

Jiilkeen Cube
Construction Bricks

RESOURCE
Glass bottles

TYPE
Designed

SIZES
Capacity 500 ml, dimensions
100 mm × 100 mm × 100 mm

DESIGNER
Petit Romain, Lyon, France

PROJECT
Jiilkeen Cube, p. 134

Jiilkeen Cubes rely on the same
structural strength of the material
as an ordinary bottle, but the shape
is re-designed to make up for the
inefficiency of spatial arrangements
of conventional cylindrical shapes.
The cubic form is achieved by
introducing a rectangular body
and pushing the bottleneck inside
this boundary as well. Through
their ability to be stacked in a
very compact way, they can be
handled just like any other brick.
As the design does not provide a
self-interlocking system, it requires
a second material functioning
as mortar.

Vacuumized PET Bottles
Construction Beams

RESOURCE
Discarded PET bottles

TYPE
Densified

SIZES
Custom

MANUFACTURER
Luft & Laune, Zurich, Switzerland

DESIGNER
Assistant Professorship of Architecture and
Construction Dirk E. Hebel, ETH Zurich/
FCL Singapore, Singapore, and Zurich,
Switzerland

PROJECT
Airless, p. 36

Vacuumized PET Bottles is a
structural building system in which
discarded plastic drinking units are
packed into a prefabricated and
airtight membrane tube. Put under a
vacuum condition of about 22 mbar,
this composite system reaches high
load-bearing capacities combined
with an extremely low density of
53 kg/m^3. Depending on the selected
membrane, the inexpensive material
is able to reach a B1 fire rating and
can be used for indoor and outdoor
large-span spatial arrangements.

TRPA Treated Recycled Plastic Aggregates
Construction Aggregate

RESOURCE
Discarded plastics

TYPE
Transformed

SIZES
Custom

MANUFACTURER AND DESIGNER
TEWA Technology Corporation,
Albuquerque, NM, USA

PROJECT
Plasphalt, p. 70

Using all types of unsorted plastic
waste, TRPA is a plastic alternative
to partially replace mineral
aggregates such as sand and gravel
in traditional asphalt cement road
pavement. In general, the produced
material is a granulate of 6 mm or
less in diameter. It replaces about
1–2% by weight, or 5–7% by volume,
of the sand and gravel in the final
mix. The end product is cheaper,
lighter, and stronger than traditional
asphalt cement.

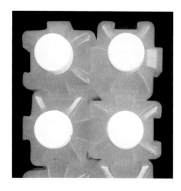

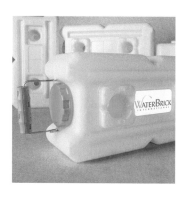

Byfusion Bricks
Construction Bricks

RESOURCE
Discarded plastics

TYPE
Transformed

SIZES
400 mm × 200 mm × 200 mm

MANUFACTURER AND DESIGNER
Byfusion Limited, Wellington, New Zealand

PROJECT
Byfusion Bricks, p. 114

Byfusion Bricks are produced from
100% post-consumer unsorted
plastics, which are shredded into
12 mm wide strips, cleaned, and
compressed into a batch mould.
In a fusion chamber, heat and
pressure fuse the material in the
capped mould into a solid block
with a density of 375–625 kg/m^3.
The compression strength (~1MPa)
of the material is relatively low
(a maximum of three stories can
be constructed with the maximum
density block type). However, it
immediately reverts to its original
shape after impact, a property
that allows for additional uses
besides construction.

UNITED BOTTLE
Construction Bricks

RESOURCE
PET bottles

TYPE
Designed

SIZES
Capacity 1,500 ml, dimensions
89 mm × 89 mm × 350 mm

DESIGNER
UNITED BOTTLE Group, Zurich
and Basel, Switzerland

PROJECT
UNITED BOTTLE, p. 140

UNITED BOTTLE introduces a new
recycling circuit for discarded PET
containers, whereby the design of
the bottles allows for a second life
cycle as a building element. Each
bottle is equipped with two inward
and two outward-oriented tucks,
allowing one bottle to be connected
to another four bottles and create
a load-bearing wall system. About
1,000 bottles are required, each at a
weight of about 40 g, to construct a
6-m^2 wall area.

WaterBrick
Construction Bricks

RESOURCE
High Density Polyethylene (HDPE)
water container

TYPE
Designed

SIZES
229 or 458 mm × 229 mm × 152 mm

MANUFACTURER AND DESIGNER
Wendell Adams, WaterBrick International,
Winter Garden, FL, USA

PROJECT
WaterBrick, p. 144

WaterBricks, once emptied of their
original contents, can enter a second
life cycle as basic building blocks.
Their design does not require any
mortar to be applied; they can be
combined almost like toy bricks.
Each unit shows a top side with at
least one positive lug and a lower
side with a corresponding cavity.
This system allows the units to be
layered and forming a robust and
interlocking structure, while the
regular opening, lid, and handle are
placed on the side, not interfering
with this feature. 1000 containers
are sufficient to construct a wall
with an area of 69 m^2.

UPM ProFi
Construction Profiles

RESOURCE
Label printer waste

TYPE
Reconfigured

SIZES
60 mm × 60 mm × custom length;
8 mm thick

MANUFACTURER
UPM Biocomposites, Lahti, Finland

DESIGNER
Shigeru Ban, Shigeru Ban Architects,
Paris, France

PROJECT
Artek Pavilion, p. 72

UPM ProFi is a wood-plastic
composite, extruded out of label
printer waste trimmings containing
60% cellulose fibres and 40%
plastic polymers. In addition to the
structural robustness and strength,
the material has a low moisture
absorption, which means it does
not require any additional surface
treatment and is suitable for outdoor
use. The absence of lignin, the
natural wood binder, prevents the
material from turning grey when
exposed to UV light. The L-shaped
profiles can be manufactured by
extrusion and injection moulding
and handled with conventional tools.

Corrugated Cardboard Bundles
Construction Blocks

RESOURCE
Discarded corrugated cardboard

TYPE
Densified

SIZES
2,000 mm × 800 mm × 700 mm

MANUFACTURER
Corrugated cardboard box plants, USA

DESIGNER
Rural Studio, Auburn University,
Newbern, AL, USA

PROJECT
Corrugated Cardboard Pod, p. 42

Corrugated Cardboard Bundles
are compressed bales made from
cardboard scrap. With a density of
about 400 kg/m³, these bales reach
high thermal as well as sound
insulation rates and can be used
as a structural material due to their
high compression strength. The high
density results in a fire-retardant
building material. Fire ratings can
be improved with additional flame-
retardant sprays or plasters.

Recycled Cardboard Bales
Construction Blocks

RESOURCE
Discarded cardboard

TYPE
Densified

SIZES
1,400 mm × 1,100 mm × 800 mm

MANUFACTURER
Paper recycling facilities,
Oberhausen, Germany

DESIGNER
Dratz & Dratz Architects,
Oberhausen, Germany

PROJECT
PHZ2, p. 44

Recycled Cardboard Bales consist
of densified cardboard scrap held
together by metal straps. Due to
their extremely high compactness,
the bales can take high amounts of
compressive strength. They are easy
to stack and can form wall elements
of up to 30 m in height without any
additional support. With a density
of approximately 400 kg/m³, the
bales show high sound and thermal
insulation qualities.

Paper Tiles
Construction Bricks

RESOURCE
Paper waste

TYPE
Reconfigured

SIZES
300 mm × 150 mm × 25 mm

MANUFACTURER AND DESIGNER
BLOCK Research Group,
ETH Zurich, Switzerland

PROJECT
Paper Tile Vault, p. 76

Paper Tiles are produced from paper
and cardboard that is repulped by
adding water to dissolve fibres and
starch into a formable mass that
can be pressed into virtually any
shape desired. The dried paper tiles
have a density of 250–450 kg/m³
and reach a compression strength
of 1.2–1.4 MPa. Waterproofing
and fireproofing properties can
be achieved by adding ingredients
such as borates to the mix, or by
lacquer coatings.

Ubuntublox
Construction Bricks

RESOURCE
Plastic waste and vetiver root waste

TYPE
Densified

SIZES
400 mm × 200 mm × 200 mm

MANUFACTURER AND DESIGNER
Harvey Lacey, New York City, NY, USA

PROJECT
Ubuntublox, p. 40

Ubuntublox are densified building
bricks made from eradicated vetiver
roots in a size of 400 mm × 200 mm
× 200 mm. They are compacted in
a hand-operated press to a density
of about 225 kg/m³. Vetiver roots are
naturally insect and fungi-resistant
and widely available. Due to the
rough surface resulting from
the compacting of the natural
fibre, the product can easily be
plastered or treated with any other
finishing material.

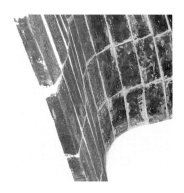

Strawjet Cables
Construction Blocks

RESOURCE
Straw waste

TYPE
Densified

SIZES
50 mm ø

MANUFACTURER
Strawjet Inc., Talent, OR, USA

PROJECT
Strawjet, p. 54

The Strawjet machine compresses wheat and rice straw or other commercial stalks into a highly compacted and extruded strand, called cable, with a diameter of 5 cm. Fed by conveyer belts, compression rollers compact the straw, which is then tightly bound by a rotating annulus with strings. The process can run continuously at a speed of 40 m per minute. The resulting product can be applied to construct building elements such as columns or beams, or simply as a highly insulating filling material.

Songwood Boards
Construction Panels

RESOURCE
Furniture industry and branch waste

TYPE
Densified

SIZES
100 mm × 2,000 mm × 10–150 mm

MANUFACTURER
Engineered Timber Resources, Boulder, CO, USA

Songwood Boards are pressed of wood by-products from furniture and pulp manufacturing plants as well as stockpiles of branch waste from the silk and industrial filtration industries. Cleaned and dried, the wood strands are partially coated in heat-activated, low-VOC glue. Depending on the desired aesthetic, the colour-sorted and dried fibres are aligned in a mould (roughly 100 mm × 150 mm) and pressed at a pressure of 1,800 tons. After this treatment, the material needs to cure at ambient conditions for 40–45 days before it can be cut and kiln-dried so that the desired profiles can be manufactured.

Green Leaf Bricks
Construction Bricks

RESOURCE
Sewage waste and scrap materials

TYPE
Reconfigured

SIZES
194 mm × 92 mm × 25 mm

MANUFACTURER
Green Leaf Brick, Charlotte, NC, USA

DESIGNER
Masonry Research Group, Massachusetts Institute of Technology, MA, USA

PROJECT
Vault201, p. 92

Green Leaf Bricks are produced from 30% processed sewage waste and recycled iron oxides, recycled glass, mineral tailings, virgin ceramic scrap – the by-products of open-pit mining operations, contents from industrial dust filtration, and a variety of other waste materials. Fired at above 1,030° C, the bricks reach a density of 2,380 kg/m^3, which results in a compression strength of 112 MPa. The material is odourless and can be used similar to any other fired brick.

Blood Bricks
Construction Bricks

RESOURCE
Discarded animal blood and sand

TYPE
Transformed

SIZES
500 mm × 120 mm × 40 mm

DESIGNER
Jack Munro, Arthur Mamou-Mani, Toby Burgess, University of Westminster, London, United Kingdom

PROJECT
Blood Brick, p. 124

Blood Bricks are produced from discharged blood residues, which are mixed with a preservative and an anticoagulant immediately after collection to allow short-term storage. This biological substance is then blended with sand at a ratio of roughly 1:4 to create a thick paste, which must be heated sufficiently to coagulate the blood and drive off excess water. This can be achieved by leaving it exposed to the sun, or by placing it in solar ovens. The bricks reach a density of 1,300 kg/m^3 and a compression strength of 115 kPa.

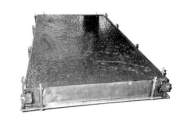

Mushroom Bricks
Construction Bricks

RESOURCE
Mushroom mycelium, straw waste

TYPE
Cultivated

SIZES
Custom

MANUFACTURER
Ecovative, Green Island, NY, USA

DESIGNER TINY MUSHROOM HOUSE
Ecovative, Green Island, NY, USA

DESIGNER HY-FI
The Living, New York, NY, USA

PROJECT
Tiny Mushroom House, p. 158 and
Hy-Fi, p. 160

Mushroom Bricks are grown from mushroom mycelium and corn stalk. The moist mixture is poured into a mould of the desired shape. Left alone in a dark space, the mixture grows into the form in the course of about 15 days. The properties of the building element can be finetuned depending on the type of mushroom and agricultural nourishment. The building elements are 100% grown and compostable. They received a Class A fire rating and can take significant compression forces.

Mycoform
Construction Bricks

RESOURCE
Mushroom mycelium, paper waste
and discarded aluminium

TYPE
Cultivated

SIZES
Custom

DESIGNER
Mitchell Joachim, Maria Aiolova, Oliver
Medvedik, Dylan Butman, Greg Mulholland,
Terreform ONE, New York City, NY, USA

PROJECT
Mycoform – Mycelia Amalgamation
Methods for Urban Growth, p. 164

The polypore fungal species *Ganoderma lucidum* (Reishi) possesses enzymes that readily digest a wide variety of cellulose-based organic by-products. The rapid growth of branching mycelia results in a dense matrix with structural properties conducive for use as a construction material. The fungal substance is encased within a strong and durable outer-layer shield of compacted material such as recycled aluminium. Computer simulations and computation can predict growth scenarios of Mycoform building blocks and climate/time control allows regulating the growth.

Fly Ash Panels
Construction Panels

RESOURCE
Residues from combustion

TYPE
Transformed

SIZES
Custom

MANUFACTURER
Natural Process Design Inc.,
Winona, MN, USA

Fly Ash Panels are produced from 99% fly ash mixed with a small amount of chemical flux. The mixture can be formed into panels and blocks by using various moulds and firing processes. The optimal panel composition consists mainly of fly ash combined with small amounts of acid, straw, plasticizers, and water. The blended acid acts as a fluxing agent, it increases the compressive strength and reduces shrinkage and cracking. The straw, an inexpensive and easily attainable natural fiber, further reduces shrinkage and cracking, acting as a reinforcement, while the plasticizer functions as a sort of lubricant, reducing water requirements in the fabrication process. Increases in the temperature (optimal range of 800–900° C) and in the duration of sintering result in higher strength capacities and decrease water permeability.

See also

FOAMGLAS T4+
Construction Blocks
Description on page 180

POLLI-Brick
Construction Bricks
Description on page 180

Enviro Board (E-Board)
Construction Panels
Description on page 181

Stropoly Straw Panels
Construction Panels
Description on page 181

Strawtec Straw Panels
Construction Panels
Description on page 181

Agricultural Waste Panels
Construction Panels
Description on page 182

Kirei Boards
Construction Panels
Description on page 189

Mycotecture
Construction Bricks
Description on page 182

SELF-SUPPORTING PRODUCTS

GreenStone
Construction Bricks

RESOURCE
Discarded glass bottles

TYPE
Reconfigured

SIZES
Custom

MANUFACTURER AND DESIGNER
Realm of Design, Henderson, NV, USA

GreenStones are produced from discarded glass bottles from the Las Vegas Strip hotels. Cleaned and pulverized, the glass is turned into particles as a substitute for silica sand in composites, while fly ash – a waste product from steel manufactures – acts as the binding agent. Mixed in the right proportions together with optional pigments and plain water, the blend is placed along the surfaces of the desired mould, creating a hollow form. A second mixture with glass fibres for structural support is applied as an additional layer creating the final GreenStone with a material density of 1,700 kg/m^3 and an average thickness of 13 mm.

Recy Blocks
Construction Bricks

RESOURCE
Discarded plastics

TYPE
Transformed

SIZES
600 mm × 300 mm × 100–150 mm

MANUFACTURER AND DESIGNER
Gert de Mulder, Hertogenbosch, The Netherlands

PROJECT
Recy Blocks, p. 120

Recy Blocks are made out of wasted polyethylene plastic bags that are carefully selected, cleaned, and arranged in a mould. Exposed to heat and compression, they form a solid building element. Due to their rectangular shape, Recy Bricks can be used to construct walls or other structures. An interconnection system is based on holes and bolts that secure the elements from shifting and connect them into a structurally active building system.

Filabot Reclaimer
Construction Filament

RESOURCE
Discarded thermoplastics

TYPE
Reconfigured

SIZES
1.7–3 mm diameter

MANUFACTURER
Filabot, Montpelier, VT, USA

The Filabot Reclaimer is a grinding unit that allows for the reuse of wasted 3D prints and other thermoplastic materials. It is a hand-powered system that reduced such plastics into shavings. These can then be turned into filament for any available 3D printer through a Filabot Extruder system using heat and pressure. This idea opens doors for up-scaled reuse of thermoplastics in the building industry.

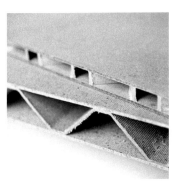

ECOR
Construction Panels

RESOURCE
Waste materials with high fibre contents

TYPE
Reconfigured

SIZES
610 mm × max 2440 mm × 2.5 mm

MANUFACTURER AND DESIGNER
Robert Noble of Noble Environmental
Technologies, San Diego, CA, USA

PROJECT
ECOR, p. 84

ECOR is a high-strength moulded
fibre composite product made out
of recycled office paper, corrugated
cardboard, kenaf fibres, sawdust
from mills, rotted wood, dehydrated
food scraps, recycled fabrics, as well
as discarded beverage containers.
In the production process of the
panels, the fibres are first mixed
with water. The resulting pulp flows
into a mould with the desired shape
(flat, corrugated, etc.) whereby the
majority of the water is removed. This
mass is then subjected to heat and
pressure, producing a fully formed
high-density panel with a density of
940 kg/m³.

vbc3000 Bricks and
Lightened Granulates
Construction Aggregate

RESOURCE
Sewage treatment sludge

TYPE
Transformed

SIZES
Custom

MANUFACTURER
vbc3000 Enterprise Innovante,
Ferrières-en-Bray, France

vbc3000 solid bricks and lightened
granulates are manufactured out
of partially dried sewage treatment
sludge (65% dryness) and clay.
Once mixed, the mass is heated
to temperatures ranging from
1,000 to 1,200° C, depending on
the clay type in use. During the
heating process the mineralization
of the organic content of the
sludge creates air pockets in the
material, thereby reducing the
weight and consequently the
density of the substance. Due to
this fact, the products are not only
lighter compared to traditional
mineral-based building materials
but also achieve excellent thermal
and soundproofing insulation
ratings. Any heavy metals present
in the sludge are trapped in the
ceramic matrix.

See also

NewspaperWood
Construction Boards
Description on page 189

Ecococon
Construction Infill
Description on page 182

INSULATING PRODUCTS

FOAMGLAS T4+
Insulating Blocks

RESOURCE
Discarded glass

TYPE
Transformed

SIZES
Panels, 450 mm × 600 mm × 30–180 mm

MANUFACTURER AND DESIGNER
Pittsburgh Corning Europe NV,
Tessenderlo, Belgium

PROJECT
FOAMGLAS T4+, p. 106

FOAMGLAS T4+ is an insulation material manufactured primarily from discarded glass and additional natural raw materials such as sand, dolomite, lime, and iron oxide. The ground-down mixture is expanded in a furnace to create a glass cell structure that gives this waterproof material an extraordinary compressive strength of 600 kPa and extremely high insulation values of 0.043 W/m^{2}K at a minimum density of 117 kg/m^3.

Reapor Recycled Poroused Waste Glass
Insulating Panels

RESOURCE
Discarded glass

TYPE
Transformed

SIZES
Custom

MANUFACTURER AND DESIGNER
Ronald Tschiersch, LIAVER GmbH & Co KG, Ilmenau, Germany, and Norbert Koenig, Fraunhofer Institute for Building Physics, Stuttgart, Germany

Reapor is produced out of Liaver Expanded Glass Granulate, a material made from discarded glass. Glass waste is fine-ground, mixed with other charges, and formed to granulate particles. These are sintered and expanded at a temperature of 750–900°C in a rotary kiln. During a second thermal process, the granules are grouted to panels of a thickness of 50 and 25 mm. The sinter necks resulting from this process provide the mineral, non-fibrous, open-porous structure with good stability and acoustic properties. The lightweight panels (270 kg/m^3) can be easily glued to walls or ceilings or fixed in a frame construction; they are resistant to humidity, non-combustible, and can be recycled.

POLLI-Bricks
Insulating Bricks

RESOURCE
PET bottles

TYPE
Transformed

SIZES
Capacity 6,000, 690, 450 ml; diameter 160 mm; height 308, 180, 118 mm

MANUFACTURER
Far Eastern Group, Taipei, Taiwan

DESIGNER
MINIWIZ, Taipei, Taiwan

PROJECT
POLLI-Brick, p. 136

POLLI-Brick is a multifunctional bottle brick with an embedded second life cycle made from 100% recycled Polyethylene Terephthalate (PET) polymer. The brick bottle is translucent, naturally insulated, and durable. The designers changed the usual round shape of a plastic bottle to a modular three-dimensional honeycomb self-interlocking form. A system constituted by a multitude of bottles can form a structural and insulating component. Lacking an interlocking feature, POLLI-Brick needs a frame structure to support it.

Shading Devices
Insulating Louvers

RESOURCE
Discarded polycarbonate and E-waste

TYPE
Transformed

SIZES
2,000 mm × 200 mm × 200 mm

DESIGNER
MINIWIZ, Taipei, Taiwan

MINIWIZ in Taiwan have developed shading devices made from recycled polycarbonate structurally enhanced with glass fibres, a by-product of e-waste recycling. The glass fibre content makes the extrusion stiffer and less prone to oscillate in the wind. The joints, produced from recycled Nylon, are produced by gas-assisted injection moulding.

Enviro Board (E-Board)
Insulating Panels

RESOURCE
Straw waste

TYPE
Densified

SIZES
2,438 and 3,658 mm × 813 mm × 57 mm

MANUFACTURER AND DESIGNER
Enviro Board Corporation,
Camden, NJ, USA

PROJECT
Enviro Board (E-Board), p. 50

Enviro Boards (E-Boards) are versatile building panels that take discarded harvest residues, such as rice or wheat straw, as their raw material resource. They are compressed without any additions into various panel sizes and shapes. Adhered with durable and waterproof papers, they are cut to length and immediately placed into a light steel wall-frame system. Equipped with this edge protection, they can be used as an interior or exterior building element. The boards are usually waterproofed with a moisture barrier and covered with any conventional outdoor surfacing material, including stucco, vinyl, shingles, or stone. As straw is also an excellent acoustic insulator, the material reduces noise by 65 decibels per panel.

Stropoly Straw Panels
Insulating Panels

RESOURCE
Straw waste

TYPE
Densified

SIZES
6,000 mm × 2,500 mm maximum × 12–200 mm

MANUFACTURER
Stropoly, Güstrow, Germany

PROJECT
Strohhaus, p. 52

Stropoly produced a wide range of compressed straw panel products that can be used in various applications including exterior walls, interior walls, and roofing structures. A sandwich of two 40 mm highly compressed straw-fibre slabs with a lightweight straw insulation filling in between provides a load-bearing structural element with high capacities of compression and bending strength, as well as a thermal conductivity of only 0.2 W/m²K. While this company has gone out of business, similar products can be found on the market.

Strawtec Straw Panels
Insulating Panels

RESOURCE
Straw waste

TYPE
Densified

SIZES
1,250–3,200 mm × 1,200 mm × 58 mm

MANUFACTURER
Strawtec Building Solutions,
Berlin, Germany

PROJECT
Sustainable Emerging City Unit (SECU), p. 56

Strawtec is a compressed straw panel product made out of untreated wheat straw, covered with recycled cardboard. Through heat exposure, the natural starch (lignum) in the wheat straw is activated and functions as natural glue, without any other chemical additions. The material has excellent physical properties, including high soundproofing and fire-protection ratings. It shows a load-bearing capacity of up to 80 kg per screw.

Ecococon Panels
Insulating Infill

RESOURCE
Straw waste

TYPE
Densified

SIZES
1,200 mm × 400–3,000 mm × 400–1,200 mm

MANUFACTURER
Ecococon Ltd., Vilnius, Lithuania

Ecococon Loadbearing Insulated Straw Panels are produced from straw bundles that are placed in parallel to each other and pressed into modular blocks. For construction purposes, these are supported by a frame structure made out of wood fibreboards. The straw panels achieve a thermal conductivity of 0.148 W/m²K and in combination with a 100 mm wood fibreboard of up to 0.111 W/m²K .

Agricultural Waste Panels
Insulating Panels

RESOURCE
Agricultural waste

TYPE
Reconfigured

SIZES
700 mm × 500 mm × 5–40 mm

DESIGNER
Berne University of Applied Sciences, Biel, Switzerland; University of Nigeria, Enugu Campus, Nigeria; Ahmadu Bello University, Zahia, Nigeria

PROJECT
Agricultural Waste Panels, p. 80

Agricultural Waste Panels are made from compacted agricultural by-products such as rice husks, groundnut shells, wheat husks, barley husks, corn stalks, corn cobs, or corn husks. They can be deployed in the fabrication of composite panels for varying applications. The raw materials are mixed with an adhesive and hot-pressed into a board. Based on the tannin from tree bark, the adhesive system is an all-organic substance especially developed for this product, while other formaldehyde-free synthetic glues can also be used. A thermal conductivity of 0.044–0.051 W/m²K makes it a viable material not only for structural applications, but also for insulation purposes.

Ultratouch Denim Insulation Batts
Insulating Infill

RESOURCE
Discarded jeans and denim fabrics

TYPE
Reconfigured

SIZES
381 / 584 mm × 1,220 / 2,320 / 9,750 mm × 51 / 89 / 140 / 203 mm

MANUFACTURER AND DESIGNER
Bonded Logic Inc., Chandler, AZ, USA

PROJECT
UltraTouch Denim Insulation, p. 90

UltraTouch Denim is a high-quality insulation material made out of natural cotton fibres, obtained from disposed jeans and denim fabrics. The material offers an effective sound absorption and a thermal performance of 0.125–0.03 W/m²K. In the production process, the shredded cotton fabrics are brought back to fibre form and treated with a borate solution to make the insulation Class A fire-resistant as well as mould and mildew-repellent. Mixed with other natural fibres, the blend is baked in a large oven and pressed into a variety of different thicknesses.

Mycotecture
Insulation Bricks

RESOURCE
Mushroom mycelium, sawdust

TYPE
Cultivated

SIZES
Custom

MANUFACTURER AND DESIGNER
Philip Ross, MycoWorks, San Francisco, CA, USA

PROJECT
Mycotecture, p. 166

Mycotecture building elements are grown from mushroom mycelium. Within 14–30 days, the fungi digest cellulose and transform it into chitin, creating bricks with a core of spongy cross-grained pulp that becomes progressively denser towards its outer skin. The skin itself is extremely hard, shatter-resistant, and can handle compression forces of more than 40 MPa. The bricks can be shaped by common wood-working tools, although considerable force is necessary to do so.

NeptuTherm Balls
Insulation Infill

RESOURCE
Beached *Posidonia oceanica* (sea balls)

TYPE
Cultivated

SIZES
Approx. 20–100 mm

MANUFACTURER
NeptuTherm e. K., Karlsruhe, Germany

NeptuTherm specializes in producing thermal insulation out of natural fibrous balls that derive from seagrass (*Posidonia oceanica*). The material can be found on the shores of the Mediterranean Sea and the west coast of Australia. The sea balls are carefully collected, dried, and tested. When approved for use, the fibres have the ability to absorb humidity from the environment, buffer it, and give it back, without any influence on thermal insulation. The thermal conductivity is as low as 0.041– 0.044 W/m^{2}K, at a density of 65–75 kg/m^3.

Seaweed Insulation
Insulation Infill

RESOURCE
Eradicated seaweed

TYPE
Cultivated

SIZES
Custom

MANUFACTURER
Ib Ungermand, Bogø Island, Denmark, and Helle Raknes Thatching, Møn Island, Denmark

DESIGNER
Vandkunsten architects, Søren Nielsen, Copenhagen, Denmark

Seaweed has several possible applications in construction. Firstly, as insulation, the material can fill out empty construction spaces in façade or roofing elements. Secondly, roofs and façades can be clad with netted pillows stuffed with this grass. The cylindrical bags used on roofs are thick and soft, while on façades they are small and hard. Interior panels can also be filled with the seaweed and upholstered with linnet fabric. Seaweed has remarkable acoustic properties as well as the ability to absorb and emit moisture, which contributes to regulate indoor climates.

See also

Alusion Stabilized Aluminium Foam Panels
Insulating Panels
Description on page 187

Ubuntublox
Insulating Bricks
Description on page 175

Byfusion Bricks
Insulating Bricks
Description on page 174

UNITED BOTTLE
Insulating Bricks
Description on page 174

Corrugated Cardboard Bundles
Insulating Blocks
Description on page 175

Recycled Cardboard Bales
Insulating Blocks
Description on page 175

Zelfo Technology Boards
Insulating Panels
Description on page 189

Strawjet Cables
Insulating Blocks
Description on page 176

Mushroom Bricks
Insulating Bricks
Description on page 177

WATERPROOFING PRODUCTS

StoneCycling
Waterproofing Tiles

RESOURCE
Demolition waste

TYPE
Transformed

SIZES
600 mm × 600 mm × 8 mm

MANUFACTURER AND DESIGNER
Tom van Soest, Eindhoven,
The Netherlands

PROJECT
StoneCycling, p. 98

StoneCycling uses a powerful blender that pulverizes glass, concrete, bricks, and even complete ceramic washbasins. Through mixing and baking these powders in various compositions, new stone-like materials are produced without adding any artificial binders or no-waste additives. The results are fire- and waterproof tiles and bricks with a variety of shapes, colours, textures, and properties.

Tuff Roof
Waterproofing Panels

RESOURCE
Discarded Tetra Pak cartons

TYPE
Reconfigured

SIZES
2,250 mm × 950 mm × 4 mm

MANUFACTURER AND DESIGNER
Daman Ganga Paper Mill,
Gujarat, India

PROJECT
Tuff Roof, p. 66

Tuff Roof corrugated sheets are produced from unseparated Tetra Pak cartons, a combination of paper, polyethylene, and aluminium. Next to their very high flexion resistance (7,630 kPa) and zero water absorption, the sheets are fire-retardant, corrosion-free and at 6 kg/m^2 extremely light. Also, spaces covered with Tuff Roof sheets show a 25% lower heat gain compared to conventional roofing materials.

BioGlass
Waterproofing Panels

RESOURCE
Discarded glass

TYPE
Transformed

SIZES
2,800 mm × 1,250 mm × 20 / 23 mm

MANUFACTURER
Coverings Etc, Miami, FL, USA

BioGlass is made out of 100% discarded glass material without any additions, colorants, or additives. It is available in six natural colours with a density of 2,400 kg/m^3 and a heat conductivity of 1.04 W/m^{2}K. The material can be cut on site with water-cooled diamond tools and is water-, stain-, chemical-, and fireproof.

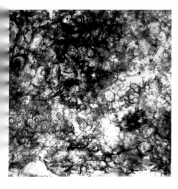

Cristalejo (Recycled Crystal Glass)
Waterproofing Tiles

RESOURCE
Discarded crystal glass cullet

TYPE
Transformed

SIZES
200 mm × 200 mm × 20 mm

DESIGNER
Fernando Miguel Marques,
Lisbon, Portugal

Recycled Crystal Glass is produced from 100% pre-consumer crystal glass cullet waste – broken glass hull is also used to lower the melting temperature of the raw material – from Portugal's largest producer of lead crystal glass. The resulting glass product can be applied as tiles or panels, which – due to the presence of lead – cannot be recycled in the normal system. The production process of Cristalejo allows for partial or total staining.

GR Green Slate, GR Green Cedar Tiles
Waterproofing Tiles

RESOURCE
Discarded milk bottles, plastic bags, and limestone waste

TYPE
Transformed

SIZES
457 mm × 254 mm × 6 mm

MANUFACTURER AND DESIGNER
GR Green Building Products Inc.,
Vancouver, BC, Canada

PROJECT
GR Green Slate, GR Green Cedar, p. 116

GR Green Slate and Cedar Tiles are produced out of polyethylene milk bottles and plastic bags into roofing tiles for the construction industry. A typical roof construction recycles about 4,400 milk bottles and 44,000 plastic bags in a zero-waste process that uses 20% polyethylene and 80% recovered limestone. The tiles cost half the price of, yet look similar to, regular slate tiles and they come with a 50-year warranty. The tiles can be nailed for easy installation and are maintenance-free.

Nappy Roofing
Waterproofing Tiles

RESOURCE
Discarded absorbent hygiene products

TYPE
Transformed

SIZES
1,100 mm × 320 mm × 6 mm

MANUFACTURER AND DESIGNER
Knowaste with Light Weight Tiles Ltd.,
Bromsgrove and Lydney, United Kingdom

PROJECT
Nappy Roofing, p. 118

Nappy Roofing utilizes absorbent hygiene products that contain plastic materials, fibres, and super-absorbent polymers. Sterilized, shredded, and separated, these elements are used to create a three-part roofing system: the roofing sheets, ridge tiles, and side flashings. All of them are available in different colours and surface structures. Compared to a traditional clay tile, they are extremely light-weight (750 kg/m^3), UV-resistant, and non-corrosive. In addition, the material is easy to install and shows good thermal insulation and sound absorption qualities.

ReMaterials Roof Panels
Waterproofing Panels

RESOURCE
Packaging and agricultural waste

TYPE
Reconfigured

SIZES
610 mm × 610 mm × 25 mm

MANUFACTURER AND DESIGNER
Hasit Ganatra and Swad Komanduri,
ReMaterials, Ahmedabad, India

PROJECT
ReMaterials Roof Panels, p. 82

ReMaterials Roof Panels are produced out of shredded cardboard, blended together with water into pulp. Organic fibres are added as a reinforcement material. The paste is placed into moulds, compressed cold, and heated to reduce the moisture content. Finally, the boards are coated with a waterproofing paint. With a bending strength of 6.85 kPa, the lightweight panels are an alternative to corrugated iron or cement sheets for roofing applications.

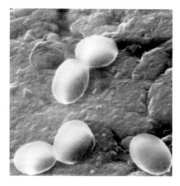

Bacteria-based
Self-healing Concrete
Waterproofing Sealing Material

RESOURCE
Bacteria

TYPE
Cultivated

SIZES
Custom

MANUFACTURER AND DESIGNER
Henk M. Jonkers, Microlab,
Delft University of Technology,
The Netherlands

PROJECT
Bacteria-based Self-healing Concrete,
p. 156

Bacteria-based Self-healing Concrete
uses a metabolic conversion of
calcium lactate to calcium carbonate
to seal occurring cracks. This
biochemically mediated process, in
other words the waste product of the
bacteria, results in efficient sealing
of sub-millimetre-sized cracks.
For effective self-healing, both the
bacteria and a bio-cement precursor
compound, their nourishment,
are to be integrated in the material
matrix before pouring, being
activated only at the moment when
a crack appears.

See also

Alkemi Boards
Waterproofing Panels
Description on page 187

CRT Glass Tiles
Waterproofing Tiles
Description on page 187

World Bottle (WOBO)
Waterproofing Bricks
Description on page 173

Jiilkeen Cube
Waterproofing Bricks
Description on page 173

Dapple Sheets
Waterproofing Panels
Description on page 188

Flexisurf Sheets
Waterproofing Panels
Description on page 188

Origins Sheets
Waterproofing Panel
Description on page 188

WaterBrick
Waterproofing Bricks
Description on page 174

UPM ProFi
Waterproofing Profiles
Description on page 174

Recycled Cardboard Bales
Waterproofing Blocks
Description on page 175

FINISHING PRODUCTS

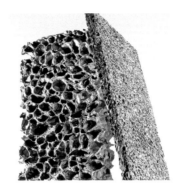

Alkemi Boards
Finishing Panels

RESOURCE
Discarded aluminium scrap

TYPE
Reconfigured

SIZES
920 / 1,220 mm × 1840 / 2440 mm × 13 mm

MANUFACTURER
Renewed Materials, LLC,
Cabin John, MD, USA

Alkemi is a recycled surface material composed of post-industrial scrap waste (60% by volume). It is made from fine flake aluminium milling scrap, which commonly burns up as a heavy smoke pollutant when exposed to conventional aluminium recycling. Combined with a resin, the composite hardens into a versatile finishing material in many variations of colour, form, and size.

Alusion Stabilized Aluminium Foam Panels
Finishing Panels

RESOURCE
Discarded aluminium

TYPE
Transformed

SIZES
2,440 mm × 1,220 mm × 12.7 / 25.4 / 43.2 mm

MANUFACTURER AND DESIGNER
Cymat Technologies Ltd., Mississauga, ON, Canada

PROJECTS
Alusion – Stabilized Aluminium Foam Panels, p. 102

Alusion Panels use heated, liquified aluminium with a temperature way above its melting point to pour it into a casting apparatus, where air is injected into the hot mass. It continuously foams onto a production line that cures the mass into a material layer to create strong (414 MPa) yet lightweight panels (density 110–550 kg/m^3). These are similar in appearance to a metallic sponge and can be cut into any desired form and length.

CRT Glass Tiles
Finishing Tiles

RESOURCE
Discarded cathode ray tubes

TYPE
Transformed

SIZES
50 mm × 100 / 200 mm × 9.5 mm or diameter 20 mm × 9.5 mm

MANUFACTURER AND DESIGNER
Fireclay Tile, San Francisco, CA, USA

PROJECTS
CRT Glass Tiles, p. 104

CRT Glass Tiles utilize cathode ray tube glass from electronic waste. This requires a very detailed chemical analysis of the glass to exactly determine its contents and to guarantee that it is safe to use. Chunks of the front part of the tubes are crushed to demagnetize the material, starting a multi-step process that ultimately produces glass particles small enough to melt when exposed to heat. After the glass is sorted, it is cast into moulds, resulting in very dense (6,500 kg/m^3) and strong (900 MPa) tiles.

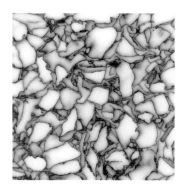

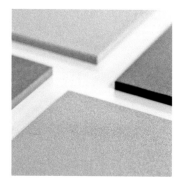

Dapple Sheets
Finishing Panels

RESOURCE
Discarded High Density Polyethylene (HDPE)

TYPE
Transformed

SIZES
1,000 mm × 2,000 mm × 12 / 20 mm

MANUFACTURER
Smile Plastics, The Remarkable Factory,
Worcester, United Kingdom

Dapple is produced from recycled high-molecular-weight polyethylene waste, which is used extensively for machined components in the food manufacturing industry. This waste can be transformed through application of heat and pressure into a unique board material. It can be applied to manufacture table tops and cupboard doors, external and internal cladding materials, and waterproof surface protections for bathrooms and wet areas.

Flexisurf Sheets
Finishing Panels

RESOURCE
Polyvinyl chloride waste

TYPE
Transformed

SIZES
457 / 610 / 1,524 mm × 457 / 610 / 1,524 / 2438 mm × 3–6 mm

MANUFACTURER AND DESIGNER
Yemm & Hart Green Materials,
Marquand, MO, USA

Flexisurf is produced from discarded swimming pool covers, industrial roofing membranes, and automobile upholstery trim scraps. These materials are granulated and fed into a sheet extruder where colour pigments are added. The resulting product is an alternative for conventional flooring materials made out of waste. The material is stain, chemical, weather, impact and puncture-resistant as well as non-corrosive. It is produced in sheets or interlocking tiles.

Origins Sheets
Finishing Panels

RESOURCE
Discarded milk jugs and soap bottles

TYPE
Transformed

SIZES
609 / 1,219 / 1,422 / 1,524 mm × 1,219 / 2,438 / 3,048 / 3,708 mm × 3–50 mm

MANUFACTURER AND DESIGNER
Yemm & Hart Green Materials,
Marquand, MO, USA

Origins is produced from polyethylene plastic bottles, a material resource found just about everywhere on the planet. The bottles run through a comprehensive purification and shredder process before they are compression-moulded into flat panels. The look of the material resembles an aesthetic of a frozen liquid substance that yields to the specific colour patterns. Material specifications are equal to pure High Density Polyethylene (HDPE) with a density of 952 kg/m^3.

Ripietra
Finishing Tiles

RESOURCE
Wood and plastic waste

TYPE
Transformed

SIZES
400 mm × 400 mm × 40 mm

MANUFACTURER
Studio Grassi Design slr,
Gambettola (FC), Italy

Ripietra Tiles look like natural stone plates but are created entirely from polyethylene derived from municipal solid waste and wood collected from industrial processing. The plastic parts are washed and cut up into small pieces, while the wood parts are ground, dried, and transformed into fibres. The mixture is processed by extrusion and moulding. This organic fibre-reinforced plastic composite is strong, sturdy, and resistant to environmental impacts and chemicals.

NewspaperWood
Finishing Boards

RESOURCE
Discarded newspapers

TYPE
Densified

SIZES
max 140 mm × 380 mm × custom thickness

MANUFACTURER AND DESIGNER
Mieke Meijer with Vij5, Eindhoven,
The Netherlands

PROJECTS
NewspaperWood, p. 46

NewspaperWood is produced out
of paper waste. Soaked with glue
and wrapped in a radial movement
along a linear axis, it forms a thick
role of paper layers with a density
of 560 kg/m³. When a finished
NewspaperWood log is cut, the
layers of paper appear like annual
growth rings of a tree and therefore
resemble the appearance of grown
wood. The material can be cut,
milled, drilled, nailed, and sanded
and generally treated like any
other type of wood. Sealed from
the outside, it can be turned into
a waterproof substance.

Rocco Sheets
Finishing Panels

RESOURCE
Discarded newspapers

TYPE
Reconfigured

SIZES
910 mm × 10,980 mm × 2 mm

MANUFACTURER AND DESIGNER
La Casa Deco, Manila, Philippines

Rocco is a wall covering veneer
made from discarded newspapers.
In the process of production, the
newspapers are cut and bonded with
a water-based glue to a paperboard
surface. When cut into strips, these
can be woven into a veneer including
a polyester thread. A final coating
protects Rocco wall covering from
external impacts and influences.
Its properties resemble a Class A
fire resistance.

Zelfo Technology Panels
Finishing Panels

RESOURCE
Waste materials with high fibre contents

TYPE
Transformed

SIZES
Custom

MANUFACTURER
Zelfo Technology GmbH,
Schorfheide-Chorin, Germany

Zelfo Technology provides an energy
and water-efficient processing
method for the defibrillation of
lingo-cellulosic fibre waste materials.
The technology refines the fibres
in an undamaged way into a slurry
with high contents of solids. The
fibre mix can then be pressed into
a range of self-binding panels.
These composites are recyclable
and biodegradable, free of binders
or adhesives, and can be produced
in various shapes and densities
(400–1,500 kg/m³).

Kirei Boards
Finishing Panels

RESOURCE
Sorghum straw waste

TYPE
Reconfigured

SIZES
305 / 910 mm × 1,820 mm ×
6 / 10 / 20 / 30 mm

MANUFACTURER
Kirei USA, Solana Beach, CA, USA

Kirei Board is a strong and
lightweight substitute for
wood products used in interior
applications. The boards are
manufactured from reclaimed
sorghum straw and formaldehyde-
free adhesive agents. With a density
of 357–533 kg/m³ and an internal
bond of 1.5 kg/cm², these boards
can hold up to 25 kg load per screw.
Kirei Boards have a fire rating of
Class C, but can be treated so to
reach Class A.

Decafe Tiles
Finishing Tiles

RESOURCE
Discarded coffee grounds

TYPE
Densified

SIZES
300 mm × 300 mm × 20 mm

MANUFACTURER AND DESIGNER
Raul Lauri Design Lab, Alicante, Spain

PROJECTS
Decafe Tiles, p. 60

Decafe Tiles are a composite material produced from disposed coffee grounds and a natural binding agent, pressed under heat influence into the desired shape, using preformed moulds. The designers are keen to retain the original coffee colour and aroma in their products to remind the senses of the emotional aspects and collected stories of this waste material. The product is meant be used indoors as a finishing material to keep this unique characteristic.

Natura 2
Finishing Panels

RESOURCE
Eradicated water hyacinth plants

TYPE
Reconfigured

SIZES
910 mm × 10,980 mm × 2 mm

MANUFACTURER AND DESIGNER
La Casa Deco, Manila, Philippines

PROJECTS
Natura 2, p. 86

Natura 2 is a wall covering material made from recovered wasted water hyacinth plants. In the process, the stalk is collected and dried, de-fibered, and glued atop a paperboard for stability. Once trimmed into strips of regular size and properties, the material is connected into standard rolls by manual weaving. Depending on the colour of the stalks and the desired final appearance, different shades of polyester thread can be used in the loom. A final water-based coating, to a certain extent, protects the wall covers from external impact and influences.

Prisma 2
Finishing Panels

RESOURCE
Capiz shell scrap

TYPE
Reconfigured

SIZES
910 mm × 10,980 mm × 2 mm

MANUFACTURER AND DESIGNER
La Casa Deco, Manila, Philippines

Prisma 2 wall coverings are produced from the abundant scrap of capiz shells. The flakes are placed on a paperboard by using a water-based adhesive and roller brush. Strips of this paperboard are woven manually into a veneer by using a handloom. There are different shades of polyester thread that can be used. A water-based final coating protects Prisma 2 wall covering products from external influences. Class A fire-resistant, the material should not be exposed to high moisture or direct UV light.

Wine Cork Tiles
Finishing Tiles

RESOURCE
Discarded wine cork stoppers

TYPE
Reconfigured

SIZES
300–900 mm × 300–900 mm × 4.8 (veneer) or 6–152 (sheet) mm

MANUFACTURER AND DESIGNER
Yemm & Hart Green Materials, Marquand, MO, USA

PROJECTS
Wine Cork Tiles, p. 88

Wine Cork Tiles are produced from whole cork stoppers. Placed next to each other, the voids in between are filled with recycled granulated cork, a by-product of the cork production. This mixture is combined with a food-grade polyurethane binder, heated, and pressed into blocks before being finally cut into sheets or veneer. Wine Cork Tiles have a density of 320 kg/m^3, are fire-resistant and 100% formaldehyde-free.

Tire Veneer Tiles
Finishing Tiles

RESOURCE
Re-treaded automobile and truck tires

TYPE
Transformed

SIZES
610 mm × 100 mm × 4 mm

MANUFACTURER AND DESIGNER
Yemm & Hart Ltd., Marquand MO, USA

PROJECTS
Tire Veneer Tiles, p. 122

Tire Veneer Tiles are produced from grinder dust of old tires, mixed with a polyurethane binder and placed into a mould. Heat and pressure are applied to create a solid block with a density of 1,041 kg/m^3 of refurbished rubber, which is sliced or veneered into thin material sheets. These 4 mm thick sheets can be cut in any desired shape, creating for example an interlocking tile system. Aesthetic appeal is given to the material by adding colourful non-recycled rubber granules.

Electrostatic Dust Attractor
Finishing Façade Element

RESOURCE
Airborne dust particles (smog)

TYPE
Cultivated

SIZES
Custom

MANUFACTURER
City of Bangkok

DESIGNER
R&Sie(n) François Roche and Stephanie Lavaux, Bangkok, Thailand

PROJECTS
Dustyrelief, p. 168

The Electrostatic Dust Attractor harvests airborne particles from the air in Bangkok for the façade of a proposed art gallery. It consists of a metal mesh which through an electrostatic mechanism attracts these particles. This apparatus 'glues' the small waste elements together, forming a hairy fur. This procedure will repeat itself whenever the electricity is turned off or rain washes down the particles, whereby they can be collected and recycled again for other purposes.

See also

StoneCycling
Finishing Tiles
Description on page 184

GreenStone
Finishing Bricks
Description on page 178

BioGlass Panels
Finishing Panels
Description on page 184

Cristalejo (Recycled Crystal Glass) Tiles
Finishing Tiles
Description on page 185

GR Green Slate, GR Green Cedar Tiles
Finishing Tiles
Description on page 185

Recy Blocks
Finishing Bricks
Description on page 178

ECOR
Finishing Panels
Description on page 179

Songwood Boards
Finishing Panels
Description on page 176

NOTES

INTRODUCTION
pages 7–19

1 Daily Chart, 'A rubbish map', *The Economist online*, accessed on-line 02/04/2014, http://www.economist.com/blogs/graphicdetail/2012/06/daily-chart-3.

2 Angélil, Marc; Siress, Cary (2010). 'Re; Going Around in Circles', in Ruby, Ilka and Andreas. *Re-inventing Construction*, Ruby Press, Berlin, Germany, pp. 248–264.

3 Bataille, Georges (1967). *La part maudite*, translated into English by Hurley, Robert (1988). *The Accused Ssare. An Essay on General Economy*, Urzone Inc., New York City, USA (reference by Angélil, Marc and Siress, Cary).

4 Mayr, Walter (2014). 'The Mafia's Deadly Garbage: Italy's Growing Toxic Waste Scandal', *Spiegel online*, accessed on-line 03/04/2014, http://www.spiegel.de/international/europe/anger-rises-in-italy-over-toxic-waste-dumps-from-the-mafia-a-943630.html.

5 Garbology, 'Difference Engine: Talking Trash', *The Economist online*, accessed on-line 02/04/2014, http://www.economist.com/blogs/babbage/2012/04/garbology-0.

6 Stein, Chris (2013). 'Inside Ghana's wasteland', *Aljazeera online*, accessed on-line 29/04/2014, http://www.aljazeera.com/indepth/features/2013/10/inside-ghana-electronic-wasteland-2013103012852580288.html.

7 Schluep, Matthias; Manhart, Andreas; Osibanjo, Oladele; Rochat, David; Isarin, Nancy; Mueller, Esther (2011). 'Where are WEee in Africa?, The Basel Convention E-Waste Africa Programme', Châtelaine, Switzerland, accessed on-line 25/03/2014, http://www.oeko.de/oekodoc/1372/2011–008-en.pdf.

8 See: Mayr, Walter (2014). 'The Mafia's Deadly Garbage: Italy's Growing Toxic Waste Scandal', *Spiegel online*, accessed on-line 03/04/2014, *http://www.spiegel.de/international/europe/anger-rises-in-italy-over-toxic-waste-dumps-from-the-mafia-a-943630.html.*

9 Leonard, Annie (2010). *The Story of Stuff: The Impact of Overconsumption on the Planet, Our Communities, and Our Health – And How We Can Make It Better*, Free Press, New York City, USA.

10 United States Environmental Protection Agency (2014). 'Municipal Solid Waste Generation, Recycling, and Disposal in the United States: Facts and Figures for 2012', accessed on-line 23/03/2014, http://www.epa.gov/osw/nonhaz/municipal/pubs/2012_msw_fs.pdf.

11 'Plastic bags and plastic bottles – CO_2 emissions during their lifetime', Timeforchange.org, accessed on-line 27/04/2014, http://timeforchange.org/plastic-bags-and-plastic-bottles-CO2-emissions.

12 Sarantis, Heather (2002). *Business Guide to Paper Reduction*, ForestEthics, San Francisco and Belingham, USA, cited from Liedtke, C. (1993). *Material Intensity of Paper and Board Production in Western Europe*, Fresenius Environmental Bulletin, Freising, Germany.

13 Stahel, Walter R. (1982). *The Product-Life Factor*, winner of the 1982 Mitchell Prize, Houston Area Research Center (HARC), The Woodlands, Texas, USA.

14 Clift, Roland; Allwood, Julian (2011). 'Rethinking the economy', *TCE: The Chemical Engineer*, issue 837, p. 30, London, UK.

15 Ellen MacArthur Foundation (2014). *Towards the Circular Economy*, Report Volume 3, Isle of Wight, UK, accessed on-line 28/03/2014, http://www.ellenmacarthurfoundation.org/business/reports.

16 Special report: waste, 'Less is more, The ultimate in waste disposal is to tackle the problem at source', *The Economist online*, accessed on-line 03/04/2014, http://www.economist.com/node/13135425?zid=313&ah=fe2aac0b11adef572d67aed9273b6e55.

17 Papanek, Victor (1971). *Design for the Real World*, Pantheon Books, New York City, USA.

18 Fitzgerald, Frances (1973). *Fire in the Lake, The Vietnamese and the Americans in Vietnam*, Macmillan, London, UK.

19 Barbalace, Kenneth (2003). 'The History of Waste'. EnvironmentalChemistry.com, accessed on-line 20/01/2014, http://EnvironmentalChemistry.com/yogi/environmental/wastehistory.html.

20 Worrell, William A.; Vesilind, P. Aarne (2011). *Solid Waste Engineering*, Cengage Learning, 2nd edition, Stamford, USA.

21 Canguilhem, Georges (1991). *The Normal and the Pathological*, Zone Books, New York City, USA.

22 Kumar, Supriya (2012). 'Global Municipal Solid Waste Continues to Grow', Worldwatch Institute, accessed on-line 25/01/2014, http://www.worldwatch.org/global-municipal-solid-waste-continues-grow.

23 ZWIA, Zero Waste International Alliance (2009), accessed on-line 26/01/2014, http://zwia.org/standards/zw-definition.

24 McDonough, William; Braungart, Michael (2002). *Cradle to Cradle: Remaking the Way We Make Things*. North Point Press, New York City, USA.

25 Ruby, Ilka and Andreas (2010). 'Mine the City', in *Re-inventing Construction*, Ruby Press, Berlin, Germany, pp. 243–247.

26 Graedel, Thomas. 'Urban Mining, Recycling Embodied Energy', greenbuilding.world-aluminum.org , accessed on-line 22/01/2014, http://greenbuilding.world-aluminium.org/facts/urban-mining.

27 Sommer, Sarah (2010). 'Müllberge zu Goldgruben', Manager magazine online, accessed on-line 25/01/2014, http://www.manager-magazin.de/unternehmen/energie/a-727834.html.

28 Crow, James Mitchell (2008). 'The concrete conundrum', *Chemistry World*, London, UK, pp. 62–68.

29 Di Maio, Francesco (2013). 'Buildings rising from the Ashes', youris.com, accessed on-line 25/01/2014, http://www.youris.com/Energy/Ecobuildings/Buildings_Rising_From_The_Ashes.kl.

30 Joachim, Mitchell (2013). 'Turning waste into building blocks of the future city', BBC Online News, accessed on-line 06/02/2014, http://www.bbc.com/future/story/20130524-creating-our-cities-from-waste.

31 Kumar, Supriya (2012). 'Global Municipal Solid Waste Continues to Grow', Worldwatch Institute, accessed on-line 25.01.2014, http://www.worldwatch.org/global-municipal-solid-waste-continues-grow.

32 An introduction to the concepts, strategies, and practices of adaptive reuse, by Liliane Wong, will be published also by Birkhäuser.

CITY AND REFUSE
pages 21–25

1 Mitchell Joachim, Maria Aiolova, Melanie Fessel, Philip Weller, Ian Slover, Emily Johnson, Landon Young, Cecil Howell, Andrea Michalski, Sofie Bamberg, Alex Colard, and Zachary Aders for Terreform ONE (Open Network Ecology), Ecological Design Group for Urban Infrastructure, Building, Planning and Art.

2 United States Environmental Protection Agency (2008). *Report on the Environment: Highlights of National Trends*, http://www.epa.gov/roehd/pdf/roe_hd_layout_508.pdf.

3 Rogers, Heather (2006). *Gone Tomorrow: The Hidden Life of Garbage*, The New Press, New York City, USA, pp. 54–67 and 104–132.

4 Cohen, Steve (2008). 'Wasted: New York City's Garbage Problem', *New York Observer*, April 3, 2008.

5 Parks Commissioner Robert Moses, NYC Proposal for Development at Fresh Kills, November 1951.

6 Disney/Pixar Animation Studios, *WALL-E*, 2008.

7 "Cities are not machines and neither are they organisms, and perhaps resemble them even less – Rather then communities of non-thinking organisms undergoing inevitable phases until they reach a certain iron limit – cities are the product of beings capable of learning. Culture can stabilize or alter the habitat system, and it is not clear whether we wish it to be otherwise." Lynch, Kevin (1984). *Good City Form*, MIT Press, Cambridge, USA, pp. 26–27.

8 McDonough, William (1998). 'Waste Equals Food: Our Future and the Making of Things', in Laddon, Judy; Atlee, Tom; Shook, Larry (eds.). *Awakening: The Upside of Y2K*, Printed Word, pp. 5–57.

9 John F. Kennedy, speech at The American University, Washington, D.C., June 10, 1963. BrainyQuote.com. Xplore Inc, 2010. http://www.brainyquote.com/quotes/quotes/j/johnfkenn124671.html.

10 Dyson, Freeman (1998). *Infinite in All Directions*, Harpercollins, New York City, USA.

11 Dawidoff, Nicholas (2009). 'The Civil Heretic', *New York Times*, March 25, 2009.

12 Krieger, Alex; Saunders, William S. (eds.) (2009). *Urban Design*, University of Minnesota Press, Minneapolis, USA.

HANDS OFF: URBAN MINING
pages 27–31

1 The 2014 report on the Berlin housing market, published by the Berlin Investment Bank, is available under: www.ibb.de/wohnungsmarktbericht.

2 In 2014, the Senate of Berlin has introduced a fund for the construction of affordable housing (Wohnungsneubaufonds) with a yearly budget of 64 million Euros. Similar to the former social housing programme, it will support the investors and ensure an affordable rent for a minimum of 20 years and up to 30 years. The expected number of affordable apartments resulting from the programme is 1,000 per annum, considerably lower than the demand. http://www.stadt entwicklung.berlin.de/wohnen/wohnungsbau/de/foerderung/index.shtml

3 These areas can be identified thanks to the 2013 Rent Index (Mietspiegel) published by the Berlin Senatsverwaltung, which registers price ranges of existing lease contracts in Berlin and is available under: http://www.stadtentwicklung.berlin.de/wohnen/mietspiegel/

4 In comparison with the second-generation social housing programmes that started in 1961, which involved large housing associations and private and public housing societies, the buildings of the earlier Aufbauprogramm were based on smaller building credits for individual investors. Hardly any comprehensive records were taken at the time and data have still to be collected from various sources.

5 Wikipedia, accessed on-line 02/03/2014, http://de.wikipedia .org/wiki/ Sozialer_Wohnungsbau _in_ Berlin#cite_note-1.

6 Kompetenzzentrum Großsiedlungen e.V., accessed on-line 02/03/2014, http://www .gross-siedlungen.de.

DENSIFIED
pages 33–61

1 Desroches, Reginald; Ergun, Ozlem; Swann, Julie (2010). 'Haiti's Eternal Weight', *The New York Times*, accessed on-line 21/03/2014, http://www .nytimes.com/2010/07/08/opinion/08desroches.html?_r=0.

2 Hoornweg, Daniel; Bhada-Tata, Perinaz (2012). 'What a waste: a global review of solid waste management', *Urban Development Series; Knowledge Papers No. 15,* World Bank, Washington, D.C., USA, accessed on-line 02/04/2014, http://documents. worldbank.org/curated/en/2012/03/16537275/waste-global-review-solid-waste-management.

3 Weiser, Christian; Zeller, Vanessa; Reinicke, Frank; Wagner, Bernhard; Majer, Stefan; Vetter, Armin; Thraen, Daniela (2013). 'Integrated assessment of sustainable cereal straw potential and different straw-based energy applications in Germany', *Applied Energy*, accessed on-line 21/03/2014, http://www.ufz.de/index.php?en=32109.

4 Jenkins, Brian M.; Turn, Scott Q.; Williams, Robert B. (1991). 'Survey documents open burning in the San Joaquin Valley', *California Agricultural Magazine*, vol. 45, #4, July/August 1991, accessed on-line 23/03/2014, http://california agriculture.ucanr.org/landingpage .cfm?article=ca.v045n04p12& fulltext=yes.

5 Food and Agricultural Organization of United Nations: Economic and Social Department: The Statistical Division 2012 (last updated on February 07, 2014), Faostat.fao.org.

RECONFIGURED
pages 63–93

1 'Tetra Pak to Double Carton Recycling' (2011), *Environmental Leader: Environmental and Energy Management News*, accessed on-line 21/03/2014, http://www.environmentalleader .com/2011/04/22/tetra-pak-to-double-carton-recycling.

2 NAPA: National Asphalt Pavement Association. 'Asphalt Pavement Overview', accessed on-line 14/03/2014, https://www .asphalt pavement.org/index. php?option= com_content&view =article&id=14&Itemid=33.

3 National Asphalt Pavement Association and European Asphalt Pavement Association (2011). *The Asphalt Paving Industry: A Global Perspective* (2nd edition), accessed on-line 12/03/2014, http://www.eapa .org/userfiles/2/Publications/GL101–2nd-Edition.pdf.

4 'The future of recycling waste from label printing' (2013), accessed on-line 12/03/2014, http://www.paperandprint.com/flexotech/features/flexo-2013/october-2013/04–10–13-the-future-of-recycling-waste-from-label-printing.aspx.

5 United States Environmental Protection Agency (last updated on February 28, 2014), accessed on-line 15/03/2014, http://www .epa.gov/wastes/conserve/materials/paper.

6 United States Environmental Protection Agency (last updated on February 28, 2014), accessed on-line 10/03/2014; http://www.epa .gov/wastes/nonhaz/municipal/index.htm.

7 'Floating aquatic macrophytes-Water hyacinths', *Food and Agricultural Organization of United Nations: Economic and Social Department: The Statistical Division, 2012.*

8 'Global wine consumption set to increase by 2 billion bottles' (2012), *Western Farm Press*, accessed on-line 14/03/2014, http:// westernfarmpress.com/grapes/ global-wine-consumption-set-increase-2-billion-bottles.

9 'Jeans market rises to the occasion' (2007), just-style.com, accessed on-line 10/03/2014, http://www.just-style.com/analysis/jeans-market-rises-to-the-occasion_id99156.aspx.

10 'New York City's Wastewater', NYC Environmental Protection, accessed on-line 14/03/2014; http://www.nyc.gov/html/dep/html/wastewater/index.shtml.

TRANSFORMED
pages 95–125

1 Hendriks, Ch. F.; Janssen, G. M. T. (2001). 'Reuse of Construction and Demolition Waste in the Netherlands for Road Construc-tions', *Heron*, vol. 46, 2001, no. 2, p. 109–117, accessed on-line 28/03/2014, http://heronjournal .nl/46–2/4.pdf.

2 'Global Metal Flow', *alu: Aluminium for Future Generations*, accessed on-line 27/03/2014, http://recycling.world-aluminium .org/review/global-metal-flow.html.

3 United States Environmental Protection Agency (2011). 'Electronics Waste Management in the United States Through 2009', accessed on-line 27/03/2014, http://www.epa.gov/osw/conserve/materials/ ecycling/docs/fullbaselinereport 2011.pdf.

4 FEVE: The European Container Glass Federation (2012). 'Glass recycling rate', accessed on-line 23/06/2014, http://feve.org/index .php?option=com_content&view =article&id=lo&Itemid=11.

5 Palmer, Brian (2013). 'Recycling of plastic lags because recovery is hard and new production is cheap', *The Washington Post*, accessed on-line 25/03/2014, http://www.washingtonpost.com/national/health-science/recycling-of-plastic-lags-because-recovery-is-hard-and-new-production-is-cheap/2013/02/04/78ca1b92-6953-11e2-ada3-d86a4806d5ee _story.html.

6 'Market Study: Polyethylene-HDPE' (2013), *Ceresana: Market Intelligence. Consulting*, accessed on-line 20/03/2014, http://www .ceresana.com/en/market-studies/plastics/polyethylene-hdpe.

7 Summers, Chris (2012). 'What should be done about plastic bags?', *BBC News Magazine*, accessed on-line 21/03/2014, http://www.bbc.com/news/magazine-17027990.

8 Casey, Taylor (2010). 'Plastic bags: your two cents' worth', *The Daily Iowan*, accessed on-line 20/03/2014, http://www .dailyiowan.com/2010/06/17/Opinions/17547.html.

9 'Scrap Tyres: Basic Information' (last updated November 14, 2012), accessed on-line 20/03/2014, http://www.epa.gov/epawaste/conserve/materials/tires/basic.htm

DESIGNED
pages 127–145

1 McDonough, William; Braungart, Michael (2002). *Cradle to Cradle: Remaking the Way We Make Things*, North Point Press, New York City, USA. Both the quote and the steel example are taken from this source.

2 One of the more famous ones is Calico in the Mojave desert in Southern California, USA.

3 Information from flaska.com, accessed on-line 12/03/2014, http://www.flaska.eu/less-waste-2.

CULTIVATED
pages 151–171

1 'All about Fungus', accessed on-line 15/03/2014, http://www .100thmonkeymushrooms. com/learn/kids-educational/all-about-fungus.

ILLUSTRATION CREDITS

Aerni, Georg 52/6

Adams, Wendell 145, 174/3

Artek 73

Assistant Professorship Dirk E. Hebel (Carlina Teteris) 34, 57/2, 160/1, 177/1, 181/4

Assistant Professorship Dirk E. Hebel (Eszter Fulesdi): based on drawings by Fireclay Tile 105/4; based on drawings by Pittsburgh Corning Europe NV 108/5; based on images by Artek 75; based on images by Ecovative Design 159/2; based on images by Harvey Lacey 40/2; based on images by Hasit Ganatra 83/3; based on images by Strawjet 54; based on information and drawings by Byfusion Limited 114/2–3; based on information by John Habraken 131/3; based on information by Knowaste 119/4; based on information by StoneCycling 100/4; based on information by Yemm & Hart Green Materials 88/1, 123/3

Assistant Professorship Dirk E. Hebel: based on drawings by The Living 160/2; based on images by Wendell Adams 144; based on information by Erik Bowers 70/2, 71/5; based on information by John Habraken 132/5–6, 133/7

Assistant Professorship Dirk E. Hebel (Georg Hana) 38, 39/9–10

Bäcker, Anja 45/4

Barkow, Amy | Barkow Photo 161, 162

Berne University of Applied Sciences 62, 80, 81, 182/2

BLOCK Research Group 76–79, 175/3

Bonded Logic Inc. 90, 91, 182/3

Böttcher, Ulrike 148/5

Bowers, Erik 70/1, 71/3–4, 173/4

Braungart, Michael (EPEA GmbH 2008) 15

Buster, Noreen 155/2, 172/1

Bueno, Alvaro 32, 42/1–2, 175/1

Byfusion Limited 115/4

Coverings Etc 184/2

Cymat Technologies Ltd. 96, 102, 103, 187/2

Daman Ganga Paper Mill 67, 69/7

de Laurens, Erik 147/4

de Mulder, Gert 120, 178/2

Donath, Dirk, Prof. Dr., and EiABC Addis Ababa 57/3, 59/7–9

Dratz & Dratz Architects 44/2–3, 45/5–6

Dry, Carolyn 177/3

Dyer, Brady 94, 114/1, 115/5–6, 174/1

Ecococon Ltd. 182/1

Ecovative Design 18, 147/2, 153, 158, 159/3–4

Enviro Board Corporation 50, 51, 181/2

FCL Singapore 10

Filabot Reclaimer 97

Fireclay Tile 104, 105/5, 187/3

Ganatra, Hasit 82, 83/4, 185/4

GR Green Building Products 116, 117, 185/2

Grod, Wassilij 148/7

Gulley Tryforos, Charlotte 88/2

Hahn, Dorothee, and Daniela Mehlich 26 ; 30

Hebel, Dirk E. 36/1, 173/3

Heineken Experience 128/1, 131/2, 173/1

Heisel, Felix, based on information provided by Worldwatch Institute 8, 9

Heisel, Felix 56

Hilbertz, Wolf 154, 155/3

Holtz, Amy, Gabriel Comstock, Andrew Olds 42/4, 43/6

Hursley, Timothy 42/3, 43/5

Jerusalem, Felix 52/1–5, 181/3

Jetten, Christine 121/3–4

Jonkers, Henk M. 156, 157/2–3, 186/1

Kirei USA 189/4

Knowaste 118, 119/5–7, 185/3

Koenig, Norbert 180/2

Kokkonen, Ville 65, 72, 74/7–8

Klooster, Thorsten, and Heike Klaussmann 149

La Casa Deco 87/2,3,5, 189/2, 190/3

Lacey, Harvey 40/1, 41, 175/4

Lauri, Raul 60, 61, 190/1

Lechner, Julian 146

Lohmann, Julia 147/3

Marcus, Frank 157/4

Masonry Research Group 92/2–3, 93/4

Meacham, Fabiana 93/6–7

Miguel Marques, Fernando 185/1

MINIWIZ 136–139, 180/3, 181/1

Müller, Ulrich, Dr. 148/6

Munro, Jack 124, 125, 176/4

NeptuTherm 183/1

New Territories / R&Sie(n) 110–113, 152, 168–171, 172/2, 191/2,

Noble, Robert, of Noble Environmental Technologies 84, 85, 179/1

Pittsburgh Corning Europe NV 106, 107, 108/4, 109, 180/1

Petit, Romain 134, 135, 173/2

Peijnenburg, Ruud 121/5

Pihler, Morten 183/2

Random House LLC 12

Realm of Design 178/1

Renewed Materials, LLC 187/1

Riehle, Tomas 44/1, 175/2

Ross, Philip 150, 166, 167, 182/4

Sewnet, Helawie 58/6

Smithsonian Institution. Image credits: VAULT201: Design team: John Ochsendorf, Philippe Block, Lara Davis, Florence Guiraud Doughty, Scott Ferebee, Emily Lo, Mallory Taub, Sze Ngai Ting, Robin Willis, Masonry Research Group, Massachusetts Institute of Technology. Installation crew: Masoud Akbarzadeh, Michael Cohen, Samantha Cohen, Lara Davis, Samuel Kronick, Fabiana Meacham, Mallory Taub, Sze Ngai Ting. LEARNING LANDSCAPE: Emily Pilloton, Heleen de Goey, Dan Grossman, Kristina Drury, Neha Thatte, Matthew Miller, and Ilona de Jongh, Project H Design. INDI 002, ALAR 002, AND AZHA CUSTOM WALLPAPERS: (left to right). Jee Levin and Randall Buck, Trove. RETURN TO SENDER ARTISAN ECO-CASKET: Greg Holdsworth, Return to Sender Eco-Caskets 92/1

SongWood 176/2

StoneCycling 98, 99, 100/5, 101, 184/1

Strawjet Inc. 55, 176/2

Studio Grassi Design Srl 188/4

Taub, Mallory 93/5, 176/3

Terreform ONE 20–25, 164, 165, 172

The Bancroft Library, University of California, Berkeley (Tom Kelly) 17

The Living 163

Trudo, Whitney 178/3

UNITED BOTTLE Group Cover, 126, 128/2, 140–143

UPM Biocomposites 74/6, 174/4

urbz.net 64, 68, 69/8

van den Berg, Rinus 130, 132/4, 133/8

vbc3000 Enterprise Innovante 179/2

Vij5 46–49, 189/1

Williamson, Colin 188/1

Wisniewska, Marta H. 6, 35, 36/2, 37, 39/8, 58/4–5, 66, 86, 87/4, 88/3–5, 122, 123/2, 174/3, 184/2, 188/2, 188/3, 190/2, 190/4, 191/1

Zelfo Technology 189/3

ABOUT THE AUTHORS

Dirk E. Hebel is Assistant Professor of Architecture and Construction at the Swiss Federal Institute of Technology (ETH) in Zurich, Switzerland, and at the Future Cities Laboratory in Singapore, a research program of ETH Zurich in South-East Asia. Prior to that, he was the founding Scientific Director of the Ethiopian Institute of Architecture, Building Construction and City Development (EiABC) in Addis Ababa, Ethiopia. His research and practice focus on unusual and alternative building materials such as air (*DISCOVERIES*, an exhibition for the Foundation Lindau Nobel Laureates, and *ON_AIR*, an installation for Kunst-Werke Berlin), water (as the project manager for the Blur Building for EXPO.02 in Switzerland), or plastic bottles (as in the award-winning project UNITED BOTTLE). Hebel is the author of numerous books, lately *SUDU: HOW TO CONSTRUCT A SUSTAINABLE URBAN DWELLING UNIT* (under preparation at Ruby Press, Berlin) and *CITIES OF CHANGE: ADDIS ABABA* (with Marc Angélil, Birkhäuser, 2010). He published *DEVIATIONS* (with Marc Angélil, Birkhäuser, 2008), an experiment in architectural design pedagogy, and *BATHROOM UNPLUGGED* (with Jörg Stollmann, Birkhäuser, 2005). He was awarded the New York Van Alen Institute Fellowship, the Red Dot Design Award for Best Conceptual Design, the SMART Innovation Grant Singapore, and the LANXESS Award Singapore.

Marta H. Wisniewska is a researcher at the Chair of Architecture and Construction Dirk E. Hebel at the Swiss Federal Institute of Technology (ETH) in Zurich and the Future Cities Laboratory Singapore, a research program of ETH Zurich in South-East Asia. Her research focuses on the development of alternative building materials for the application in developing territories from locally available resources, with a special focus on waste. She conducted a seminar "Constructing Waste", addressing questions of designed waste materials. Prior to her engagement at ETH Zurich, Wisniewska was working as a lecturer and architectural program coordinator at the Ethiopian Institute of Architecture, Building Construction and City Development (EiABC) in Addis Ababa. Her work has been published in various magazines and books, such as *Building Ethiopia* (EiABC, Addis Ababa), *Construction Ahead* (Butterfly Publishers, Addis Ababa), and *Architektura & Biznes* (RAM, Krakow).

Felix Heisel is a researcher at the Chair of Architecture and Construction Dirk E. Hebel at the Swiss Federal Institute of Technology (ETH) in Zurich and the Future Cities Laboratory Singapore, a research program of ETH Zurich in South-East Asia. His research addresses the activation of organic fibers for the building industry on an industrial scale. Before joining ETH Zurich, he was a lecturer and architectural program coordinator at the Ethiopian Institute of Architecture, Building Construction and City Development (EiABC) in Addis Ababa. Together with Bisrat Kifle, Heisel is the author of the movie series '_Spaces', a cinematic investigation of the cultural and social habitat of Ethiopia. His work was published in various magazines and books, such as *Building Ethiopia* (EiABC, Addis Ababa), *Construction Ahead* (Butterfly Publishers, Addis Ababa), and *TEC21* (SIA, Zurich). Felix Heisel has won several awards, including the SMART Innovation Grant Singapore and the Bauhaus.SOLAR Award 2012.

ABOUT THE CONTRIBUTORS

Dr. Mitchell Joachim [jo-ak-um], is a Co-Founder of Terreform ONE. He is an Associate Professor at New York University (NYU) and The European Graduate School (EGS) in Switzerland. He was formerly an architect at Gehry Partners, and Pei Cobb Freed. He is a TED Senior Fellow and has been awarded fellowships with Moshe Safdie and the Martin Society for Sustainability at the Massachusetts Institute of Technology (MIT). He was chosen by *Wired* magazine for "The Smart List: 15 People the Next President Should Listen To". *Rolling Stone* magazine honored Joachim in "The 100 People Who Are Changing America". Mitchell won many awards, including the AIA New York Urban Design Merit Award, Victor Papanek Social Design Award, Zumtobel Group Award for Sustainability and Humanity, History Channel Infiniti Award for City of the Future, and the *Time Magazine* Best Invention with MIT Smart Cities Car. *Dwell* magazine featured him as "The NOW 99" in 2012. He earned a Ph.D. at Massachusetts Institute of Technology, MAUD at Harvard University, and M.Arch. at Columbia University.

Jörg Stollmann lives and works in Zurich and Berlin. He is co-founder of urbaninform.net with Rainer Hehl and Professor at the Chair for Urban Design and Urbanization at the Technische Universität Berlin. His work focuses on cooperative design strategies as well as socially and environmentally sustainable urban development. Among his research projects in the field of education and urban development is the Akademie einer neuen Gropiusstadt, Soko Klima. From 2002 to 2008, he was principal of INSTANT Architects with Dirk Hebel. He taught at the ETH Zurich in the MAS Landscape Architecture and directed the MAS Urban Design. Jörg Stollmann graduated from the Berlin University of the Arts and Princeton University. He received awards and fellowships of DAAD, Graham Foundation, German Academy Rome, Red Dot Award, and the Van Alen Institute in New York.

Dr. Sascha Peters is the founder and owner of HAUTE INNOVATION – Material and Technology in Berlin, Germany. In the context of the services offered by his company, he focuses on accelerating innovation processes and turning technological developments in materials into marketable products. Along with leading technology companies such as BMW, Ottobock, Audi, and Evonik, his clients also include public institutions such as the Hessen Ministry of Economics, Technologiestiftung Berlin, and the European Commission. Peters has authored numerous specialist publications. He lectures throughout Europe and runs workshops on innovative materials, sustainable materials, and energy technologies. In recent years he has held teaching positions at several German universities, focusing on the subjects of material technologies, sustainable production, and construction.

INDEX OF PRODUCTS AND PROJECTS

Agricultural Waste Panels 80, 177, 182

Airless 36, 173

Alkemi Boards 186, 187

Alusion Stabilized Aluminium Foam Panels 102, 183, 187

Artek Pavilion 72, 174, 186

Bacteria-based Self-healing Concrete 156, 186

BioGlass 184, 191

Biorock 154, 172

Blood Brick 124, 176

Byfusion Bricks 114, 174, 183

CONBOU High Heel Table 148

Corrugated Cardboard Bundles 42, 175, 183

Corrugated Cardboard Pod 42, 175, 183

Cristalejo (Recycled Crystal Glass) 185, 191

CRT Glass Tiles 104, 186, 187

Dapple Sheets 186, 188

Decafe Tiles 60, 190

Dustyrelief 168, 191

Dye-sensitized Solar Cells Integrated into Concrete 149

Ecococon Panels 179, 182

ECOR 84, 179, 191

Electrostatic Dust Attractor 191

Enviro Board (E-Board) 50, 177, 181

Ex-presso 146

Filabot Recycler 178

Fish Scale Project 147

Flexisurf Sheets 186, 188

Fly Ash Panels 177

FOAMGLAS T4+ 106, 177, 180

GR Green Slate, GR Green Cedar Tiles 116, 185, 191

Green Leaf Bricks 176, 191

Green Stone 178

Hy-Fi 160, 177, 183

Jiilkeen Cube 134, 173, 186

Kirei Boards 177, 189

Maize Cob Board 148

Mushroom Bricks 158, 160, 177, 183

Mushroom Surfboard 147

Mycoform 164, 177

Mycotecture 166, 177, 182

Nappy Roofing 118, 185

Natura 2 86, 190

NeptuTherm Balls 183

NewspaperWood 46, 179, 189

Oki Naganode 147

Olzweg 110, 172

Origins Sheets 186, 188

Paper Tile (Vault) 76, 175

PHZ2 44, 175, 183, 186

Plasphalt 70, 173

POLLI-Brick 136, 177, 180

Prisma 2 190

Reapor Recycled Poroused Waste Glass 180

Recy Blocks 120, 178, 191

Recycled Cardboard Bales 44, 175, 183, 186

ReMaterials Roof Panels 82, 185

Ripietra 188

Rocco Sheets 189

Seaweed Insulation 183

Shading Devices 181

Songwood Boards 176, 191

StoneCycling 98, 184, 191

Strawjet Cables 54, 176, 183

Strawtec Straw Panels 56, 176, 181

Strohhaus 52, 177, 181

Stropoly Straw Panels 52, 177, 181

Sustainable Emerging City Unit (SECU) 56, 176, 181

Tiny Mushroom House 158, 177, 183

Tire Veneer Tiles 122, 191

TRPA Treated Recycled Plastic Aggregates 70, 173

Tuff Roof 66, 184

Ubuntublox 40, 175, 183

UltraTouch Denim Insulation 90, 182

UNITED BOTTLE 140, 174, 183

UPM ProFi 72, 174, 186

Vacuumized PET Bottles 36, 173

Vault201 92, 176

vbc3000 Bricks and Lightened Granulates 179

Waterbrick 144, 174, 186

Wine Cork Tiles 88, 190

World Bottle (WOBO) 130, 173, 186

Zelfo Technology Panels 183, 189

Zerbrechlich 148

INDEX OF MANUFACTURERS AND DESIGNERS

Adams, Wendell, WaterBrick International, Winter Garden, FL, USA 144, 174, 186

Ahmadu Bello University, Zahia, Nigeria 80, 177, 182

Aiolova, Maria, Terreform ONE, New York City, NY, USA 164, 177

Ban, Shigeru, Architects, Paris, France 72, 174, 186

Bauhaus University, Weimar, Germany 56, 176, 181

Berne University of Applied Sciences, Biel, Switzerland 80, 177, 182

Biorock Inc., MA, USA 154, 172

BLOCK Research Group, ETH Zurich, Switzerland 76, 175

Bonded Logic Inc., Chandler, AZ, USA 90, 182

Böttcher, Ulrike, Berlin, Germany 148

Burgess, Toby, University of Westminster, London, United Kingdom 124, 176

Butman, Dylan, Terreform ONE, New York City, NY, USA 164, 177

Byfusion Limited, Wellington, New Zealand 114, 174, 183

Coverings Etc, Miami, FL, USA 184

Cymat Technologies Ltd., Mississauga, ON, Canada 102, 183, 187

Daman Ganga Paper Mill, Gujarat, India 66, 184

de Laurens, Erik, London, United Kingdom 147

de Mulder, Gert, 's-Hertogenbosch, The Netherlands 120, 178, 191

Dratz & Dratz Architects, Oberhausen, Germany 44, 175, 183, 186

Ecococon Ltd., Vilnius, Lithuania 182

Ecovative Design, Green Island, NY, USA 147, 158, 160, 177, 183

Engineered Timber Resources, Boulder, CO, USA 176

Enviro Board Corporation, Camden, NJ, USA 50, 177, 181

Ethiopian Institute of Architecture, Building Construction and City Development (EiABC), Addis Ababa, Ethiopia 56, 176, 181

Far Eastern Group, Taipei, Taiwan 136, 177, 180

Filabot, Montpelier, VT, USA 178

Fireclay Tile, San Francisco, CA, USA 104, 186, 187

Fraunhofer Institute for Building Physics, Stuttgart, Germany 180

Goreau, Thomas J., Dr., Biorock Inc., MA, USA 154, 172

Grod, Wassilij, Berlin, Germany 148

Grassi, Studio, Design slr, Gambettola (FC), Italy 188

GR Green Building Products Inc., Vancouver, BC, Canada 116, 185, 191

Green Leaf Brick, Charlotte, NC, USA 92, 176

Habraken, John, Amsterdam, The Netherlands 130, 173, 186

Hebel, Dirk E., Assistant Professorship of Architecture and Construction, ETH Zurich / FCL Singapore, Switzerland / Singapore 36, 56, 173, 176, 181

Heineken International (Breweries company), Amsterdam, The Netherlands 130, 173, 186

Hilbertz, Wolf, Dr., Biorock Inc., MA, USA 154, 172

Jerusalem, Felix, Zurich, Switzerland 52, 177, 181

Joachim, Mitchell, Terreform ONE, New York City, NY, USA 164, 177

Jonkers, Henk, Microlab, Delft University of Technology, The Netherlands 156, 186

Kirei USA, Solana Beach, CA, USA 189

Klooster, Thorsten, University of Kassel, Germany 149

Klussmann, Heike, University of Kassel, Germany 149

Knowaste, Bromsgrove, United Kingdom 118, 185

Koenig, Norbert, Fraunhofer Institute for Building Physics, Stuttgart, Germany 180

Kompetenzzentrum Holz, Linz, Austria 148

La Casa Deco, Manila, Philippines 86, 189

Lacey, Harvey, New York City, NY, USA 40, 175, 183

Lauri, Raul, Design Lab, Alicante, Spain 60, 190

Lechner, Julian, Berlin, Germany 146

LIAVER GmbH & Co KG, Ilmenau, Germany 180

Light Weight Tiles Ltd., Lydney, United Kingdom 118, 185

Lohmann, Julia, London, United Kingdom 147

Luft & Laune, Zurich, Switzerland 36, 173

Mamou-Mani, Arthur, University of Westminster, London, United Kingdom 124, 176

Masonry Research Group, Massachusetts Institute of Technology, Cambridge, MA, USA 92, 176

Medvedik, Oliver, Terreform ONE, New York City, NY, USA 164, 177

Meijer, Mieke, Eindhoven, The Netherlands 46, 179, 189

Miguel Marques, Fernando, Lisbon, Portugal 185

MINIWIZ, Taipei, Taiwan 136, 177, 180, 181

Mulholland, Greg, Terreform ONE, New York City, NY, USA 164, 177

Müller, Ulrich, Dr., Kompetenz-zentrum Holz, Linz, Austria 148

Munro, Jack, University of Westminster, London, United Kingdom 124, 176

MycoWorks, San Francisco, CA, USA 166, 177, 182

Natural Process Design Inc., Winona, MN, USA 177

NeptuTherm e. K., Karlsruhe, Germany 183

New-territories / R&Sie(n), Paris, France 110, 168, 172, 191

Noble Environment Technologies, Robert Nobel, San Diego, CA, USA 84, 179, 191

Paper recycling facilities, Oberhausen, Germany 44, 175, 183

Petit, Romain, Lyon, France 134, 173, 186

Pittsburgh Corning Europe NV, Tessenderlo, Belgium 106, 177, 180

R&Sie(n), Paris, France 110, 168, 172, 191

Raknes, Helle, Thatching, Møn Island, Denmark 183

Realm of Design, Henderson, NV, USA 178

ReMaterials, Hasit Ganatra and Swad Komanduri, Ahmedabad, India 82, 185

Renewed Materials, LLC, Cabin John, MD, USA 187

Ross, Philip, MycoWorks, San Francisco, CA, USA 166, 177, 182

Rural Studio, Auburn University, Newbern, AL, USA 42, 175, 183

Smile Plastics, The Remarkable Factory, Worcester, United Kingdom 188

Strawjet Inc., Talent, OR, USA 54, 176, 183

Strawtec Building Solutions, Berlin, Germany 56, 176, 181

Stropoly, Güstrow, Germany 52, 177, 181

Terreform ONE, New York City, NY, USA 164, 177

TEWA Technology Corporation, Albuqerque, NM, USA 70, 173

The Living, New York City, NY, USA 160

Tschiersch, Ronald, LIAVER GmbH & Co KG, Ilmenau, Germany 180

Ungermand, Ib, Thatching, Bogø Island, Denmark 183

UNITED BOTTLE Group, Zurich and Basel, Switzerland 140, 174, 183

University of Nigeria, Enugu Campus, Nigeria 80, 177, 182

UPM Biocomposites, Lahti, Finland 72, 174, 186

van Soest, Tom, Eindhoven, The Netherlands 98, 184, 191

Vandkunsten architects, Søren Nielsen, Copenhagen, Denmark 183

vbc3000 Entreprise Innovante, Ferrières-en-Bray, France 179

Vij5, Eindhoven, The Netherlands 46, 179, 189

WaterBrick International, Winter Garden, FL, USA 144, 174, 186

Yemm & Hart Green Materials, Marquand, MO, USA 88, 122, 188, 190, 191

Zelfo Technology GmbH, Schorfheide-Chorin, Germany 189

ACKNOWLEDGEMENTS

The authors would like to express their sincere
gratitude to all manufacturers, designers,
companies, and contributors featured in this
book for their involvement and dedicated support.
Further, we would like to offer our thanks to
the Singapore-ETH Centre (SEC) for Global
Environmental Sustainability and the Future
Cities Laboratory (FCL), particularly SEC Director
Prof. Dr. Peter Edwards, Founding SEC Director
Prof. Dr. Gerhard Schmitt, SEC Managing Director
Dr. Remo Burkhard, FCL Scientific Director
Prof. Dr. Stephen Cairns, and FCL Program Leader
Prof. Kees Christiaanse, as well as the Department
of Architecture of ETH Zurich, specifically Dean
Prof. Hubert Klumpner. We would also like to
extend our gratitude to Binocular, the graphic
designers of this book. Our special thanks go to
the editor for the publisher, Andreas Müller,
who made this book possible through his great
dedication and creative input.